Tax For Dummies

C000241666

Income Tax

Personal allowances	2007–8	2008–9
Under 65	£5,225	£5,435
65 to 74	£7,550	£9,030
75 upwards	£7,690	£9,180
Age allowance limits*	£20,900	£21,800

*The higher personal allowance paid to those aged 65 and over is reduced for income at and above this level by £1 for every £2 of income until the extra age allowance rate comes down to the personal allowance for under 65s.

Taxable Income Bands

Band	2007–8	Band	2008–9
10% (starting rate)	£0–2,230	10% (savings income only)	£0–2,320
22% (basic rate) / (20% savings rate)	£2,231–34,600	20% (basic rate)	£0–36,000
40% (higher rate)	£34,601 or more	40% (higher rate)	£36,001 or more

National Insurance Contributions

Employees 2008–9

Weekly earnings	Rate
Up to £105	0%
£105.01 to £770	11% (9.4% if contracted out of the state second pension)
£770.01 or more	1% on earnings above this level

Self-employed 2008–9

Limit below which Class 2 not payable	£4,825
Class 2 rate	£2.30 per week
Class 4 rate	8% on profits between £5,435 and £40,040 and 1% on sums above the upper limit

Corporation Tax

Rate	2007–8	2008–9
Full rate	30%	28%
Small companies rate	20%	21%

The small companies rate is payable by companies with taxable profits up to £300,000. The full rate is payable on taxable profits above £1.5 million.

For Dummies: Bestselling Book Series for Beginners

Tax For Dummies®

Cheat Sheet

Value Added Tax

Rates	Payable on
0%	books, newspapers, children's clothes, most food items
5%	domestic gas and electricity/energy-saving materials
17.5%	most items (standard rate)

Traders must register for VAT if their annual sales exceed £67,000 (from April 2008) for the previous 12 months or expect to go over this level within the next 30 days. Traders whose sales fall below £65,000 (from April 2008) may (but aren't obliged to) deregister for VAT.

Capital Gains Tax

Annual exemption	2007–8	2008–9
	£9,200	£9,600

Inheritance Tax

Band	2007–8	2008–9
Nil rate band	£300,000	£312,000
40% rate band	£300,001 or more	£312,001 or more

Stamp Duty

Property purchase price	Rate
Up to £125,000	0%
£125,001 to £250,000	1%
£250,001 to £500,000	3%
£500,001 and over	4%

Tax is paid at the rate applicable to the purchase price on the whole amount.

For Dummies: Bestselling Book Series for Beginners

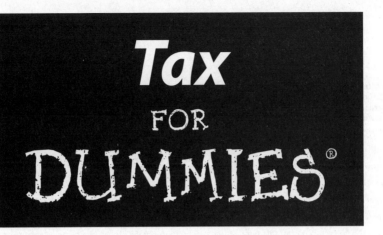

by Sarah Laing

John Wiley & Sons, Ltd

Tax For Dummies®
Published by
John Wiley & Sons, Ltd
The Atrium
Southern Gate
Chichester
West Sussex
PO19 8SQ
England

E-mail (for orders and customer service enquires): cs-books@wiley.co.uk

Visit our Home Page on www.wiley.com

For general information on our other products and services, please contact our Customer Care Department within the U.S. at 800-762-2974, outside the U.S. at 317-572-3993, or fax 317-572-4002.

For technical support, please visit www.wiley.com/techsupport.

Wiley also publishes its books in a variety of electronic formats. Some content that appears in print may not be available in electronic books.

British Library Cataloguing in Publication Data: A catalogue record for this book is available from the British Library

ISBN: 978-0-470-99811-3

Printed and bound in Great Britain by TJ International, Padstow, Cornwall

10 9 8 7 6 5 4 3 2 1

WILEY

About the Author

Sarah Laing is a Chartered Tax Adviser and a member of the Chartered Institute of Taxation. She has been writing professionally since joining CCH Editions in 1998, as a senior technical editor, where she contributed to a range of highly regarded tax publications. She became Publishing Manager for the tax and accounting portfolio in 2001 and later went on to help run CCH's conferences and courses business. She originally worked for the Inland Revenue in the Newbury and Swindon tax offices before moving out into practice in 1991. She has worked for both small and 'Big 5' firms, and now works as a freelance author providing technical writing services for the tax and accountancy profession. Sarah is the News Editor and a director of TaxationWeb Limted (www.taxationweb.co.uk) which provides free information and resources on UK taxes to taxpayers and professionals.

Author's Acknowledgements

Although I've been writing about tax for many years, writing *Tax For Dummies* has proved to be one of the greatest challenges I have faced. Tax affects us all, and is undoubtedly one of the most complicated, yet most talked about, topics. I hope that you'll find this book easy to navigate and more digestible than other reference material. The objective of this book is to provide an easy-to-use, straightforward commentary on many common tax issues and problems, with the emphasis on practical rather than theoretical points.

I would like to thank everyone at Wiley for their hard work, patience, and dedication during the production of this book.

Thank you also to my husband Nev, who has helped me through another writing project. You're a star! Thank you also to my parents, Averil and Vivian. Your continual love and support is invaluable.

Finally, many thanks to you the reader, for picking up and reading this book. Keep it close to hand and personalise it for your own use. Highlight relevant points and add notes in the margin. I hope that you find it useful.

Publisher's Acknowledgements

We're proud of this book; please send us your comments through our Dummies online registration form located at www.dummies.com/register/.

Some of the people who helped bring this book to market include the following:

Acquisitions, Editorial, and Media Development

Project Editor: Steve Edwards

Development Editor: Charlie Wilson

Content Editor: Nicole Burnett

Commissioning Editor: Alison Yates

Copy Editor: Andy Finch

Proofreader: Kim Vernon

Technical Editor: Andrew Lymer

Publisher: Jason Dunne

Executive Editor: Samantha Spickernell

Executive Project Editor: Daniel Mersey

Cover Photos: © Getty Images/Mike Kemp

Cartoons: Ed McLachlan

Composition Services

Project Coordinator: Erin Smith

Layout and Graphics: Reuben W. Davis, Alissa D. Ellet, Melissa K. Jester

Proofreader: David Faust

Indexer: Cheryl Duksta

Brand Reviewers: Jennifer Bingham, Carrie A. Burchfield

Contents at a Glance

Table of Contents

Introduction

● ●

*A*s Scarlet O'Hara pointed out in Margaret Mitchell's *Gone with the Wind*: 'Death, taxes, and childbirth! There's never any convenient time for any of them.' But inconvenient and unwelcome as tax is, you just can't afford to be in the dark about this subject. Everyone needs to know about tax because paying the correct amount of tax when it's due is compulsory. Failing to do so brings a range of penalties from a simple fine to a long spell in prison.

These days, avoiding having to deal with HM Revenue & Customs (HMRC) at some stage in your life is difficult. Two generations or so ago, only the minority of people paid tax. Most people earned their weekly cash wage packet and that was that. Now, practically no one escapes the taxman's net. You can be a customer of the tax system as an employee, employer, self-employed worker, parent, and consumer. You generally start paying income tax and national insurance as soon as you start work and some people carry on paying tax well beyond the grave. And many state benefits are now administered by HMRC, so if you are lower paid or out of work, you need to make contact with HMRC for any claims.

The UK tax system is complicated and ever-changing. However, one factor remains unaltered – we need taxes to pay for public services such as hospitals, schools, roads, and fire and police services. Yet, we would all rather have more money in our own pocket to spend on our families and ourselves. Reading this book helps you to square this circle by using many legitimate ways to ensure that you pay the taxman the minimum amount possible, and not a penny more.

About This Book

Tax For Dummies is designed to give you an understanding of the UK tax system and help you pay the right amount of tax for your situation. It contains many tax-saving tips to help you legally reduce your tax bill and plenty of warning points to help you avoid the pitfalls.

But *Tax For Dummies* isn't just about saving tax. In this book I show you how the system works and your role in it. I tell you where you can find more information, often at no cost. I give you hints and tips on how to deal with HM Revenue & Customs (HMRC) and provide guidance on how to file your own self-assessment tax return.

Conventions Used in This Book

To help you navigate through this book, I set up a few conventions:

- ✓ *Italics* are used for emphasis and to highlight new words or defined terms.
- ✓ **Bold faced** text indicates the key concept in a list.
- ✓ `Monofont` is used for Web and e-mail addresses.

What You're Not to Read

This book is primarily an action guide to dealing with your taxation affairs. The text in grey boxes throughout the book contains information that's interesting but not essential. So, you can choose to read a sidebar if the topic appeals to you, but if you skip over it, you aren't missing out on anything you really need to know.

Foolish Assumptions

While writing this book I made some assumptions about you:

- ✓ You aren't a tax professional. If you are, you have plenty of reference books and manuals to choose from and are far too experienced to be reading a basic guide to the tax system.
- ✓ You don't need hand-holding to fill in your annual self-assessment tax return. I don't go through the self-assessment form step-by-step because the HMRC guidance that accompanies the tax return is very comprehensive and easy to follow. Instead, I offer tips that you can put to use beforehand so that you can fill in the form easily and quickly, and hopefully save some of your hard-earned cash.
- ✓ You don't want tax to be an all-consuming pastime. You want to know just enough to make sure that you pay the right amount and claim what you are entitled to.
- ✓ You want to know the pitfalls as well as the plus points when it comes to organising your finances to minimise tax. This applies particularly to investment choices, and deciding whether to give assets away to children and grandchildren.
- ✓ You're willing to seek professional advice if you're unsure about anything. You don't make financial decisions lightly, and if you need more info than I provide in the book, you'll get some support from the professionals and organisations I suggest.

How This Book Is Organised

This book has six major parts, each on a different theme. Each part is divided into chapters relating to the theme, and each chapter is subdivided into individual sections relating to the chapter topic. Additionally, check out the table of contents at the start of this book and the detailed index at the end to help you pinpoint a specific area of interest.

Here's an outline of what you can expect to find out about in each part.

Part 1: Tax Facts

This part is essential for understanding the tax system in the UK. I take you through the legal framework and the internal workings of HM Revenue & Customs (HMRC). I help you get to grips with self assessment and what it means for you. I also tell you how to organise your paperwork and how to work out how much tax you owe.

Part II: Tax through Your Ages

In this part, I look at how tax affects you in your personal life. I examine tax-efficient savings and investments and how to take advantage of the tax breaks on offer. I look at the tax implications of having kids and getting on the property ladder, and I also include a run through of inheritance tax issues that may affect your estate after your death.

Part III: Pensions and Benefits

This part tells you how to maximise your pension pot in the most tax-efficient way and explains the state retirement pension and surrounding tax issues. Then I look at other state benefits that HMRC administers, and outline which ones you can expect to receive if you've paid national insurance and which ones you have to pay tax on.

Part IV: Working for Someone Else

This part concentrates on being an employee, looking at the Pay As You Earn (PAYE) system in detail and telling you how to check your tax and national insurance payments. In addition, I guide you through which employment-related perks are taxable and which are tax-free.

Part V: Working for Yourself

Working for yourself can be the best, or worst, thing you ever do. Getting organised and setting up properly for tax from the start hopefully helps to set you on the path to success. In this part I help you decide which business structure is best for you. I show you what you can claim for tax purposes and help you understand how your tax bill is calculated. Finally, I take you through the practicalities of turning a business into a limited company.

Part VI: The Part of Tens

This part is an essential ingredient in any *For Dummies* book. Each of the three chapters contains ten succinct, must-know points. In this part, I sum up tax-saving ideas and give you a rapid revision course on how to deal with HMRC. The final chapter gives a quick romp through the most important things to keep in mind when you run your own business.

Icons Used in This Book

Within each chapter you find the following icons pointing you to particular types of information that you may find immediately useful:

This icon contains true-to-life examples to help illustrate a point. These examples are designed to give you a better understanding of how to put the theory into practice, but if you already have a grasp of the topic, you can skip over them.

Keeping in mind the tips that this icon highlights can make your tax life easier.

The bull's-eye highlights things you can do to minimise your tax bill and general advice on how best to arrange your tax affairs.

This icon marks pitfalls, traps, and other things that you definitely shouldn't do if you want to stay on the right side of HMRC.

Where you see this icon you know that the accompanying text is a little more complex. If you're struggling to get to grips with the detail, feel free to move on.

Where to Go from Here

You can read this book in several ways. You can start at the front cover and read all the way through to the end. Reading the book this way gives you a good understanding of the UK tax system because it covers all the main taxes (income tax, capital gains tax, inheritance tax, corporation tax, stamp duty, VAT, and national insurance).

Alternatively, you can pick a topic that interests you and go straight to it. This book is set up so you read the bits that interest you in self-contained sections. If you do want to skip about the book, I recommend that you read Part I first. This gives you a good foundation for understanding the whole taxation process. But of course, you can read it in any way you want – it's *your* book.

Wherever you go from here, whenever you find a piece of advice or a warning that applies to you, copy it, and then fix it to the fridge with a magnet, or pin it up on your notice board, and then don't forget to act on it. And as you read through this book, why not make pencil notes on your tax form to help you when you come to complete the form for real? Being informed and planning well ahead is the best tax advice anyone can give you.

Part I
Tax Facts

'The taxmen never give up, do they?'

In this part . . .

*D*o you find the subject of taxation decidedly taxing?
Does working out your tax bill leave you nursing a
pounding headache? Never fear — this part is just for you
and gently eases you into the basics of the UK tax system.
Think of this part as the foundation stone on which you can
build and broaden your knowledge — or the code-breaker
that helps you understand the taxman's gobbledegook.

In this part I tell you how the tax system works, what you
have to do to keep on the right side of the law, and how to
make life easier for yourself by getting properly organised.
I also explain the self assessment system, so that you have
a good understanding of how to complete the right forms,
calculate your tax bill, and pay anything you owe on the
right date (so avoiding any nasty fines).

Chapter 1

Thinking About Tax

● ●

In This Chapter

▶ Getting to grips with the main taxes

▶ Understanding how you pay HMRC

▶ Being tax-efficient with savings and investments

▶ Thinking about retirement and benefits

● ●

*M*uch as you may hate paying it, tax is a fact of life. The government relies on taxing your income and savings in order to pay for the public services such as the National Health Service, education, and the police. And try as you may (and I certainly don't recommend that you do), you can't hide from HM Revenue & Customs (HMRC).

Many people have no direct contact with the HMRC whatsoever. If your earnings are about average and you don't have a second home, overseas investments, a second job, or any of a number of other sources of income, you may never meet the taxman. Your employer, banks, or investment companies often pay any tax liabilities you have on your behalf. But even if you don't currently have direct contact with HMRC, you may need to in the future, and so getting to grips with the basics of tax is important.

Chapter 2 gives you an overview of the legalities of the UK tax system. But to get you started, this chapter looks at which taxes we pay, why, and how, and introduces you to key areas in which you can save tax.

Looking at Types of Tax

When I refer to 'tax', I'm really over-simplifying a vast and complex system for collecting the money that the government needs to pay for all the services, such as hospitals, schools, and the police, which the country needs. Tax doesn't just refer to the money that your employer deducts from your pay packet, it can also be payable when you buy goods or services (VAT), when you die (inheritance tax), or when you give something away (capital gains tax). Here is a summary of the main taxes you're likely to encounter during your lifetime:

- ✔ **Capital gains tax** is generally charged on the profit you make when you sell (or give away) certain assets such as shares and properties. From 6 April 2008, capital gains tax is payable at a flat rate of 18 per cent. Prior to 2008–9 rates of up to 40 per cent were payable. See Chapter 6 for more information on capital gains tax.

- ✔ **Corporation tax** is payable by incorporated companies on their business profits. Rates vary between 21 per cent for small companies up to 28 per cent for companies with profits over £1.5million. Chapter 17 examines incorporation and corporation tax.

- ✔ **Council tax** is paid on your residence whether you own it or rent it. Discounts apply to people living on their own. The amount you pay depends on where you live and the value of the property you live in. Chapter 7 explains more.

- ✔ **Income tax** is charged on earnings you receive from an employer, or profits you make if you're self-employed and run your own business. You also have to pay income tax on most income you receive from savings and investments. Some state benefits, such as the state retirement pension, are also chargeable to income tax. Income tax is currently charged at 10 per cent, 20 per cent, 32.5 per cent, and 40 per cent.

- ✔ **Inheritance tax** is charged on the value of your estate when you die. Your *executors* (the people who sort out your affairs when you die) pay inheritance tax and it's subject to a tax-free nil rate band (£312,000 for 2008–9). You can transfer any unused inheritance tax nil-rate band on a person's death to the estate of his or her surviving spouse or civil partner who dies on or after 9 October 2007. Take a look at Chapter 8 for more on inheritance tax.

- ✔ **National insurance** is a tax on those who work and the people for which they work: Both employees and employers have to pay. Special rules apply for self-employed people. You can pay national insurance even if you don't earn enough to pay income tax. Paying voluntary contributions may enhance a future entitlement to state benefits. The rates are quite complicated, but most people pay 11 per cent across most of their earnings from work. Chapter 12 deals with employees' national insurance and Chapter 15 deals with the special self-employment rules.

- ✔ **Stamp duty** is paid on most property transactions and most stock market deals. Rates range from 1 per cent to 4 per cent depending on the value of the property being purchased. The tax doesn't rise evenly – stamp duty is payable at 3 per cent on transactions up to £500,000 and at 4 per cent over £500,000. So you pay tax of £14,970 when you buy a property for £499,000 (£499,000 × 3 per cent) and £20,040 on a property of £501,000 (£501,000 × 4 per cent) – so just a £2,000 increase in property price can mean an extra £5,070 in tax! Flick to Chapter 7 for more on stamp duty.

✔ **Value Added Tax (VAT)** is charged by registered businesses on most business transactions. VAT is also charged on the provision of most labour services. The end result is a sales tax on many items and services you buy. The current standard rate of VAT is 17.5 per cent, but some items, such as the installation of mobility aids for the elderly and related supplies of the mobility aids themselves, is charged at the reduced rate of 5 per cent. Chapters 15 and 16 deal with registering and deregistering for VAT.

The tax system is rather complicated and much of that complexity derives from trying to make it fair. In aiming for fairness, the system taxes different types of income in different ways, and consequently, the way in which a transaction is structured affects the overall tax bill. Where differences in tax treatment exist, the scope for tax planning arises. This causes problems where the tax planning becomes interpreted as tax abuse or avoidance. The government then legislates to prevent the perceived abuse and, in doing so, causes the system to become yet more complicated, triggering more complicated tax-planning schemes. And so it goes on.

When you're feeling grumpy about the level of taxes you pay, bear in mind that if the government lowers tax rates then it has less money to spend on public services. Therefore, services may be cut or the government has to borrow to fund them. If it borrows, interest rates go up, which impacts on your mortgage payments, credit cards, and any other loans you may have.

Knowing How You Pay Taxes

HMRC is responsible for the collection of all taxes (apart from council tax and business rates, which local authorities administer) through two systems: self assessment and Pay As You Earn (PAYE).

As the name suggests, *self assessment* means that you calculate your own tax liability and pay any tax due. HMRC may check your calculation at a later date by way of a random or formal enquiry. HMRC refers to this process as the 'pay now, check later' approach. Only one in three taxpayers has to fill in a self-assessment tax return form, which equates to around nine million people.

Most people pay income tax through the PAYE scheme. Under this scheme, your employer deducts tax and national insurance contributions (NICs) and pays them over to HMRC on your behalf. The money goes straight out of your pay packet without you ever having to think about tax.

Unfortunately life isn't that simple for others. Millions of people taxed under PAYE also have to fill out a self-assessment tax return each year. This process may be because they are receiving benefits from their employer, such as a company car or medical insurance, or they may have vast amounts of savings, two houses, offshore investments, income from a hobby, or any other number of income sources that the tax authorities need to know about.

Chapter 3 examines the self-assessment system and tells you how and when to pay your tax bill, and Chapter 12 takes you through PAYE. For more details on HMRC, flick to Chapter 2.

Keeping Money in Your Pocket

You're entitled to arrange your finances so that you pay the minimum tax possible. (Just make sure that you don't stray into the realms of tax evasion, which is illegal – Chapter 2 explains this aspect fully.) So, with a little know-how, you can maximise your income and minimise your tax bill.

Saving tax on savings

Here's a cheery thought: Lowering your tax bill doesn't have to involve complex money manoeuvres. For starters, making savings can be as simple as changing your bank account. For example, you may put £1,000 into a bank account that pays you, say, 5 per cent interest and pay no tax on the interest you earn. At the other end of the scale, you may save the same amount at the same rate and have to pay tax at 40 per cent on the interest you earn – the difference depends on the type of savings scheme you opt for.

And if you think that the taxman is out to milk you dry, think again. HMRC may actually want to give you back the tax that your bank or building society automatically takes from you. Your bank or building society takes tax off your interest at a rate of 20 per cent. However, if you pay tax on less than £2,320 (for 2008–9) of your income, including your interest, you have to pay tax only at the starting rate for savings income of 10 per cent. So you can claim back the tax taken off your interest that is more than you need to pay.

If you think you've paid too much tax on your bank and building society interest, make a claim by 31 January 2009 and you can go back as far as the tax year 2002–3 – so your bank or building society may repay your interest on five years' worth of interest.

If you want some more tips on how to keep more of your savings in your pocket, head over to Chapter 6.

Giving money away

When you give money to someone, you want to make sure that both you and the grateful recipient pay the least possible tax on the money. By making sensible financial choices you can ensure that less money finds its way into HMRC's wallet.

If your child is under 18 and you give him money, according to HMRC that money still belongs to you, not your child. Therefore, HMRC taxes you on the interest the money in your child's bank account earns. But you can benefit from a small exemption to this rule: You don't pay tax if the annual interest on all the savings accounts is less than £100 per parent per child. Within the £100 level, the interest is taxed as belonging to the children, and they can usually reclaim tax deducted on it by the bank or building society using form R85. So you can give your lucky children some tax-free money each year.

As well as thinking about money you give to your children, consider any charitable donations you make. If you're a taxpayer, you can donate money under the government's Gift Aid scheme. Through Gift Aid, not only does the charity itself receive more money (an extra 25 pence for every pound you donate), but you, the donator, can also claim tax relief on making one-off or regular gifts of any amount if you're a higher rate taxpayer.

Skip to Chapter 6 for more on making tax-efficient gifts.

Investing in property

More people than ever are investing in property – from snapping up buy-to-let properties or renting out their spare room, through to buying second homes or even dabbling in property development. In times of such a volatile stock market, only time will tell whether these investments pay off, but for the time being, lots of opportunities exist to save tax when investing in property.

Owning a home remains an attractive investment for tax purposes. If your property is worth over a certain amount (currently £125,000) you pay stamp duty when you buy your property, but provided you live in it and don't rent it out, you generally pay no tax when you sell. For example, say you have £50,000 in the bank. If you leave that money in the bank it gathers interest (great), but you pay tax on that interest (not so great). If you invest that money in property, however, HMRC doesn't make a penny out of that £50,000.

If you rent out a property (or properties) HMRC treats the income you receive from it as investment income and not as earnings from a trade. Generally, therefore, you aren't entitled to as many reliefs and allowances as someone who trades but, on the plus side, you don't have to pay NICs on any profits you make from a property rental business.

The rent-a-room scheme allows you to receive up to £4,250 a year tax-free for renting out a room in your home. You don't need to be the homeowner to take advantage of the scheme – it applies equally to rented properties.

Chapter 7 gives you more details on the tax implications (and savings you can make) when buying and selling property.

Receiving pensions and benefits

You have to think about tax throughout your working life, and I'm afraid that nothing changes when you retire. Pensions are generally treated as earnings and are usually taxed based on entitlement in the tax year.

Tax advantages are to be had in paying into a pension scheme or policy during your working life. Contributions or premiums (up to certain limits) attract tax relief at your top rate of income tax (currently 40 per cent). Your employer can also pay into your pension and receive tax relief. When you retire you can get a tax-free lump sum (within permitted limits) and non-taxpayers can obtain basic rate tax relief on personal pension contributions of up to £3,600 per tax year. Have a look at Chapter 9, which gives lots of information on pensions.

In addition, your NICs mean that during your lifetime you're entitled to receive benefits from the government. Some benefits are taxable and some aren't – you need to know how each is treated for tax purposes so that you can include it, or disregard it, in your income tax calculation. Chapter 11 gives an overview of both taxable and non-taxable benefits.

Chapter 2

Understanding the Legal Framework

*T*ax in the UK can seem fiendishly complicated. But that's no reason to shut this book in despair and resign yourself to a lifetime of confusion. With a little guidance and understanding you can navigate the complexities of tax law and make sure that you get the best from HM Revenue & Customs (HMRC) – and pay the least possible amount of tax. This chapter helps you to understand the legalities of the UK tax system.

Laying Down and Interpreting the Law

By law, the government is responsible for levying taxes. The following sections take you through the basics of how the government makes tax law, and how HMRC and the court system interpret the law.

Laying down the law

The government usually introduces new tax laws through *statutes*, the technical name for *bills* (legal documents) that go through Parliament for debate and come out the other end as *acts* (which are law). The government uses one particular statute – the Finance Act – each year to make changes to all areas of tax law and to impose income tax.

The evolution of income tax

Income tax was originally introduced as a temporary measure by Prime Minister William Pitt to help pay for the Napoleonic wars in 1799. Unfortunately, as the name suggests, income taxation brought with it the necessity that taxpayers had to reveal the extent of their income, which was most unpopular as people didn't want to reveal how much they earned (or didn't earn as the case may be!). So when Henry Addington re-introduced income tax in 1803, he chose a method of classifying income by its source and charged each source of income separately. Using this method, no one was able to ascertain a taxpayer's total income without examining each separate income source.

Income tax was last introduced by Sir Robert Peel in 1842 as a three-year temporary measure, but it has been with us ever since.

Each year the government follows a process. First, the chancellor presents the pre-budget report (usually in December), which sets out growth forecasts for the coming year. A consultation period follows, during which the government works out how much money it needs to raise to balance the books. The chancellor presents the final figures to Parliament in his budget speech (usually in March).

Following the chancellor's budget speech, the government publishes the Finance Bill. This bill goes through various committee and debate stages in Parliament and any necessary changes are made. Towards the end of July the Queen signs off the bill, and then the Finance Bill then becomes the Finance Act.

Interpreting the law

HMRC often issues statements in which it makes known its views on the correct interpretation of statute, or the way in which it proposes to apply certain rules. For example, in particular situations it may announce a relaxation of the law or *concession*, which you can apply as a courtesy from HMRC but you can't use to avoid tax.

In addition to HMRC's interpretation, courts can make rulings that affect tax law. If you're in dispute with HMRC you normally take the matter to the *special commissioners* or the *general commissioners*, who provide independent tribunal hearings. The special or general commissioners try to make a decision based on both the facts of a particular case and the strict letter of the law. Findings of fact are final, but the commissioners' findings on law aren't conclusive and you can appeal against them to the High Court.

If a dispute arises between a trader and HMRC, the trader may appeal to a VAT tribunal. Decisions in VAT tribunal cases are on the public record and so provide important guidance as to the effects of the legislation. Some VAT tribunal cases have been the subject of appeal to the higher courts in the UK, and also of referrals to the European Court of Justice, providing further guidance. In addition, decisions of the European Court of Justice on matters referred to it from other member states can be of relevance as UK law is often bound by general European Community law.

Getting to Know HMRC

HMRC was formed on the 18 April 2005, following the merger of the former Inland Revenue (which collected *direct* taxes such as income tax, capital gains tax, and inheritance tax) and HM Customs and Excise (which collected *indirect* taxes such as Value Added Tax or VAT, fuel duties, and import duties). The basic rationale behind the merger of the departments was to improve communications and make things simpler for the taxpayer.

HMRC's basic duty is to ensure that the correct tax is paid at the right time, including the payment of taxes received by HMRC or the entitlement to benefits paid out. HMRC's responsibilities include:

- Administering national insurance (HMRC collects the money in, although the main benefit paid out, the state retirement pension, is paid by the Department for Work and Pensions).

- Collecting customs duties and enforcing border and frontier controls.

- Collecting interest and repayments on student loans from the government's Student Loans Company.

- Collecting taxes, including income tax, capital gains tax, and inheritance tax, as well as stamp duty, VAT, and corporation tax on companies.

- Enforcing the national minimum wage and investigating employers who try to pay below that level.

- Overseeing the work and spending of business support teams – local organisations set up to encourage new and small businesses.

- Paying benefits and credits, including child benefit, child tax credit, and working tax credit.

- Valuing land for council tax and other purposes.

HMRC collects tax through two systems:

- ✔ **Pay As You Earn (PAYE):** Your employer deducts tax and national insurance contributions (NICs) and pays them over to HMRC on your behalf. Chapter 12 explores PAYE.

- ✔ **Self assessment:** You calculate your own tax liability, communicate this liability to HMRC on a tax return, and pay any tax due. Chapter 3 gives you the low-down on self assessment.

Seeing Who Is Liable for Tax

Individuals in the UK usually pay tax on:

- ✔ Income arising in the UK, whether or not you're resident in the UK

- ✔ Income arising outside the UK if you're treated as resident in the UK

- ✔ Any gains or profits you make when you dispose of assets anywhere in the world if you're resident or ordinarily resident in the UK

Special rules apply in certain circumstances, but generally the amount of income tax and capital gains tax you have to pay depends on whether you're resident and/or ordinarily resident in the UK, and in some cases on your domicile. If you find the terms 'resident', 'ordinarily resident', and 'domicile' as clear as mud, fear not. The following sections explain each term in detail, and the criteria you must fit to be worthy of such titles and thus pay tax in the UK.

Establishing your residence

The following sections explore how UK law defines your residency for tax purposes.

Defining resident and ordinarily resident

If you're physically present in the UK for 183 days or more in the tax year, HMRC defines your status as *resident*. HMRC accepts no exceptions to this rule. You count the total number of days you spend in the UK – you can come and go several times during the year or spend one stay of 183 days or more. Days of departure and arrival are counted as days of residence in the UK for tax purposes.

Visitors with other criteria can also be considered by HMRC to be resident. As a shorter-term visitor, you may still be treated as resident for the year if you visit the UK regularly. If you're in the UK for fewer than 183 days in a tax year, but after four tax years your visits during that time average 91 days or more each tax year, you're counted as resident. If this situation applies to you, HMRC treats you as resident in the UK from the start of the fifth year. However, if it's clear when you first come to the UK (for example, because you have set work commitments) that you intend making such visits and you do actually make the visits, HMRCs treat you as resident from 6 April of the first year you come. Any days you spend in the UK for exceptional circumstances beyond your control (for example, because you or a member of your immediate family were ill) don't count.

If you're resident in the UK year after year, you're treated as being *ordinarily resident* here. As a shorter-term visitor, you can also be treated as ordinarily resident if you come to the UK regularly and your visits average 91 days or more a tax year. Any days spent in the UK for exceptional circumstances beyond your control, for example due to illness, aren't normally counted. The date from which HMRC treats you as ordinarily resident depends on your intentions and whether you actually carry them out. You're ordinarily resident:

- ✔ From 6 April of the tax year of your first arrival, if it is clear when you first come here that you intend visiting the UK regularly for at least four tax years.

- ✔ From 6 April of the fifth tax year after you have visited the UK over four years, if you originally came with no definite plans about the number of years you intend to visit.

- ✔ From 6 April of the tax year in which you decide you'll be visiting the UK regularly, if you make that decision before the start of the fifth tax year.

In a tax year, you can be any combination of the following:

- ✔ **Resident and ordinarily resident in the UK:** If you usually live in this country and only go abroad for short periods – for example, on holiday or on business trips.

- ✔ **Resident but not ordinarily resident in the UK:** For example, if you normally live outside the UK but are in this country for 183 days or more in the year.

- ✔ **Ordinarily resident but not resident in the UK:** For example, you usually live in the UK but have gone abroad for a long holiday and do not set foot in the UK during that year.

Residing in two (or more) countries

You can be resident or ordinarily resident in both the UK and in another country (or countries) at the same time. Being resident or ordinarily resident in another country doesn't mean that you can't also be resident or ordinarily resident in the UK.

Strictly speaking, you're taxed as a UK resident for the whole of a tax year if you're resident here for any part of it. But if you leave or come to the UK part way through a tax year, HMRC may agree to split the tax year.

Working abroad

If you leave the UK to work full-time abroad under a contract of employment, you're treated as not resident and not ordinarily resident, and therefore not liable to UK income tax, if you meet all the following conditions:

- ✔ Your absence from the UK and your employment abroad both last for at least a whole tax year

- ✔ During your absence, any visits you make to the UK:

    • Total less than 183 days in any tax year

    • Average less than 91 days a tax year

The average is taken over the period of absence up to a maximum of four years. Any days spent in the UK because of exceptional circumstances beyond your control, for example the illness of yourself or a member of your immediate family, don't normally count for this purpose.

If you meet all the conditions, you're treated as not resident and not ordinarily resident in the UK from the day after you leave the UK to the day before you return to the UK at the end of your employment abroad. You are treated as coming to the UK permanently on the day you return from your employment abroad and as resident and ordinarily resident from that date.

Ascertaining your domicile

Domicile is important for tax purposes because people who are resident (see the preceding section 'Establishing your residence') but not domiciled in the UK receive special tax treatment for their overseas income and capital gains.

Domicile is a general law concept and, as such, is a little complex. I can't list all the factors that affect your domicile, but in the following sections I explain a few of the main points to help you ascertain your domicile. I then summarise the special tax treatment that applies to non-UK domiciled individuals.

Breaking down domiciles

Broadly speaking, you're domiciled in the country where you have your permanent home. Domicile is distinct from nationality or residence and you can only have one domicile at any given time.

You normally acquire a *domicile of origin* from your father when you're born: It need not be the country in which you're born. For example, if you're born in France while your father is working there, but his permanent home is in the UK, your domicile of origin is in the UK.

Until you have the legal capacity to change it, your domicile follows that of the person on whom you're legally dependent. If the domicile of that person changes, you automatically acquire the same domicile (a *domicile of dependency*), in place of your domicile of origin.

You have the legal capacity to acquire a new domicile (a *domicile of choice*) when you reach the age of 16. To do so, you must broadly leave your current country of domicile and settle in another country. You need to provide strong evidence that you intend to live there permanently or indefinitely. Living in another country for a long time, although an important factor, is not enough in itself to prove you have acquired a new domicile.

Looking at the rules for non-domiciled residents

People who are resident in the UK but not domiciled here receive special tax treatment in respect of income and gains arising outside the UK. In general, if you're non-UK domicile, you're only charged UK tax on money you bring to the UK – known as the *remittance basis*.

However, from 6 April 2008 a non-domiciled individual who has been UK tax resident for seven or more years can only use the *remittance basis* for taxation of her overseas income if she pays an additional tax charge of £30,000 a year. Years of residence before 6 April 2008 are taken into account. If the charge isn't paid, the individual has to pay tax as though she were resident, ordinarily resident, and domiciled in the UK.

In addition, from 6 April 2008 someone who is a UK tax resident, but not domiciled or not ordinarily resident, and who claims the remittance basis for taxing overseas income, is only able to claim personal allowances, married couple's allowance, and blind person's allowance against their total taxable income, if their unremitted foreign income is below £2,000 a year.

Claiming Allowances and Reliefs

UK residents and non-residents who are classed as UK taxpayers are entitled to certain allowances and reliefs, based on their personal circumstances, which reduce the amount of tax charged on income.

Knowing who can claim

UK residents can claim allowances and reliefs (visit the earlier section 'Establishing your residence' for a definition of 'resident'). If you aren't resident in the UK, you can claim tax allowances if you're a

- ✔ Citizen of a state within the European Economic Area (EEA), that is Austria, Belgium, Denmark, Finland, France, Germany, Greece, Iceland, Italy, Liechtenstein, Luxembourg, Netherlands, Norway, Portugal, Republic of Ireland, Spain, and Sweden

- ✔ Civil servant in a territory under the protection of the British Crown

- ✔ Commonwealth citizen (including a British citizen)

- ✔ Former resident of the UK and you live abroad for the sake of your own health or the health of a member of your family who lives with you

- ✔ National and/or a resident of a country with which the UK has a double taxation agreement that allows such a claim

- ✔ Present or former employee of the British Crown (including a civil servant, member of the armed forces, and so on)

- ✔ Resident of the Isle of Man or the Channel Islands

- ✔ UK missionary society employee

- ✔ Widow or widower of an employee of the British Crown

If you become, or cease to be, resident in the UK during a tax year, you can't claim full allowances and reliefs for the year of arrival or departure.

Making the claim

UK residents who are employees have tax deducted at source from their wages or salaries under the Pay As You Earn (PAYE) system. The employer deducts tax on the basis of code numbers issued for each employee by HMRC. These codes take account of the tax allowances and reliefs to which each individual is entitled.

Other UK residents may need to make claims for allowances and reliefs. UK residents may be sent a tax return. If you get one, you can use it to claim your allowances and reliefs. If you don't get a tax return, you can contact your tax office and ask them to send you one (tax office contact details can be found on the HMRC Web site at www.hmrc.gov.uk).

If you aren't resident in the UK but you fit the criteria to claim allowances and reliefs, contact HMRC on 0845 070 0040 (unless you're an employee of the British Crown or receive a pension for Crown service, in which case contact HMRC Cardiff 4 Foreign Section on 02920 325000).

To make a claim for tax allowances, you must do so within 5 years 10 months from the end of the tax year to which the claim relates. For example, to claim for the tax year 2006–7 (6 April 2006 to 5 April 2007), you have until 31 January 2013.

Distinguishing between Avoidance and Evasion

Every year solicitors, tax practitioners, and accountants try to come up with new ways to exploit loopholes in the tax legislation in order to legally reduce the tax bills of their usually well-off clients. Therefore, of course, every annual budget and pre-budget report published by the government has a section entitled 'Protecting tax revenues'. These sections contain a new round of anti-avoidance legislation aimed at closing down the loopholes and making sure that the Treasury coffers are filled to the max each year.

But even though the government tries to limit tax avoidance, such avoidance is perfectly legal. In the 1936 tax case *Inland Revenue Commissioners vs. Duke of Westminster*, the judge concluded that 'Every man [women rarely paid tax in those days] is entitled if he can, to order his affairs so the tax attaching under the appropriate act is less than it otherwise would be'. Therefore, translating the legalese, you can legally take advantage of every tax-break going. Tax evasion, however, is strictly illegal and can cause you to end up in one of Her Majesty's less choice establishments as an enforced guest of the taxpayer.

The distinction between avoidance and evasion is as follows:

- ✔ **Avoidance is legal:** For example, arranging your savings so that you don't draw interest or dividends on shares until some future date when your tax rate falls is legal. So too is claiming the cost of a computer and computer software for use in your business if you run your own company.

- ✔ **Evasion is illegal:** Stashing money in an offshore tax haven and denying that you know anything about it is illegal. So too is claiming the cost of the computer and software that you gave to your son for Christmas to do his homework and play games on.

Clamping down on avoidance schemes

At one time the courts saw their task in terms of applying the tax law to a given set of facts (referred to as the *form* of the transaction) and they were in general unwilling to go behind the legal issues on the surface. However, during the 1970s the tax avoidance industry grew to the extent that by the 1980s the courts were forced to take on a more complex approach and look at what was really behind a tax-avoidance scheme (referred to as the *substance* of the transaction). The most famous cases that resulted from this change in approach were *WT Ramsay Ltd vs IR Commrs* and *IR Commrs vs Burmah Oil Co Ltd*. The later case of *Furniss (HMIT) vs Dawson* further explored the court's new approach.

Two decades later and HMRC still uses this principle to look at the reality of tax returns. The basic test is whether someone would carry out a particular transaction or practice if no tax considerations or advantages were to be had. If the answer is yes, everything will probably be fine. If the scheme is perceived to exist only to obtain a tax advantage, HMRC may well challenge it under the *Ramsay* or *Furniss* principles.

Looking After Your Records

Every taxpayer in the UK who fits the criteria for self assessment (see Chapter 3 for details) must abide by an important law: You must keep the records you need to back up your tax return. If you don't keep records, HMRC has no way to verify how much you earned and what you spent.

Everyone who files a self-assessment tax return has to keep personal financial records for one year following the annual 31 January filing date. However, if you're self-employed or have any earnings on top of your main job, you have to keep records for five years after the 31 January filing date – so six years altogether.

HMRC charges penalties of up to £3,000 for failing to keep the records that back up your tax return. In addition, falsifying your records, or intentionally destroying records, is a criminal offence.

Basically, you need to keep any information and documents that support your tax return by law, and keeping any other records that may prove useful in the future is also a good idea. The exact records you need to keep depend on the types of income or gains, tax deductible expenses, personal allowances, and other deductions and reliefs you put on your tax return or claim. Here are a few examples of records to keep in a safe place:

- ✔ **Personal records:** Keep details from banks and building societies about the interest on your account(s). If you receive a state pension, keep any documents you receive from the Benefits Agency. Hold on to any tax credit vouchers relating to dividends received on shares you own.

- ✔ **Employment records:** If you work for someone else, keep information you get from your employer about your pay and tax deducted, benefits in kind, expenses payments, and any share scheme arrangements.

- ✔ **Self-employment records:** Keep records or all income you receive and any expenditure you incur in connection with your business. Flick to Chapter 16 for more on business record-keeping.

Chapter 3

Self Assessing

*M*any people pay their tax without having any direct contact with the taxman, because their employers collect tax on earnings through the Pay as You Earn (PAYE) system and banks deduct tax from their savings. However, other people have to fill out an annual *self-assessment tax return* for HM Revenue & Customs (HMRC). On this form you fill in the details of your income and tax-deductible expenses for the year. You then work out how much tax you owe, if any, based on the figures shown on your self-assessment return.

This chapter helps you keep more of your hard-earned money in your pocket. How? Well, you make fewer mistakes when you understand the tax filing and payment process. Errors can prove to be very costly: Not only can you lose out on tax rebates, benefits, and tax credits, but you may face severe penalties for mistakes and interest on late payments. HMRC operates a strict regime, and you need to comply with the rules.

Knowing Who Does Self Assessment

How do you know whether you need to submit a self-assessment tax return? Well, if any of the following apply to you, expect to receive a self-assessment tax return from HMRC:

- ✔ You're self-employed or a company director.

- ✔ You receive income that has not had UK tax deducted from it, for example gross bank or building society interest or benefits-in-kind (perks, such as company cars) that you receive from your employer.

- ✔ You pay tax at the higher rate on investment income.

- ✔ You receive income from investment property, such as a buy-to-let property or holiday accommodation.

- ✔ You have capital gains above the annual exempt limit.

In many cases HMRC knows whether you need to complete a self-assessment return and it automatically sends one to you. For example, if you have a company car your employer tells HMRC when you first have use of it, and if you receive interest on a savings account without anything taken off for tax (gross interest) the account provider notifies HMRC of the amount they paid you. Having said that, it is your responsibility to notify HMRC by 5 October after the end of each tax year of any new sources of taxable income you received. You risk having to pay a penalty if you don't notify HMRC of changes in your tax status by this date.

If you think you need to complete a self-assessment return for a particular year, but haven't been sent one, contact the HMRC Self Assessment helpline as soon as possible on 0845 900 0444.

Understanding the Process

Under the self-assessment system you're responsible for completing your own tax return and sending it to HMRC. Individuals and trustees are generally required to send HMRC their tax return, together with a self-assessment calculation of their income tax and capital gains tax, by 31 January following the end of the tax year.

HMRC immediately processes the return and makes basic checks to ensure the accuracy of your calculations. Unless you hear otherwise from HMRC, you pay anything you owe based on the figures shown in your self-assessment return – HMRC refers to this system as 'process now, check later'. If you file your return on time and then realise that you made a mistake, you have a year from the filing date to make any amendments. When you make changes to your return, you have to pay interest on any amounts owing, but you don't face anything more serious unless HMRC finds evidence that shows your original return was fraudulent or negligent.

To encourage compliance and honesty, HMRC has a formal system for picking out cases for further examination, so if you're dishonest in completing your tax return, you're likely to be caught. HMRC corrects any obvious errors or mistakes, but for more serious problems it may start an enquiry (see the later section 'Dealing with Enquiries'). HMRC has a year to give notice of its intention to examine and audit your return (although once an enquiry into your tax affairs is under way, HMRC can look back at your records for the previous six years, and even longer in cases of fraud). Thereafter, unless something else comes to HMRC's attention (known as making a *discovery*), the return and the tax liability becomes final and conclusive.

Remembering the Important Dates

The tax year runs from 6 April to 5 April. HMRC realises that most people are paid monthly, and so it works on the basis that 31 March is the end of the tax year for many employees. However, the 5 April year-end date still applies to many investment-related matters such as individual savings accounts or capital gains tax.

Here are some of the key dates in the tax year:

- ✔ **6 April:** The start of a new tax year. Shortly after this date HMRC sends a tax return or Notice to Complete a Tax Return (SA316) to anyone who fits the criteria for self assessment.

- ✔ **31 May:** The deadline for receiving form P60 (which shows your previous year's earnings, tax, and national insurance contributions) from your employer, if you're employed. You need this information to fully complete your tax return.

- ✔ **31 July:** The deadline to note in order to avoid a second automatic penalty of £100 if your tax return for the previous year was due back by 31 January but hasn't been sent in. You may also be charged a second automatic 5 per cent surcharge if you were due to pay tax on 31 January and it has not been paid in full by 31 July. If you're self-employed, your payment on account is due by this date (see the later section 'Paying Your Tax Bill' for details of payment on account).

- ✔ **5 October:** The deadline for notifying HMRC that you had new sources of income such as self-employment earnings during the previous tax year so they can send you a tax return to complete. You risk having to pay a penalty if you don't notify HMRC of changes in your tax status by this date.

✔ **31 October:** The deadline for completing a paper tax return for 2007–8 onwards, if you want HMRC to calculate your tax for you and tell you what to pay by 31 January 2009. You must also send your return by this date if you want HMRC to collect unpaid tax through your PAYE tax code next year rather than paying it in one lump sum on 31 January (such collection can be done only if the amount owing is less than £2,000).

✔ **30 December:** The deadline for sending back your tax return over the Internet if you want HMRC to collect tax through your PAYE tax code when you owe less than £2,000.

✔ **31 January:** The big deadline, by which you need to file your self-assessment return for the previous tax year. You must submit online tax returns and paper tax returns on which you calculated your own tax by this date. If you're self-employed, this date is also the deadline for making the first interim payment of tax and Class 4 national insurance contributions (NICs) against your liability for the current tax year, and the final balancing payment against your liability for the previous tax year (see the later section 'Paying Your Tax Bill' for more details). HMRC may stretch the 31 January filing date by one or two days when the deadline falls on a weekend.

✔ **1 February:** The deadline for sending back your completed tax return if HMRC had sent you a tax return by 31 October.

✔ **28 February:** The date on which you may be charged an automatic 5 per cent surcharge if you were due to pay tax for the previous tax year and haven't paid your bill in full by this date.

✔ **5 April:** The end of the tax year.

Paying Your Tax Bill

If you're employed (working for someone else) you pay tax through the PAYE system. If you have no other sources of income (such as earnings for self-employment, or bank or building society interest) you probably paid the right amount of tax and you can relax and let others sort your tax. But if you're self-employed, or do have other sources of income, chances are you need to complete a self-assessment tax return each year and pay anything you owe to HMRC. In the next sections I look at how and when you pay your tax bill if you're self-employed. I then cover the situation if you're not self-employed.

Paying your tax bill if you're self-employed

The self-assessment tax system works with two formal payments dates a year:

- ✔ **31 January:** On or by this date each year you have to pay anything you owe from the tax year that ended on the previous 5 April, plus half of what you're likely to owe for the current year. This is known as an *interim payment* or a *payment on account*. So, on or before 31 January 2009 you should have paid any outstanding balances for 2007–8 plus half of what you're likely to owe for 2008–9.

- ✔ **31 July:** On or by this date you pay a second interim payment, which is the other half of what you're likely to owe for the current tax year. So for the 2008–9 tax year (6 April 2008 to 5 April 2009), you pay half of what you're likely to owe for that tax year on 31 July 2008.

Commit these dates to memory now. Plan well in advance and make your payments promptly. That way you won't face the prospect of getting a large lump of cash together at the last minute, and you avoid incurring interest and penalty charges.

You won't have to make payments on account in January and July if your previous year's tax and Class 4 national insurance liability was less than £500, or if more than 80 per cent of your tax bill for the previous year was covered by tax deducted at source (for example, if you had any income from employment which was taxed under the PAYE scheme).

The amount of your payments on account is initially based on your total tax bill for the previous year. So, if your total tax bill for 2007–8 was £8,000, HMRC would expect payments on account for 2008–9 of £4,000 from you on 31 July 2008 and 31 January 2009.

If you believe that your tax liability for the next year will be less than your expected payments on account (because for example, there has been a dip in your business turnover, or you have incurred substantial business expenditure which means that your taxable profits for the year will be significantly reduced), you can ask HMRC to reduce your payments on account (see the HMRC self- assessment worksheet SA151c for more information at www. hmrc.gov.uk/worksheets/sa151c.pdf).

Paying your tax bill on other sources of income

The rules for paying your tax bill are slightly different if you're not self-employed but have to complete a self-assessment tax return because you fit one of the criteria set out in the earlier section 'Knowing Who Does Self Assessment'.

In the previous section, I explain that HMRC usually expects self-employed people to make payments on account twice a year. But this rule doesn't apply if you're not self-employed and 80 per cent or more of your income tax bill (not including capital gains tax) is covered by tax deducted at source – PAYE and automatic deductions from banks and building society savings interest are the most common deductions. Instead, you generally pay any income and capital gains tax you owe for the previous year in one lump sum on 31 January following the year to which it relates.

If you think you owe tax for an earlier tax year, make sure that you file your self-assessment tax return before 31 October following the end of that tax year. This is the final date on which HMRC will agree to collect that money through your PAYE code number the following year. If you don't file by this date, you have to pay the tax in one lump sum on 31 January and, if you're late paying, you have to pay interest and possibly even a penalty.

One exception to the 31 January payment deadline exists. If you're employed and you owe less than £2,000 in tax for an earlier year – for example because you first had use of a company car and the taxable amount wasn't included in your PAYE tax code number for that year – HMRC often collects the amount you owe by restricting your PAYE tax code number for the following tax year. (See Chapter 12 for details on PAYE tax codes and how they work.) The advantage of this arrangement is that you pay some of the tax you owe each time you're paid during the following year, and by the end of the next tax year you've paid everything you owe. You won't have to make a lump sum payment on 31 January and you won't have to pay any interest on the money included in your tax code number.

Paying Interest and Penalties

My advice is to commit the earlier section 'Remembering the Important Dates' to memory and get your tax return in on time – because if you miss a deadline, you pay. HMRC charges interest on late interim and balancing payments from the due date of payment to the date you actually pay the tax (and Class 4 NICs if you're self-employed). Hopefully, the following sections are enough to put you off throwing money away on interest and penalties.

Understanding interest

Interest charges result in a larger tax bill, and you can't deduct any interest you pay to HMRC from your profits for tax purposes. You pay interest in the following situations:

- ✔ HMRC has to amend your tax return for any reason.
- ✔ You pay your bill or balancing payment late.

In both cases, HMRC charges interest from the date the tax was due until the date you actually pay it. You can find details of HMRC's current interest rates online at www.hmrc.gov.uk/rates/interest.htm.

In addition, HMRC can charge surcharges, which are in addition to the interest charges and which themselves carry interest:

- ✔ If the tax due is unpaid after 28 days following the due date (normally by 28 February), you pay 5 per cent of the unpaid amount.
- ✔ If the tax is still unpaid after six months following the due date, you pay a further 5 per cent of the tax unpaid.

You can appeal against a surcharge, but you have to do so within 30 days of receiving the surcharge notice.

The good news is that as well as paying interest you can sometimes earn it. If you're due a repayment of tax, HMRC adds interest (known as a *repayment supplement*). The supplement normally runs from the date of payment (or in the case of income tax deducted at source, from 31 January following the relevant tax year) to the date the repayment is sent to you. Tax deducted at source includes PAYE, but only for the current tax year (amounts relating to previous years are excluded). If a penalty or surcharge is repaid, a repayment supplement is also added to that repayment. The repayment supplement is tax free.

Facing penalties

If you send in your tax return late, you're charged an automatic penalty – in addition to any interest surcharge – of £100. If you still haven't sent in your tax return by the next 31 July, you're charged another £100. HMRC can also charge up to £60 per day where the failure continues. If you still haven't sent in your tax return by the next 31 January (that is, a year after the filing date) HMRC can charge you a penalty of up to 100 per cent of the tax that would've been payable had the return been sent in on time. These penalties can be very expensive, so make sure that you get your return in on time.

Dealing with Enquiries

The following sections look at that dreaded occurrence: an HMRC enquiry. If HMRC notifies you that your tax return is under enquiry, don't panic! It doesn't necessarily mean that something is wrong. Further information is sometimes required to ensure that a return is correct. Returns are also selected at random for enquiry to make sure that the system is operating fairly.

Whatever the reason for HMRC's enquiry, being co-operative and open can make all the difference. In calculating the amount of any penalty, HMRC takes into account the extent to which you're help-ful and freely and fully volunteer any information about income or gains that were omitted or understated.

Going through the process

The enquiry may be concerned with one or more particular aspects of a tax return or the whole of it. The enquiry has three possible outcomes:

- ✔ If nothing is wrong, HMRC makes no amendments to the return and you don't pay anything extra.

- ✔ If the enquiry reveals that an innocent mistake was made, HMRC tells you in writing that they've completed their enquiries and amends your self assessment to the correct figures. You aren't liable to a penalty, but HMRC does charge interest on any additional tax that may be due. A surcharge penalty may also be incurred if payment is made late. (See the earlier section 'Paying Interest and Penalties'.)

- ✔ If your enquiry highlights a more serious issue, HMRC charges penalties and interest on the additional tax you owe. The next section 'Negotiating a settlement' explains what happens when HMRC believes that you were negligent or dishonest.

At the end of the enquiry, HMRC issues a *closure notice* notifying you that the investigation is complete. You then have 30 days in which to appeal against the amendments, conclusions, or deci-sions, or to pay any tax due.

Negotiating a settlement

If the enquiry reveals a problem, HMRC decides how much you must now pay. To get the best out of negotiations for your settlement, you need to understand how the process works.

Meeting with HMRC

When HMRC is ready to close its enquiries, and feels that you have outstanding liabilities, the HMRC officer normally asks you and your professional adviser, if you have one, to attend a meeting. HMRC tells you what it finds, the amount of tax it believes is owed, and how far it believes the late payment or underpayment of tax is due to fraudulent or negligent conduct on your part. HMRC listens to any explanations and then advises the maximum amount of penalties it believes is to be charged. Finally, HMRC explains that normally it asks someone in your position to offer to pay one sum for tax, interest, and penalties or surcharges, and it asks you if you're prepared to make such an offer. If you ask, HMRC suggests an amount you must pay.

Calculating your offer

HMRC calculates an offer by adding together the tax, the interest on that tax, any surcharge, and an amount for penalties. The penalty figure is a percentage of the tax underpaid or paid late. The figure can legally be 100 per cent of that amount, but in practice is always less than that in a negotiated settlement.

HMRC starts with a penalty figure of 100 per cent and reduces it by an amount depending on the following:

- ✔ The extent to which you did or didn't disclose all the details of your tax affairs

- ✔ The extent to which you did or didn't co-operate over the whole period of the enquiry

- ✔ The seriousness of the offence

HMRC can reduce the amount of penalty charged as follows:

- ✔ **Full disclosure:** If a full disclosure is made when HMRC first opens the enquiry, you can get up to a 30 per cent reduction in the penalty. If you deny until the last possible moment that anything is wrong, you get little or no reduction for disclosure.

- ✔ **Co-operation:** You can get a reduction of up to 40 per cent depending on how well you co-operate with HMRC during the enquiry. If you supply information quickly, attend interviews, answer questions honestly and accurately, give all the relevant facts, and pay tax on account when it becomes possible to estimate the amount due, you get the maximum reduction for co-operation.

✔ **Severity:** HMRC can reduce the charges by up to 40 per cent depending on the seriousness of the offence. HMRC takes into account what you did, how you did it, how long it went on, and the amounts of money involved: The less serious the offence, the bigger the reduction in the penalty.

So, if you make a full disclosure, are super co-operative, and haven't done anything too serious, the maximum reduction you may receive is 100 per cent (the maths actually adds up to 110 per cent, but clearly HMRC isn't going to be rewarding you for the error!). Evidently, it pays to be honest and helpful.

Responding to HMRC's offer

You have the opportunity to draw HMRC's attention to any matters affecting the penalty figure, to which you think it hasn't given enough weight. HMRC considers the effect of these matters on the figure it has in mind, and comments on any figure you suggest. As a result, HMRC may be able to reach an agreement straight away or after only a few days consideration.

If you agree to make an offer, you have to sign a formal letter offering to pay the agreed sum within a stated period and give or send that letter to HMRC. If HMRC is happy with it, it then issues a letter of acceptance.

The exchange of letters amounts to a legal contract between you and HMRC, and both parties are bound by its terms. If you pay under the terms of the contract, HMRC can't use formal proceedings to recover the tax, interest, surcharge, or penalties. For this reason, HMRC makes sure that the terms of the letter are precise.

When HMRC sends the acceptance letter, it includes a payslip showing the Accounts Office Network Unit to which payment should be sent. When you pay the agreed amount, the matter is at an end.

Where you agree a settlement but can't pay the full amount straight away, you may be able to arrange payment by instalments. HMRC expects as large a down payment as possible, and an agreement to pay the rest, including an amount for extra interest, by instalments over as short a period as possible. HMRC usually suggests payment by direct debit.

Knowing Your Rights

After you sign your tax return to verify it's correct, or submit it online, you have no legal right to ask HMRC to change your mind about something on the return. You do, however, have the right to know the legal basis of any challenge that HMRC makes toward you as an individual.

HMRC's rights

Broadly speaking, HMRC is legally entitled to do the following:

✔ Enquire into any tax return, or any claim or election included in the return (or made outside it), provided it follows the proper procedure within the appropriate time limit.

✔ Ask you, in writing, to produce any documents in your possession or power that it may reasonably require to determine whether your tax return is complete or correct.

✔ Enter premises with a search warrant and search there. A circuit judge (or a sheriff in Scotland, or a county court judge in Northern Ireland) must issue the search warrant and certain other taxpayer safeguards also apply.

HMRC has no power to

✔ Interview you or any other person in connection with your affairs

✔ Enter any premises without a search warrant

HMRC has the right to ask you to provide any documents that they may reasonably require to back up your self-assessment statement. This provision is bolstered by hefty penalties (up to £3,000), which can be charged if you fail to keep certain records for a specified period. Intentionally falsifying or destroying documents that HMRC requests is a criminal offence. Refer to Chapter 2 for more details on keeping records.

Your rights

You have the right of appeal against any formal decision made by HMRC. You normally have 30 days to make an appeal but HMRC may accept late appeals in certain circumstances. When HMRC doesn't settle the appeal, it is listed for hearing by the Appeal

Commissioners (an independent tribunal that hears appeal against decisions made by HMRC). Decisions of the commissioners on matters of fact are normally binding on both parties. If one party is dissatisfied, an appeal on a point of law may be made to the High Court, and then to the Court of Appeal, and finally, if leave is granted, to the House of Lords.

Appeals can be very costly and although representation before the commissioners isn't necessary, I advise that you don't appear without professional representation and a great deal of preparation.

 If you feel aggrieved with the service you receive from your tax office, you have the right to tell HMRC. Chapter 19 explains how to lodge a complaint.

Finding Help

If self assessment has you tearing out your hair in clumps, here are a few options for getting help:

- ✔ **Call HMRC:** The general advice helpline (0845 9000 444) is open during evenings and weekends, and you can also flick to the Appendix in this book for a list of specialised HMRC helplines.

- ✔ **Read up on self assessment:** HMRC provides help sheets for your self-assessment tax return and a tax calculation guide. Call the HMRC Orderline on 0845 9000 404 or go to www. hmrc.gov.uk.

- ✔ **Visit your local HMRC Enquiry Centre:** HMRC enquiry centres are open every week day. You can just drop in or make an appointment. For details of your nearest enquiry centre see http://www.hmrc.gov.uk/enq/index.htm.

- ✔ **Seek help from an accountant/tax practitioner:** Although you have to pay for this type of help, it can save you money and a lot of headaches in the longer term. Flick to Chapter 15 for more information on finding professional advice.

Chapter 4

Working Out How Much Income Tax Is Due

· ·

In This Chapter

▶ Adding up all your income

▶ Factoring in allowances

▶ Understanding tax rates and bands

▶ Working out your income tax bill

· ·

*I*f you live in the UK, HM Revenue & Customs (HMRC) generally charges income tax on your worldwide income (flick back to Chapter 2 to see how where you live can affect your tax liability). Therefore, if you fit the criteria for self assessment (refer to Chapter 3 to see if you do) you need to file a tax return each year telling HMRC how much tax you owe.

You can take the easy road and let HMRC calculate your tax for you. If you file your tax return online or you send your paper return in by 31 October, HMRC does your sums. However, if you file your paper later (by the 31 January deadline), HMRC expects you to do the maths.

Even if you do let the taxman tally up the figures, knowing how to calculate your own income tax is important. If you haven't a clue how much tax you pay, how can you budget for your tax bill or check what HMRC tells you to pay is in fact correct? But if numbers bring you out in a cold sweat, relax – this chapter explains how you work out your income tax liability, step by step.

This chapter explains how to calculate how much income tax you owe, but you also pay national insurance contributions (NICs). Chapter 12 deals with paying NICs when you're employed, and Chapter 15 explains NICs for those who work for themselves.

Going through the Calculation Steps

The tax year runs from 6 April to 5 April in the following year, so the tax year 2008–9 runs from 6 April 2008 to 5 April 2009. To work out your tax liability for a particular tax year, you need to follow these steps:

1. **Add together the amounts under the various categories of income.**

2. **Deduct certain allowable deductions and personal allowances.**

3. **Apply the tax rates in force for the tax year.**

4. **Reduce the tax calculated by certain other deductions and allowances (if available).**

This section guides you through each of the steps you take to calculate your income tax bill.

 HMRC produces a helpful Comprehensive Tax Calculation Guide (SA151), which you can download from the Web site at www. hmrc.gov.uk/worksheets/sa151c.pdf. You can also use their Tax Calculation Worksheet to help you get the rates and rate bands right (see www.hmrc.gov.uk/worksheets/sa151w.pdf).

Adding up your income

To start off your calculation, you need to add up all the earnings and other income you received during the tax year. Other income may include interest that you receive from banks and building societies, dividends from shares, or any earnings you receive from a spare-time or casual job.

The following types of income are exempt from income tax and you don't need to take them into account when adding up your income:

- ✔ Benefits payable under some sickness and unemployment insurance policies.

- ✔ Casual winnings from competitions and betting.

- ✔ Certain social security benefits (see the Appendix for a list of non-taxable state benefits).

✔ Certain types of pension (for example, to war widows, wound and disability pensions to members of the armed forces, and pensions awarded to employees disabled at work).

✔ Compensation for losing your job (up to £30,000) and statutory redundancy payments (see Chapter 12 for more detail).

✔ Damages and compensation for personal injury (including annuities or periodical payments received as damages).

✔ Housing grants.

✔ Income from certain investments (Chapter 6 explains which investments are exempt).

✔ Interest on damages for personal injuries.

✔ Interest on repayments of tax made by HMRC.

✔ Premium bond prizes.

✔ Scholarship income.

Deducting allowances

After you calculate your total income, you can make certain deductions, which reduce your overall tax bill. The most common deductions are for any losses you have made in your business (Chapter 16 explains how you can claim relief for losses) and contributions you make to pension policies (Chapter 9 covers pension payments in more detail).

After you have subtracted these deductions from your total income, you can then deduct personal income tax allowances that apply to you for the tax year. The amount of personal allowances you can deduct mainly depends on your age. So, if you're under 65 you're able to take off £5,435 (for 2008–9). If you're over 65, but less than 74, you can take off £9,030.

If you or your spouse was born before 6 April 1935, you may also be entitled to married couple's allowance. However, unlike the basic personal allowance, the married couple's allowance isn't given as a deduction from your total income, but instead is given as a reduction against your final tax bill (see the section 'Making final reductions' further on in this chapter).

Table 4-1 shows the annual income tax allowances for the current tax year and last year.

Table 4-1	Income Tax Allowances for 2007–8 and 2008–9	
Income Tax Allowances	*2007–8*	*2008–9*
Personal allowance	£5,225	£5,435
Personal allowance (aged 65–74)	£7,550	£9,030
Personal allowance (aged 75 and over)	£7,690	£9,180
Married couple's allowance (born before 6th April 1935 but aged under 75)	£6,285	£6,535
Married couple's allowance (aged 75 and over)	£6,365	£6,625
Income limit for age-related allowances	£20,900	£21,800
Blind person's allowance	£1,730	£1,800

Applying the tax rates and bands

After you add up your total income and deduct your allowances, you're left with your total taxable income. The next step is to work out how much tax you owe.

Understanding the different tax rates and bands

Each year the government sets the annual *tax rates* (how much tax you pay, expressed as a percentage rate) and the *tax bands* (the income levels at which the different tax rates apply). The tax system is progressive, which means that tax rates increase as income increases. If your income exceeds a certain limit, known as the *basic rate tax band*, you have to pay tax at a higher rate.

For 2008–9, the tax rates and bands for income tax are as follows:

- ✓ **Starting rate:** The starting rate of tax is 10 per cent and this applies to the first £2,320 of savings income only for 2008–9 onwards.

- ✓ **Basic rate:** You pay the basic rate of income tax on income up to the basic tax rate band of £36,000. The basic rate is set at 20 per cent for 2008–9 onwards.

- ✓ **Higher rate:** You pay the higher rate on any income over the basic rate tax band. The higher rate is set at 40 per cent. So, if your taxable income is £40,000, you pay income tax at 20 per cent on the first £36,000 and at 40 per cent on the remaining £4,000.

Special rates of income tax also apply to dividends. When a UK company that you hold shares in pays a dividend, you're treated as receiving the dividend *net* (after tax) of a 10 per cent tax credit. So, if the dividend you receive is £90, you're treated as having received a net dividend of £90 plus a tax credit of £10. Your *gross* (before tax) income, which is the amount you declare to HMRC, is therefore £100. If you're a basic rate taxpayer, you don't have to pay any further tax at the end of the tax year, even though the basic rate of tax is actually 20 per cent. However, if you're a higher rate taxpayer, the tax rate due on dividends is 32.5 per cent, so you may have to pay an additional amount to HMRC.

Considering savings and dividends

To ensure that certain classes of income don't escape the charge to tax at the higher rates for higher rate taxpayers, the rules provide for these classes of income to be treated as the 'top slice' of income as follows:

✔ Savings income is treated as the top slice of taxable income.

✔ Dividend income (payments you receive on any shares you hold in companies) is treated as the top slice of savings income.

HMRC treats savings and dividends as follows:

✔ If you have savings income but no dividend income, the savings income is treated as the highest part of your total income.

✔ If you have dividend income but no savings income, the dividend income is treated as the highest part of your total income.

✔ If you have both savings income and dividend income:

• The savings income and dividend income are together treated as the highest part of your total income.

• The dividend income is treated as the higher part of that total.

Of course, being tax, things aren't that simple and one or two exceptions apply to this rule. If you receive certain gains from a life insurance policy, or a taxable lump sum on termination of an employment, the income from these sources is generally treated as the highest part of your taxable income, with life insurance gains right at the top.

However, capital gains in excess of the exemption limit (£9,600 for 2008–9) are treated as the very highest part of taxable income and gains. Chapter 6 looks at tax payable on capital gains in more detail.

Making final reductions

After you work out your tax bill, you may be able to reduce it even further if you qualify for the married couples allowance or have paid tax abroad.

You also need to make sure that you give yourself credit against your final bill for any tax that you have already paid during the year, such as tax you paid through the PAYE system, tax deducted from bank and building society interest, or tax credits attaching to dividends.

Married couples allowances

If you fit the criteria for the married couple's allowance, you can subtract 10 per cent of the allowance from your final tax bill. Therefore, if you're entitled to married couple's allowance for 2008–9, you can deduct £653 from your tax bill if you (or your spouse) was born before 6 April 1935 but is under 75, and £662 if aged 75 or over.

Doubling up on tax

Someone who lives and works in the UK (referred to as a UK resident for tax purposes – refer to Chapter 2 for more on what constitutes a UK resident) is normally subject to UK tax on any foreign income she receives. Non-UK resident people generally only have to pay UK tax on income they receive from a UK source. Every country has its own set of tax rules and, depending on where the individual lives and where the money is earned, income can fall to be taxable under both UK and foreign tax law. Therefore, to prevent a UK resident person being taxed twice on the same money, you can often deduct any foreign tax paid from your UK tax bill.

If income arises in a country with which the UK has a *double taxation agreement* (broadly, an agreement between two countries that allows a credit for tax paid in one country to be offset against tax owing in another country), that income may be completely exempt from UK tax and you can ignore it when working out your self-assessment tax bill. If, however, you receive income from a country that doesn't have a double taxation agreement with the UK and you have paid foreign tax on that income, you can reduce your final tax bill by the amount of foreign tax you have paid. But you can only use foreign tax paid to reduce your UK liability down to zero – you can't use the foreign tax credit to produce a UK tax repayment.

The tax rules relating to overseas income are complex and a multitude of anti-avoidance legislation exists just to ensure that nothing escapes the tax net. If you have foreign income, think about engaging a tax practitioner who specialises in overseas matters to help make sure that you only pay what is due. Chapters 19 covers finding professional advice.

Doing the Maths

The law governing tax rates and allowances is complicated and often confusing, particularly in deciding where to add income in and where to take allowances and deductions off. The following example helps you to understand the steps set out in the previous sections so that you can apply them to your own self-assessment tax calculation.

Simone runs her own business called Motorcycle Mechanics. In the financial year 2007–8, Motorcycle Mechanics makes a loss of £5,468. Simone is also a partner in a separate partnership business, Motorcycles R Us, and for 2007–8, her share of the partnership's profit is £34,775.

Simone's income and payments for 2007–8 are as follows:	£
Loss from Motorcycle Mechanics	(5,468)
Income from Motorcycles R Us	34,775
Building society interest (after income tax deducted)	2,000
Dividends from UK companies (net of tax credit)	6,750
Interest on company loan stock (after tax deducted)	1,200
Interest paid on business bank loan	1,000

To work out her 2007–8 income tax liability, Simone first needs to know how much income she has left after deductions are made. She works this amount out as follows:

	£ **Income**
Trading profit	34,775
Net interest received (£2,000 + £1,200 = £3,200)	
+ tax deducted at 20% (Net interest received × (tax deduction interest rate ÷ (100 − tax deduction interest rate)))	

So:

(£3,200 × (20 ÷ (100 − 20)) = £800)	4,000

Net UK dividends (£6,750)

> \+ tax credit at 10% (Net dividends received × (tax deduction interest rate ÷ (100 − tax deduction interest rate)))

So:

(£6,750 × (10 ÷ (100 − 10)) = £750)	7,500
Total income	**46,275**
Deductions	
Loss relief	5,468
Interest paid on business loan	1,000
Total deductions	**6,468**
Total income minus total deductions	**39,807**

Simone is entitled to an income tax allowance. Before she works out her tax liability, she needs to deduct her allowance from her earnings. This calculation tells her the amount on which she's taxed. Here's how she does the calculation:

Total income minus total deductions − personal allowance = taxable income

So:

£39,807 − £5,225 = **£34,582**

Next, Simone needs to work out the tax payable on her income from non-savings, savings, and dividend sources. She consults the section 'Applying the tax rates and bands', earlier in this chapter, for the different rates of income tax, and approaches the calculations as follows:

Non-savings income

Tax payable at 10% on first £2,230 of income	£223.00

Tax payable at 22% on remaining income up to £32,370

(Trading profit − loss relief − personal allowance − first £2,230 of income)

£34,775 − £5,468 − £5,225 − £2,230 = £21,852

So, tax payable at 22% on remaining income of £21,852	£4,807.44

Savings income

Tax payable at 20% on remaining income up
to £32,370

> (Building society interest + interest on
> company loan stock + tax deducted on
> interest received = savings income)
>
> £2,000 + £1,200 + £800 = £4,000

So, tax payable at 20% on remaining
income of £4,000   £800.00

Dividend income

Tax payable at 10% on remaining income up
to £32,370

> (UK dividends + tax credit on
> dividends = dividend income)
>
> £6,750 + £750 = £7,500

So, tax payable at 10% on remaining
income of £7,500   £750.00

Taxable amount   **£6,580.44**

Simone now knows how much tax is payable on each of her income
streams. To get a final amount, she must remember to take out the
tax credits and tax deducted at source (in other words, the part of
this tax due on her income that has already been paid for her or is
treated as having been paid for her by the provider, or source, of
the income), as follows:

> (Interest tax credit + dividend tax credit = amount to be
> deducted)
>
> £800 + £750 = £1550

So, the final sum Simone needs to perform to work out her 2007–8
tax liability is:

> (Taxable amount – amount to be deducted = tax liability)
>
> £6,580.44 – £1,550.00 = **£5,030.44**

The tax calculation for the 2008–9 tax year will be more straightforward. Simone won't need to differentiate between savings and non-
savings income because the tax rate on both types of income is 20
per cent for basic-rate taxpayers. She will need to add up her income,
just like in 2007–8, and take off her personal allowances. Tax due on
her dividend income will still be at the 10 per cent rate but everything
else will be taxed at 20 per cent. This is as long as her total taxable income doesn't go over the basic rate tax threshold of £36,000, at which
point she would start paying tax at the higher rate of 40 per cent.

Part II
Tax through Your Ages

'I'm beginning to think that passing on
our house to the children to save tax
was a big mistake.'

In this part . . .

*A*s you travel along the path of life you have to make certain financial decisions that have a major impact on your tax bill. In this part, I deal with the tax aspects of your personal life, and show you how to make sensible choices that help you keep money in your pocket.

I look at tax-efficient savings and investments, and examine income from property investments — and that includes renting out your spare room to top up your bank balance. I also guide you through supporting children — from giving them money to claiming government support. Finally, I show you how to set your house in order before you go to that giant tax haven in the sky, in order to minimise inheritance tax issues.

Chapter 5

Supporting Children

Children are expensive creatures. You buy them another new pair of shoes and they grow out of them sooner than you can say 'And try not to scuff this pair. . .'. Their pocket money demands rise at ten times the rate of inflation, and their ever-increasing appetite threatens to eat you out of house and home. Thankfully, the government provides a range of financial support for parents and guardians, and this chapter helps you determine what help you can claim. I also guide you through the nitty-gritty of giving money to children – whether that's £10 pocket money or a £10,000 gift for when they come of age.

Getting Money from the Government

Plenty of state help is available for people with children. Support such as Child Tax Credit and Working Tax Credit are means tested, and other help, such as Child Benefit and Child Trust Funds, is available to everyone. In addition, a special relief is available to provide for foster children.

Chapter 11 has full details on the tax implications of receiving state benefits.

Claiming Child Tax Credit

Despite its name, Child Tax Credit (CTC) has little, if anything, to do with tax. In fact, CTC is a social security benefit that is paid to parents and guardians of children under 16 whose income is low enough to qualify. CTC is paid regularly, usually into the claimant's bank account, and isn't deducted from your tax bill – in fact you can get it even if you don't work or pay tax.

Understanding who's eligible

Children are eligible up to 1 September following their 16th birthday. The credit remains payable after that date for those in full-time education (excluding further education) up to the age of 19, and for up to eight weeks following the death of a child.

The usual test to be applied is that the child is living with the claimant(s). Where competing claims exist, the test is who has the main responsibility for the child. It's usual for a joint election to be made over main responsibility but, in the absence of such an election, HM Revenue & Customs (HMRC) decides on the information available.

Applying for a tax credit is always worthwhile. Many people who qualify don't get anything just because they don't bother to apply. Only parents whose joint incomes add up to £58,175 or more a year (£66,350 when a child aged under 1 year is in the household) have their applications turned down.

Making a claim

To claim CTC, contact the Tax Credits helpline (0845 300 3900) and ask for a claim pack. You can also apply online at www.hmrc.gov. uk/taxcredits.

HMRC assesses your claim by looking at your *gross income* (income before tax and national insurance contributions (NICs)). The claim pack comes with good guidance notes that show you what figures to include. You work out your gross income for tax credit by following four steps:

1. **Add up any money you receive from pensions, savings and investments, property, and abroad, and any *notional income* (this is income you may be treated as having even if you don't actually have it, such as money you've given away in order to increase your entitlement to tax credits).**

If the total is £300 or less, ignore it. If the total is more than £300, subtract £300 from the total.

2. Next, add up your earnings from your employment, state benefits income, and any other miscellaneous income that you haven't already included.

3. Add together the totals of Step 1 and Step 2.

4. If you're self-employed, add in your trading income to the total in Step 3, or if you made a loss, take off the amount of your trading loss for the year from the total in Step 3. Finally, deduct any payments you made to a pension and any payments you made to charity under the gift aid scheme, payroll giving scheme, or give-as-you-earn scheme.

Calculating how much you may get

In general, four elements make up CTC:

- **Child element:** Payable for each child in the family.

- **Disabled child element:** Paid where disability living allowance is payable or the child is registered blind.

- **Severely disabled child element:** Payable to families caring for a child with severe disability, where the highest rate of the care component of disability living allowance is payable.

- **Family element:** The basic element, paid to all eligible families. A higher family element is available for the year following the birth of a child.

Table 5-1 lays out the rates for each element for 2008–9.

Table 5-1   Child Tax Credit Rates for 2008–9

Child Tax Credit	2008–9 Annual Rates (£)
Family element	545
Family element, baby addition	545
Child element	2,085
Disabled child element	2,540
Severely disabled child element	1,020

Most parents receive £545 a year tax-free no matter how many children they have. Parents with a child under 12 months old are usually entitled to a larger amount.

Claiming every penny you can

Here are a few tips to help you claim the full amount of CTC that you're due:

✔ Send in a new claim to CTC for your newborn baby as soon as possible (if you qualify). Children under 12 months old qualify for higher payments. Claims can generally only be backdated for a maximum of three months.

✔ Make sure that you claim for older children who are still in full-time education.

The amount of CTC paid to you depends on your individual circumstances. If your circumstances change, your entitlement to CTC may also change and you may receive too little or too much money. If you receive too much, HMRC eventually asks for the money back. Make sure that you let HMRC know every time something happens that you think may affect the amount of CTC you receive.

Receiving childcare support through Working Tax Credit

Working Tax Credit (WTC) is paid to people on low incomes who satisfy certain age requirements and who work more than a certain number of hours a week. It also has a childcare element, which allows you to claim help with costs of registered or approved childcare. (HMRC leaflet 'WTC5: Help with the costs of childcare' sets out what qualifies as childcare. You can download this leaflet from the HMRC Web site at www.hmrc.gov.uk/leaflets/wtc5.pdf.)

You can generally claim the childcare element for any child up to the Saturday following 1 September after the child's 15th birthday, and the claim can be extended for one year in certain circumstances (see HMRC leaflet WTC5).

Calculating how much you may get

The amount of WTC you're entitled to will depend on your income and your circumstances – whether you're in a relationship or single, a lone parent, disabled, and so forth.

Table 5-2 lays out the rates for each element for 2008–9.

Table 5-2   Working Tax Credit Rates for 2008–9

Working Tax Credit	2008–9 Annual Rates (£)
Basic element	1,800
Couple and lone-parent element	1,770
30-hour element	735
Disabled-worker element	2,405
Severe disability element	1,020
50+ return-to-work payment (16–29 hours)	1,235
50+ return-to-work payment (30+ hours)	1,840

Table 5-3 lays out the rates for the childcare element of WTC for 2008–9.

Table 5-3   Childcare Element of Working Tax Credit Rates for 2008–9

Rates and Thresholds	2008–9 Rates (£)
Maximum eligible cost for one child	175 per week
Maximum eligible cost for two or more children	300 per week
Percentage of eligible costs	80%

To claim the childcare element you must first be eligible for WTC, and you must also fit the following criteria:

- ✔ If you're a lone parent, you must be aged 16 or over and you must work at least 16 hours a week to claim.

- ✔ If you're in a couple, you must both be aged 16 or over and both must work at least 16 hours a week, or one partner must work at least 16 hours a week and the other partner must be incapacitated, or an in-patient in hospital, or in prison (whether serving a custodial sentence or remanded in custody awaiting trial or sentence).

The childcare element can help with 80 per cent of your eligible childcare costs (which are those that you pay to a registered or approved childcare provider) up to a maximum of £175 a week if you pay childcare for one child and £300 a week if you pay child-care for two or more children. Therefore, you can get up to £140 per week (80 per cent of £175) for one child and £240 per week for two of more children.

If you employ an approved home childcare provider, such as a childminder or nanny, HMRC allows you to claim for up to 80 per cent of the gross costs of employing that person within the £175 or £300 a week limits. The costs include:

- ✔ Employer's NICs

- ✔ Costs of benefits in kind (for taxable perks; see Chapter 13)

- ✔ Any other costs associated with employing that person, such as insurance

 If you receive childcare vouchers from your employer to cover some of the costs of your childcare, you can't claim for the amount covered by the voucher (even if you make a *salary sacrifice*, which means that you receive the vouchers in return for a reduction in the amount of cash pay you receive). As a result, childcare vouchers may affect your entitlement to both the childcare element of Working Tax Credit and Child Tax Credit. HMRC has devised a help-ful calculator to help you decide whether you would be better off with tax credits or childcare vouchers. You can access the calcula-tor online at www.hmrc.gov.uk/calcs/ccin.htm.

Benefiting from child benefit

Child benefit is a tax-free monthly payment that anyone bringing up a child or young person receives. The benefit isn't affected by income or savings and so most people who are bringing up a child or young person qualify. Child benefit is paid tax-free to parents no matter what their own tax rate and it doesn't have to be declared on any self-assessment tax forms. From April 2008, the weekly rate payable is £18.80 for the eldest child and £12.55 for other children.

Child benefit is paid until the September after the child's 16th birthday but extended up to 1 September after the child's 18th birthday if he's still in full-time education. You receive child benefit for a whole extra year for a child born on 1 September than one born the day before on 31 August – so plan ahead!

If you're entitled to child benefit for a child or young person who's not your own, you may also be entitled to guardian's allowance for them if both of his parents have died or, in some circumstances, where only one parent has died. From April 2008, guardian's allowance is payable at the weekly rate of £13.45. Find out more about guardian's allowance, including information on how to claim, on the Directgov Web site (www.direct.gov.uk).

Making the most of Child Trust Funds

The Child Trust Fund (CTF) is a new long-term savings and investment account for children. Newborn babies receive money from the government, which goes into the CTF account chosen by the parents. Parents (and other relatives and friends) can add money to the account up to certain level each year, but can't withdraw any money themselves because the account belongs to the child. When the child turns 18 he can access the account, and is free to spend or invest the money further.

CTFs are tax-free, provided the person entitled to the fund is a UK resident at the time the fund is paid out. This makes CTFs a particularly attractive and tax-efficient way of saving for parents and carers wondering how they are ever going to be able to afford seemingly ever-increasing educational fees. Read on to find out more.

Understanding the basics

The following rules apply to CTFs:

- ✔ **Eligibility:** CTFs apply to children born on or after 1 September 2002. Before parents or carers can receive the CTF voucher, they must first claim and be awarded child benefit (see the section 'Benefiting from child benefit' for details). New parents should therefore ensure that they register as early as possible for child benefit in order to receive the CTF voucher promptly.

- ✔ **Government contributions:** Every eligible child receives an initial voucher worth at least £250. Children from low-income families receive an additional £250 paid directly into their accounts, making £500 in total. Further payments of £250 (or £500 for those in low-income families) are made when the child reaches the age of 7.

✔ **Additional contributions:** You can pay up to £1,200 a year into a CTF account. Both friends and family can contribute money. All payments are a gift to the child and can't be reclaimed.

✔ **Paying out:** The money can only be paid out to the child and is locked in until he's 18. On that date, the account stops being a CTF account. The young adult then has full access to the money in the account and can use it how he thinks best.

Consider carefully the best ways to use the money and even seek advice on the best ways to invest, if the child chooses to do so.

Deciding on a CTF account

Parents choose between two main types of CTF account:

✔ **Non-stakeholder:** A savings account that doesn't invest your child's money in shares. The money invested will be secure and will be returned on maturity along with interest earned. Although the money invested will earn interest, it may not grow as much as if it was invested in shares. The effect of inflation means that money in the account can actually lose value over the long term too.

The account provider will make a charge for running the account, although you won't notice this charge as it won't appear on statements – providers cover their costs when deciding how much interest to pay on savings.

✔ **Stakeholder:** Invests your child's money in shares in companies but strict rules mean that the risks associated with investments in shares are reduced. This type of account is the government's preferred way of saving because it offers a lower-risk savings plan.

A stakeholder account must meet certain requirements. Although the account provider invests in shares and securities, the government lays down strict rules to minimise the risks of losing money. For example, the money must be invested in a range of companies, in case one company performs badly, and when the child reaches 13 money in the account starts to move to lower-risk investments or assets, such as cash. The provider looks at how well shares are performing and decides how much to move over into safer investments and how quickly. This means that although your child's money may not benefit if the stock market performs well, the money is protected from stock market losses as the child approaches their 18th birthday.

> The provider's charge for running a stakeholder account is limited to no more than 1.5 per cent a year. This means that the charge can be no more than £1.50 for every £100 in the account.

Table 5-4 summarises the key differences between the stakeholder and non-stakeholder accounts.

Table 5-4	Comparing Stakeholder and Non-Stakeholder Accounts	
Stakeholder	*Non-Stakeholder*
Must make some investments in shares	Need not invest in shares
Some investments are prohibited	Almost unrestricted investment choice
Maximum provider charge is 1.5% of the account's value per year	No maximum provider charge
Minimum contribution can't exceed £10	Minimum contribution may be more or less than £10
The account must provide a lifestyling facility	Lifestyling is not compulsory

You can check how your child's money is invested. The government accepts that some people have strong views as to how their money is invested; for example, they may not agree with investments in companies that are involved in arms, tobacco, or alcohol, or they may prefer to invest in companies that sell goods according to the rules of fair trade or that work to protect the environment. Therefore, all CTF providers are required to publicise their policy about social, ethical, and environmental investments, if they have one.

Keeping track of a CTF account on behalf of a child is important. The registered contact, that is, the person who opens a CTF account for a child, is responsible for managing the account for the child, for example, keeping account statements safe, letting the relevant people know of any change of address, and changing the account or provider, depending on the child's best interests. The registered contact, and the child when he turns 16, can change account or CTF provider at any time.

Collecting fostering care relief

People who provide foster care to children and young people may qualify for *foster care relief*, which can save income tax. This relief applies to foster carers who work with local authorities (Health and Social Services (HSS) Trusts in Northern Ireland) or independent fostering providers, and doesn't apply to private fostering arrangements.

HMRC usually treats foster carers as being self-employed, which means that you fill in a self-assessment tax return (see Chapter 3) to tell HMRC how much tax you owe. To get the figures right on your tax return, you need to understand how the relief works:

✔ Below a certain limit (called the *qualifying amount*), the income you receive for foster caring (from the local authority or independent provider) is exempt from income tax.

✔ If your income from foster care exceeds the qualifying amount, you must pay income tax. You can pay this tax in one of two ways:

 • **The profit method:** You work out your 'profits' from providing foster care by totalling all your income from fostering and then deducting all allowable expenses.

 • **The simplified method:** You pay tax on any money you make that's over the qualifying amount (but this means you can't deduct expenses).

The qualifying amount is made up of two elements:

✔ A fixed amount per residence of £10,000 for a full year.

✔ An additional amount per child for each week, or part-week, that the individual provides foster care. The amounts are £200 a week for a child aged under 11 and £250 a week for a child aged 11 or older.

Giving Money to Children

As a parent or guardian you can, of course, give your children as much money as you want. However, rules do exist that prevent parents and guardians handing over large sums of money to their children in an attempt to dodge paying tax on it themselves. You can't simply switch money from your own savings account to one opened in your child's name to avoid paying tax on the interest.

Giving to under-18s

If your child is under 18 and you give him money, according to HMRC that money still belongs to you, not your child. That means HMRC taxes you on the interest the money in your child's bank account earns. But you can benefit from a small exemption to this rule: You don't pay tax if the annual interest on all the savings accounts is not more than £100 per parent, per child, per tax year. Child Trust Funds are ignored for this purpose. And, it doesn't matter whether your children are your own or adopted, or whether you live with them – the exemption still applies.

As long as the £100 limit isn't exceeded, HMRC treats any interest earned on the gift as belonging to the child. Therefore, when the child's total income for the year is less than the annual personal tax-free allowance (£5,435 for 2008–9) a parent or guardian can reclaim any tax deducted from the child's savings by the bank or building society by completing HMRC form R85 (see Chapter 6 for more details).

The £100 exemption is a concession, not a tax relief, which means that once the £100 limit is exceeded, even by one penny, the entire sum is taxed as though it belonged to the parent or guardian. The only exception to this rule is if a 16 or 17 year old gets married – rather a drastic measure to avoid paying tax!

Paying out to over-18s

You can give youngsters aged 18 and over as much as you like without income tax worries because, unlike under 18s, they count as legal adults in their own right and are legally responsible for their own tax affairs. However, once the money is given, you can't ask for it back – the money has to be really given away and not just parked in your child's bank account to dodge tax.

Setting up a trust

You may want to put a gift aside for your child and control his access to the gift. For example, rather than give Callum a gift of £10,000 at the age of 8 (and then watch as he clears out an entire toy shop), you probably prefer him to receive the gift when he's older and wiser and can put the money to good use – perhaps to get on the property ladder or to go to university. Therefore, you put the £10,000 in a *trust*, a legal devise that holds property and investments for someone else (the *beneficiary*), without giving them actual control.

Get legal advice if you're considering setting up a trust to make sure the effect of the trust is actually what you wanted it to be. Any reputable solicitor should be able to help.

Going through the basics

For tax purposes, a gift into a trust has to be irrevocable. You can't give property or money away to a child with conditions attached, which mean that it can be returned to you some time in the future.

Parents and grandparents often use trusts to pass money down the generations. Most trusts are set up through wills or by making lifetime gifts (head over to Chapter 8 for more details).

You can differentiate between items held in a trust, such as shares or property, and the income that they produce. Therefore, you can leave the income from the trust to one person (trustee A) and the *capital assets* (the shares, property, and such like that you originally put into the trust) to another person (trustee B) when the first person (trustee A) dies. This arrangement may help in situations where you want to provide an income for your child or grandchild but you don't want to give the child control over the capital assets that produce that income.

Setting up a trust can help beneficiaries use their personal tax allowances. However, HMRC checks to ensure that the arrangement is a genuine one and that the trust hasn't just been set up to profit from lower tax rates while the former owner of the assets secretly continues to enjoy them.

Understanding trust terms

If you're thinking of setting up a trust, a broad understanding of the ins and outs of trust vocabulary helps you to communicate with solicitors, accountants, and financial advisers. Here are a few of the main terms:

- **Beneficiary:** The person who benefits from the trust. Beneficiaries are personally liable for tax on income they receive from trusts, but not for tax on the income the trust itself owes – the trust has to account for and pay that.

- **Settlor or donor:** The person who puts the assets into the trust to create it. In Scotland, this person is called a *trustor* or *grantor*.

- **Trustee:** The person responsible for the administration of the trust. The trustees have to file tax returns and are responsible for paying any tax the trust owes. The usual arrangement is to have between two and five trustees. When you set up a trust, you choose the trustees or use a specialist trustee firm. Trustees are allowed to charge for their services and their fees need to be taken into consideration against any potential tax savings.

Examining types of trusts

Different types of trusts have different types of benefits. Here are the main ones:

- ✔ **Bare trust:** In this type of trust the beneficiary is absolutely entitled to the trust property (money, a house, a painting, and so on) and income at any time. The beneficiary decides how much income he receives, and can claim the trust property whenever he wants. In these circumstances the trustee's powers are purely administrative.

  A very basic form of bare trust is a bank account opened by an adult for a child where the adult operates the account until the child is 18. The child can enjoy the tax benefits through-out childhood, including the ability to reclaim tax deducted on the interest paid into the account.

- ✔ **Interest in possession trust:** If you're the beneficiary of this type of trust, you have the right to the trust's income for life. You're a *life tenant*. That means the trustees pass all the trust's income, after deducting their expenses and tax, straight to you. Usually, you don't have rights over the trust's property and at a certain point in the future, such as when you die, the property passes to another person.

- ✔ **Discretionary trust:** In this type of trust, the trustees have the power (the discretion) to decide how and when the benefici-aries are to benefit, for example when they receive any money and how much.

Special rules exist for gifts held in trust for 'vulnerable beneficiar-ies', which the law takes to mean someone classed as disabled and receiving a disability living allowance or attendance allowances, or incapable of managing their affairs or administering their property under the Mental Health Act 1983. Under the legislation certain trusts with vulnerable beneficiaries pay no more tax on the income that accrues for the benefit of vulnerable beneficiaries than the beneficiary would pay if the income had arisen directly in their own hands.

Chapter 6

Making Tax-Efficient Investments

*V*arious categories of savings and investments exist that are classed as 'tax efficient' or have tax exemptions attached to them. This chapter takes you through both tax-free and tax-efficient investment options. I also look at how charitable donations can give you a tax break, and explain what tax you may have to pay on your investments (and how to ensure that you minimise your tax bill).

Whenever you consider any tax-efficient investment, always weigh up possible future changes to the tax system. Keep an eye on current trends and consider seeking independent financial advice before making investments.

Receiving Tax-Free Income from Investments

The following investments are exempt from tax:

✔ Income from Individual Savings Accounts (ISAs)

✔ Income from personal equity plans (PEPs) (including interest paid on cash held unless more than £80 of interest is withdrawn)

✔ Accumulated interest on National Savings (including index-linked) Certificates

✔ Interest and terminal bonuses under Save As You Earn (SAYE) schemes (see Chapter 14 for more on this type of scheme).

✔ Interest awarded as part of an award of damages for personal injury or death

✔ Dividends on ordinary shares in a Venture Capital Trust

For some other types of investments, the income is taxable but usually paid *gross* (that is, with no tax taken off). Examples include National Savings Bank interest, and interest on Government Stocks.

If you hold savings or investments in joint names, you're liable to tax only on your share of the income. Income from savings or investments held jointly by husband and wife or civil partners is usually split equally, but you can make an election for the income to be split on an unequal basis if you want, in order to reduce your household's tax bill. An election can't be backdated and doesn't apply to life insurance policies, life annuities, or capital redemption policies (a regular premium policy that provides a lump sum benefit when it matures).

Investing Tax-Efficiently

What qualifies as a tax-efficient investment depends on the circumstances of a particular individual. An exemption from capital gains tax (CGT) is of no benefit to an individual who can confidently expect to have the full annual exempt amount available each year. Similarly, tax relief is not important to non-taxpayers. This section takes you through the basics of tax-efficient investing, so you can determine which options can help you maximise your money.

Looking at popular investments

The following sections explore a few of the more popular vehicles that offer various tax breaks.

Individual Savings Accounts (ISAs)

ISAs are a great option for tax-efficient saving because income and gains are exempt from tax. Here are the rules that govern ISAs:

✔ Investment limits into ISAs increased from 6 April 2008. You can now invest up to £3,600 per tax year into a cash ISA, and up to £7,200 per tax year into a stocks and shares ISA, subject to an overall annual subscription limit of £7,200 to both ISAs.

✔ Investments can be made to a maxi-ISA or up to three mini-ISAs: one for stocks and shares (limited to £3,000 a year), one for cash (limited to £3,000), and one for life assurance (limited to £1,000). You can't invest in a maxi-ISA and a mini-ISA in the same year.

✔ Spouses and civil partners each have their own subscription limits.

✔ Withdrawals may be made at any time without loss of tax relief, but once a withdrawal is made a further deposit can't be made to make up for it once deposits have already been made up to the allowed limits.

✔ The original investment (up to £9,000) of a maturing TESSA can be invested in a TESSA-only ISA in addition to any investments in a mini- or maxi-ISA.

National Savings

The various National Savings schemes offering gross returns have become more attractive now that tax at 20 per cent is deducted at source from most other forms of saving income. The forms of National Savings are varied. Current products include:

✔ **National Savings Certificates:** These accounts may be linked to inflation or be fixed-interest accounts. Typically, a minimum investment of £100 and a maximum of £15,000 applies (£30,000 if a husband and wife separately hold £15,000). These accounts have fixed terms of two, three, or five years. Purchases and sales don't need to be shown on income tax returns, and all returns are tax-free.

✔ **National Savings Capital Bonds:** Capital Bonds are held for five years and offer a rising return in steps according to the period for which they are owned, with the higher interest paid in the last 12 months. No interest is earned if you withdraw your money in the first year. The minimum purchase is £100, and the maximum investment is £1 million. Interest on a bond is calculated and added to the account on each anniversary of the date of purchase without deduction of income tax. However, the interest is subject to income tax and must be included in your self-assessment tax return for the year in which it is earned. Interest is paid gross when the bond is cashed in.

✔ **National Savings Income Bonds:** The minimum investment in these bonds is £500 and the maximum is £1 million in total. No fixed investment term applies and interest rates are variable, with tiered rates. These bonds give investors a regular monthly income at a competitive (variable) interest rate. The interest is paid gross but is taxable.

✔ **National Savings Investment Account:** This deposit account can be run through the post office. Minimum investment is £20, maximum £100,000 plus accumulated interest. Interest is variable. The interest is paid gross but is subject to income tax.

✔ **National Savings Easy Access Savings Account:** This fairly low interest-earning account is run through post offices. Anyone over the age of 11 can hold an account. The minimum opening deposit is £100 and the maximum investment is £2 million (£4 million for joint investors). Withdrawals may be made using a cash card at most ATM cash machines or over the counter at post offices. Interest is paid gross but is taxable.

✔ **National Savings Premium Bonds:** Premium Bonds come under the National Savings scheme, but can't really be called an investment. You buy a bond and in return for foregoing any interest, you enter a prize draw that gives you a chance of a substantial win. The minimum investment is £100 and the maximum holding is £30,000. Winnings are tax-free. The odds against a £1 bond winning in a particular month are approximately 21,000:1. The size of each month's prize fund is set by allocating the equivalent of one month's interest on the total value of all Premium Bonds. The annual rate is 3.8 per cent from 6 March 2008.

✔ **National Savings Children's Bonus Bonds:** Individuals can invest on behalf of children under 16 a minimum of £25 up to a maximum of £3,000 per child. A bonus is added on the fifth anniversary of purchase, and all returns are totally exempt from UK income tax, even if funded by a parent.

✔ **National Savings Pensioners Guaranteed Income Bonds:** Those aged 60 or over can invest in this product. The minimum purchase is £500 and £1 million may be invested in total. Interest rates are guaranteed for the length of the Bond's term. Interest is paid gross but is taxable.

Life assurance

Life assurance payouts are generally exempt from tax on both the income arising from the funds invested and on any lump sums. In practice, investment in life policies fall into two categories:

✔ Building up a fund, typically over ten years, after which the policy matures and pays out.

✔ Providing a fund to pay at death, typically to fund inheritance tax or to write the policy in trust for someone else's benefit after the investor's death and, in doing so, pass the fund free of inheritance tax to the next generation.

Purchased annuities

When you purchase an *annuity*, you pay over a lump sum in order to receive a monthly income over a set period of time. Generally, the monthly sum paid from a purchased annuity is treated as if it were two separate payments: a capital content which is tax-free, and an income payment on which you pay income tax at the lower rate of 20 per cent. The original investment is divided into these two elements at the date of the first payment – your financial adviser can give you more information on how you apportion the annuity.

A purchased annuity can be structured so that the monthly payments increase each year in line with inflation. This arrangement doesn't affect the calculation of the division between the deemed capital element and the income element. Inflationary increases in the annuity paid are automatically treated as income and are therefore liable to income tax.

Collecting valuables

If you make a profit on investments in antiques, jewellery, stamps, coins, paintings, works of art, and so on, you may be liable to pay CGT. Everyone is entitled to an annual exemption from CGT (£9,600 for 2008–9) so you don't have to pay tax on any profits you make below that limit. A helpful CGT exemption for *chattels* (an old-fashioned term for personal property items) also exists, which is currently £6,000 per item in addition to the annual exemption.

The chattels exemption comes with conditions. If a set of items is broken down to try to avoid CGT (for example, a pair of candlesticks sold individually), HMRC can treat two or more transactions as one. And the chattels exemption only applies if collecting is an investment activity: If HMRC rule that a trade has developed, profits are subject to income tax.

Betting and racehorses

Winnings from betting (including pool betting, lotteries, or games with prizes) are normally paid free of tax and aren't subject to income tax or CGT.

Profits arising from investing in racehorses usually arise from prize money and from the sale of the horse during or after its racing career. These profits are taxable. Under current law, not more than 12 people may share in joint (syndicated) ownership with each shareholder contributing to the purchase, training, maintenance, and running costs. You can, however, sell your shares to other shareholders (they must have first refusal) or to outsiders.

Investment may also be made into syndicated stallions (where a group of people club together to buy stallions for breeding and make income from breeding fees). The rules aren't as strict as for racehorse syndication. Frequently, up to 40 shareholders form a syndicate, which is run by a committee.

You only pay CGT on the sale of a horse when it has been used for business purposes. Seeking a deduction in your accounts for the costs of purchasing and keeping horses (for example, for advertising and promotional purposes) may be unwise if they are likely to make a fortune racing or at stud.

Investing on the stock market

Anyone who successfully invests on the stock market benefits from the *capital growth* (growth in your original investment) of the share, dividends paid (usually half-yearly by quoted companies – those listed on the Stock Exchange), and perhaps perks such as a discount on company goods.

Investors receive cash dividends to which a tax credit attaches (see the later section 'Taxing dividends'). These investors are liable to income tax on the cash they receive plus the tax credit. Higher rate taxpayers are liable to tax at the rate of 32.5 per cent on dividend income, but those liable to tax only at the basic rate have no further tax to pay.

When you make a profit on the sale of shares, you may be liable to pay CGT (see the later section 'Dealing with capital gains tax'). However, if you make a loss when you sell shares, you can set the loss off against any other gains you may have made in the same tax year – an excess of losses can be carried forward for use in future years against future gains.

Investing in the stock market is always risky, but investment in unquoted companies is especially so. Consequently, HMRC offers various tax reliefs for such investments, such as the Enterprise Investment Scheme (EIS) and Venture Capital Trusts (VCTs).

To find out more about investment options, check out Tony Levene's *Investing For Dummies* (Wiley).

Enterprise Investment Scheme (EIS)

The Enterprise Investment Scheme (EIS) is a series of tax reliefs designed to encourage investments in small companies that aren't listed on the stock exchange (called *unquoted companies*). Investments in unquoted companies often carry high risks so the tax reliefs are designed to offer some compensation for that risk.

The company has to fit strict criteria for it to qualify as an EIS company. For example, it must have less than 50 full-time employees and assets of less than £7 million.

You can claim tax relief at the basic rate of tax (20 per cent) on investment of up to £500,000 (from 6 April 2008) per tax year in an EIS company (the minimum subscription is £500). Once you have invested your money you receive shares in the EIS company, which must be held for at least three years. You can claim income tax relief on your investment immediately (although the relief is withdrawn if you sell your shares within three years). You make this claim via your self-assessment tax return form (see Chapter 3 for more on self assessment). Also, you don't have to pay any CGT on any profit you make on the eventual sale of your shares after this three-year period has expired.

If you make a loss (called a *capital loss*) when you eventually sell your shares, you can set it against any other income or *capital gains* (profits you make on the sale of assets) you have in the same tax year. Shrewd investors often use EIS investments to shelter from the taxman other capital gains they have made. If you make a profit on the sale of an asset (called a *disposal*), you normally have to pay capital gains tax on it. However, you can defer payment of your CGT liability by reinvesting those profits in an EIS company. You have to make the EIS investment in the period one year before and three years after you make the disposal of your capital asset. Because CGT is payable at 18 per cent (from 6 April 2008), and 20 per cent income tax relief can be claimed on the investment in the EIS company, you can get overall tax relief of 38 per cent on your investments. You have to remember, though, that the CGT due on the original disposal is only being deferred and will probably become payable in the future, for example if you eventually sell your shares in the EIS company for a large profit.

Venture Capital Trusts (VCTs)

Tax relief is available at 30 per cent to individuals aged 18 or over who invest in shares in Venture Capital Trusts (VCTs). These companies are quoted on the stock exchange and invest in other qualifying unquoted companies trading wholly or mainly in the UK. As a tax shelter, after taking the tax relief into account, the return from this investment can be excellent. If you buy shares worth £100,000 and sell them for the same amount five years on, you still earn a tax refund of £30,000. But if you instead sell your shares at a profit, the net return may be spectacular given that any profit you make on that disposal is free of CGT. Much is dependent on you being able to make your exit easily and at a good price, which makes this a high-risk investment.

Buying into unit trusts

A *unit trust* is simply a fund of stocks and shares held by a company (a trustee) for the benefit of the investors. The investor holds a certain number of units, depending on the size of his investment. Holding units in a policy is just an easy way of obtaining a spread of investments across a range of companies. This approach can spread the risk for the investor, but does reduce the opportunity for speculative (higher risk) gain. Some trusts offer a regular income, others capital growth, and some a mixture of both. The units are easily marketable in normal conditions and prices for buying and selling are published daily. Several unit trust groups also offer savings plans.

Authorised unit trusts are exempt from CGT on gains made within the trust. Depending on the type of income, some unit trusts may prefer to be unauthorised and taxed as trusts (authorised trusts are severely restricted in their types of investment).

Dividends paid to unit holders carry a tax credit and higher rate taxpayers are liable to pay additional tax at the higher rate where applicable. Any gain made by the investor on disposal of the units is subject to capital gains tax.

Saving for school fees

Obviously the cost of private education varies from school to school and also depends on whether your child is a day pupil or a boarder, but as a rough guide, the approximate total cost for 15 years' education is around £150,000 for a day pupil and £215,000 for a boarder. The key to saving for school fees, therefore, is to plan early using a range of tax-efficient investments.

You can use virtually any savings plan that builds a pot of money as a school fees savings plan, but you must start early and stay as flexible as possible. Whether a particular investment is suitable for you depends on your attitude to risk, the investment term, and the taxation situation. Some of the investments that are typically used for saving school fees include Individual Savings Accounts (ISAs), fixed term annuities, and National Savings (see the earlier section 'Looking at common investment options' for details on these). In addition, Educational Trusts and Composition Fees, which you pay to the school of your choice, have tax advantages, but only if the child eventually goes to that school. The rules regarding these types of trusts are highly complicated and quite inflexible.

Investing overseas

You're usually able to open a bank account in a foreign currency at a UK bank as well as in a foreign country. The interest is chargeable to UK income tax if received by a UK resident. If you hold an account abroad, interest is paid according to local rules and you're taxed on it as you received it in the UK. If the interest is paid from abroad and tax is deducted in accordance with the laws of the country in which the account is held, this tax can usually be offset against the UK tax liability.

If you make an exchange gain by converting foreign currency to sterling, the gain is normally chargeable to capital gains tax (CGT) if you're resident or ordinarily resident in the UK (check out Chapter 2 for the rules on residency). You can claim relief for any losses you incur (for example, due to the fluctuation in exchange rates). CGT does not apply if you bought the currency to meet personal expenditure outside the UK, for example, to spend while you were on holiday or a business trip. CGT is covered in more detail in the section 'Dealing with capital gains', later in this chapter.

Some of the plans that are marketed as 'school fees' savings plans are often no more than a series of rather expensive endowments (a type of life insurance designed to pay out a lump sum at the end of its term). Generally, an endowment has to run for at least ten years to get value for money. If the start of your child's education is less than ten years away, you shouldn't be considering an endowment-based plan.

Giving to Charities

Donating money to a charity doesn't just help donkey sanctuaries, sick children, and local community projects; you can actually save money as well if you're a UK taxpayer. The Government's Gift Aid scheme ensures that the charity gets the maximum benefit from your gift, and can offer you tax relief for your donation.

Understanding Gift Aid

Under Gift Aid you can claim tax relief on making one-off or regular gifts to charity. No lower or upper limit applies on donations upon which tax relief may be claimed. Under the scheme, the payment you make is treated as paid *net* (that is, as if basic rate income tax had been deducted at source). The basic rate tax deemed to have been deducted by you is clawed back by HMRC if your income tax and CGT liability for the year is insufficient to match the tax retained. If you're a higher rate taxpayer, you can claim additional relief against income tax or capital gains tax, as appropriate.

If you make a donation of £100 under the Gift Aid scheme and you're a basic rate taxpayer, the charity is able to claim back tax of £25 from the Government (for 2008–9). Therefore, the charity receives £125, but it costs you only £100. Between 2008–9 and 2010–11 the Government will pay the charity an extra 2 per cent supplement, so the charity would actually receive £128.20 for your £100 donation. If you're a higher rate taxpayer, you can claim 20 per cent (the difference between the higher rate of tax at 40 per cent and the basic rate of tax at 20 per cent) as a tax deduction on the total value to the charity of your donation. So, you can reclaim higher rate relief of £25 (20 per cent of your gross donation of £125). You make this claim on your self-assessment tax return (see Chapter 3 for details on this form).

For tax-saving purposes, you can elect for a donation to be treated as paid in the previous tax year. The election must be made to HMRC by the date on which your tax return was submitted for the previous tax year and, in any event, no later than 31 January following that tax year. An election can only be made if the gift can be paid out of taxed income or gains of the previous tax year.

Making a claim through Gift Aid

When you make a donation to charity, you're normally asked to consider making your donation using Gift Aid. If you agree, the charity gives you a simple form to complete declaring that you want to make donations under Gift Aid. You should complete a separate declaration form for each charity you want to donate to, but one form can cover every gift made to the same charity.

You can also donate tax repayments arising from your self-assessment return to a chosen charity. The charity must be included in a list maintained by HMRC for this purpose, which can be accessed on the HMRC Web site (www.hmrc.gov.uk).

Giving through your employer's payroll

Some employers operate *payroll giving schemes*. Under this type of scheme an agreed deduction is taken from your pay before tax is calculated, which means that you obtain the tax relief included in the donation at your top rate of tax. For example, for 2008–9, if you donate £5 to charity and you pay tax at the basic rate, you pay only £4 to donate because you save the 20 per cent of basic rate tax. If you're a higher rate taxpayer, it only costs you £3.

The main benefit of payroll giving is to create a regular flow of funds for the benefit of the charity or charities of your choice. No upper limit applies for tax relief on donations – you can give as much as you like under the scheme.

Paying Tax on Investment Income

This section outlines how HMRC tax your savings income (and how you may be able to claim some tax back), and explains how capital gains tax (CGT) works.

Deducting tax from savings

For 2007–8, savings income (other than dividends – see the later section 'Taxing dividends') is taxed at:

- ✔ Starting rate of 10 per cent up to £2,230
- ✔ Basic rate of 20 per cent up to £34,600
- ✔ Higher rate of 40 per cent on anything over £34,600

For 2008–9, the rates are as follows:

- ✔ Starting rate of 10 per cent up to £2,320
- ✔ Basic rate of 20 per cent up to £36,000
- ✔ Higher rate of 40 per cent on anything over £36,000

If your non-savings income (such as earnings and pensions) is over the new starting rate for savings income in 2008–9, then the 10 per cent rate is not available.

Savings income includes interest from banks and building societies, interest distributions from authorised unit trusts, interest on *gilts* (fixed rate bonds issued and guaranteed by the UK government), and other securities including corporate bonds and purchased life annuities. This income is taxed in the tax year in which you receive it and you don't get any relief for expenses.

In most cases, banks and building societies deduct tax at the 20 per cent lower rate from gross interest earned on an account before paying it over to the account holder. This amount is known as a *net* payment. Basic rate taxpayers have no further tax to pay. Higher rate taxpayers are, however, liable to tax at the 40 per cent tax rate and therefore have to pay an additional amount to HMRC through their self-assessment tax return each year (refer to Chapter 3 for the lowdown on self assessment).

Claiming back tax on savings

If you're a non-taxpayer, or on a low income, you don't have to pay tax on interest you receive from bank and building society accounts, and if you have paid some, you can claim it back. Sadly, a large proportion of people who can apply for a tax rebate don't do so and needlessly hand over cash that is rightfully theirs. The main groups who qualify for tax rebates include pensioners, non-working spouses, and children.

Completing form R85

Nearly everyone who lives in the UK is allowed to earn or receive income of around £100 each week before tax has to be paid. If your income is below this limit and you have money in a bank or building society account that earns interest, you may be paying tax when you don't have to.

If you calculate that your annual income is lower than your tax-free income limit you should complete form R85, *Getting your interest without tax taken off*, obtained from most banks and building societies or from the HMRC Web site at www.hmrc.gov.uk/forms/r85.pdf. By completing form R85 you tell your bank or building society that you don't have to pay tax.

If your income goes up and that means that you should start paying tax, you must tell each bank or building society with whom you have an account. They aren't responsible for checking that the information you have given on form R85 is true or up to date. HMRC can charge a penalty of up to £3,000 for fraudulent or negligent self-certification.

If you open a new account you need to complete another form R85 so that the interest you receive on it may be paid without any tax being taken off.

Getting money back with R40

To claim back tax taken off bank and building society interest you should complete form R40, which you can download from the HMRC Web site at www.hmrc.gov.uk/forms/r40.pdf. Send it to your tax office, or if you don't have a tax office, contact the HMRC Repayment Claim Office on 0845 366 7850.

You need to keep any certificates or bank statements showing the amount of tax taken off your interest to help you complete the claim form. Another reason why you should keep your certificates (or other records) in a safe place is that HMRC may ask to see them in order to check the accuracy and completeness of your claim. You should keep the certificates (or other records) for two years from the end of the tax year for which your claim is made, because you may be liable to a penalty if you don't do so.

You have five years from 31 January after the end of the tax year for which you're claiming back tax to make your claim. So if you realise in January 2009 that you've been paying tax on your savings interest unnecessarily, you can ask for a rebate for all the years back to 6 April 2002. Simply fill in form R40. You have to complete a form for each year that you're claiming a rebate, so have a supply of pens ready!

Taxing dividends

Special rates of tax apply to *dividends* (a distribution of income from a company in which you hold shares) and other savings income. HMRC treats your dividend income as the very top slice of your income. You pay tax at 10 per cent up to the basic rate limit of £36,000 (for 2008–9) and 32.5 per cent thereafter.

When a UK company pays out a dividend, it withholds tax at the rate of 10 per cent from the payment. The company pays this tax over to HMRC on behalf of the shareholders. So although you don't have anything to do with it, when you receive your dividend you're also effectively given a credit for the tax that the company paid over on your behalf. The dividend you receive is known as the *net dividend* (because you receive it net of tax). The tax that you effectively (but not actually) paid is known as a *tax credit*. If your taxable income doesn't exceed the basic rate limit you don't have to pay any further tax on dividends you receive. If you're a higher rate taxpayer, you have to pay an additional 22.5 per cent (that is, 32.5 per cent less the 10 per cent tax credit) tax on your dividend income and you do this annually through your self-assessment tax return.

If you're a non-taxpayer, you can't receive a refund for the tax paid on your behalf on your dividends. This tax is effectively lost.

Dealing with Capital Gains Tax (CGT)

Capital gains tax (CGT) is a tax on capital gains. *Capital* is wealth in the form of money or property that is used to make more wealth and a *gain* is an increase in the value of that wealth. You normally only have to pay CGT when you no longer own an asset; that is, when you sell it or give it away (the technical term used when you get rid of an asset is making a *disposal*). The following sections explore what you pay CGT on, and how much you pay.

Assessing non-taxable items

Some assets are exempt for capital gains tax purposes. For example, you don't have to pay CGT on:

- ✔ Assets held in an Individual Savings Account (ISA) or Personal Equity Plan (PEP)
- ✔ Betting, lottery, or pools winnings
- ✔ Cash held in sterling
- ✔ Foreign currency held for your own or your family's personal use
- ✔ Investments in forestry and woodlands
- ✔ Jewellery, paintings, antiques, and other personal effects that are individually worth £6,000 or less
- ✔ Life insurance policies (although CGT is payable by the insurance company internally so, although the liability isn't actually passed on to you, because it is a cost of the insurance company, effectively you pay it anyway)
- ✔ National Savings including certificates and Premium Bonds
- ✔ Personal injury compensation
- ✔ Profit for selling your own medals for valour
- ✔ Shares held on behalf of employees in share incentive schemes up to the date the employee is entitled to full ownership
- ✔ Shares in special schemes such as Enterprise Investment Schemes and Venture Capital Trusts
- ✔ Tangible moveable property (that is, assets that have a physical existence) with an expected life of 50 years or under (for example, racehorses) and all tangible moveable property worth less than £6,000
- ✔ UK government gilts and most corporate bonds
- ✔ Your only or main home (not counting any property that you rent). If you have more than one property, you can choose which one is your main residence and not liable to CGT – flick to Chapter 7 for more on investing in property.
- ✔ Your private car and classic cars (which generally means a car that is 15 years old or more with a market value of £15,000 or more; so not that decrepit Robin Reliant you insist is a classic. . .)

Understanding liability to CGT

CGT is usually paid on profits you make by selling various types of assets including properties (but generally not the house you live in as this counts as your main residence and is exempt from CGT), stocks and shares, paintings, and other works of art, but it may also be payable in certain circumstances when you give something away. CGT is not due when you die and pass assets on but inheritance tax may be payable on the value of the assets you leave behind (Chapter 8 deals with inheritance tax).

Typically, you have made a gain if you sell an asset for more than you paid for it. The gain is what is being taxed, not the amount you receive. So, if you bought shares for £500 and sell them later for £2,000, you have made a gain of £1,500 (£2,000 – £500), and that is the amount liable to capital gains tax.

If you give an asset away, you normally look at what the asset is worth, not what you get for it if you sell it. The same is true when you sell the asset for less than its full worth in order to give away part of the value.

Some years ago you bought a small flat for your son to live in and you paid £100,000 for it. The flat is now worth £150,000, but you're feeling extremely generous and you give it to your son. You're treated as having made a gain of £50,000 (£150,000 less £100,000). Even if your son pays you £60,000 for the flat, you're still treated as making a gain of £50,000.

You may also have to pay CGT if you dispose of part of an asset or exchange one asset for another. In addition, CGT may be payable if you receive a lump (known as capital) sum of money from an asset without disposing of it, for example, if you receive compensation when an asset is damaged.

If you sell or give an asset to your husband or wife or your civil partner, while you're legally married and living together, CGT doesn't apply – transactions between spouses and civil partners are exempt. However, if your spouse or partner later sells the asset, she may have to pay CGT at that time on the gain you made while you had it, as well as any gain that belongs to her because they got the asset. She needs to know how much you originally paid for the asset or the value of it when you first acquired it.

Working out how much CGT is due

For the years up to and including 2007–8 capital gains tax is calculated at 20 per cent or 40 per cent of the gain. The rate you pay depends on the level of your other income for the year. In general, your CGT liability is added to your other taxable income and you pay tax on the whole lot. If you aren't liable to higher rate tax, you pay CGT at 20 per cent; if you're liable to higher rate tax, you pay at 40 per cent. Of course, you can pay partly at basic rate and partly at the higher rate. (Chapter 4 covers working out your tax liability in detail). For disposals made on or after 6 April 2008, CGT is payable at a new single rate of 18 per cent.

Reducing your CGT bill

You can reduce you liability to CGT in several ways. Here are a few tips:

- ✔ **Annual exemptions:** You're entitled to an annual exemption (£9,600 for 2008–9), which means that you pay no tax on gains up to that amount each year. If you're married or have a civil partner he or she also has an annual exemption, so for jointly held assets, you have scope for exempting £19,200 (for 2008–9) worth of gains. Remember that your annual exemption is good only for the current tax year – use it or lose it. If you're planning to make a series of disposals, you may want to consider the timing of sales between two or more tax years to use up as much and as many annual exemptions as possible.

- ✔ **Expenses:** You pay CGT only on your *net gains* (usually the profits you make, less the cost of the asset and any other allowable expenses). Therefore, you can deduct costs such as stockbroker commissions and legal expenses connected with property or share purchases. You can also deduct the selling costs.

- ✔ **Taper relief:** Taper relief (which may be claimed up to and including 2007–8) may reduce the amount of the gain chargeable to CGT (and hence reduce the effective rate of tax payable on the gain). The amount of relief available depends on the length of time an asset has been held since that date, and whether the asset is classified as a business or non-business asset for taper relief purposes. Maximum business assets taper relief is available if the business asset has been held for two years, and the maximum non-business asset taper relief is available if the non-business asset is held for ten years. For disposals on or after 6 April 2008, taper relief is no longer available (even if assets were held before this date) and the chargeable gain is liable to tax at the new rate of 18 per cent (subject to the deduction of allowable losses, any other reliefs, and the annual exemption allowance).

- ✔ **Entrepreneurs' relief:** This relief applies from 6 April 2008 and effectively replaces taper relief. If you've been running your business for at least one year you should be entitled to relief if you dispose of the business (or part of it), or if you sell your business assets when you stop trading. The first £1 million of gains that qualify for relief are charged to CGT at the effective rate of 10 per cent. If you make gains of more than £1 million, you have to pay capital gains tax at the normal 18 per cent rate. The relief is subject to a maximum lifetime limit of £1 million, so if you start and stop several businesses throughout your working life, you need to keep track of your gains because you can only get relief on the first £1 million of gains. You can't get the relief if you run a property letting business, although furnished holiday lettings do qualify for the relief (see Chapter 7).

Taking account of losses

In the unfortunate event that you make a loss on the sale of your assets, you can offset it against any other gains you make in the same year or in the future. A strict order applies for setting-off losses. To start, you deduct the losses arising in the tax year from any other chargeable gains for the same year. You must deduct all your losses for the year, even if this results in chargeable gains after losses below the level of the annual exempt amount. If the allowable losses arising in the tax year are greater than the total chargeable gains for the year, you can carry forward the excess losses to be deducted from chargeable gains in future years.

If chargeable gains remain after you deduct the allowable losses arising in the year, you deduct unused allowable losses brought forward from an earlier year. You only deduct sufficient allowable losses brought forward to reduce the chargeable gains after losses to the level of the annual exempt amount. Any remaining losses brought forward are carried forward again without limit, to be deducted from chargeable gains in future years.

In 2007–8, Gerald has total chargeable capital gains of £12,000 and allowable capital losses of £10,000. He deducts all the losses from the gains (£12,000 – £10,000) and doesn't have any losses left to carry forward. As the remaining chargeable gains (£2,000) are below the annual exemption (£9,200), no CGT is payable.

In the following year – 2008–9 – Gerald makes another £12,000 chargeable gain and allowable losses of £15,000. He deducts all the losses (£15,000 – £12,000) and carries forward the remaining unused loss of £3,000. He has no chargeable gains left for the year and therefore has no CGT to pay.

In 2007–8, Edward makes total chargeable gains of £14,000 and has allowable losses of £3,000. He also has unused allowable losses available from an earlier year of £8,000. He deducts the current year losses first from his gains (£14,000 – £3,000), which leaves a chargeable gain of £11,000. Next, he deducts £1,800 of the losses brought forward, to take his chargeable gains down to £9,200 (the rate of the annual exemption for 2007–8). He can then carry forward the remaining unused losses of £6,200 (£8,000 – £1,800) to be used against chargeable gains arising in future years. As his chargeable gains after losses don't exceed the annual exempt amount for 2007–8, Edward doesn't have to pay any CGT.

Shares in companies that are worthless because they've gone bust may still be useful. If HMRC classes the shares as being of *negligible value* (that is, worth nothing), you should be able to claim relief for your losses. If you paid £10,000 for shares in a company that went bust, you have £10,000 worth of losses to offset against gains made elsewhere. If you're a higher rate taxpayer, this amount may be worth up to £4,000.

HMRC publishes a Negligible Value list containing details of shares, stocks, and bonds formerly listed on the London Stock Exchange, which have been officially declared of negligible value (go to `www.hmrc.gov.uk/cgt/negvalist.htm`). You can make a claim for tax relief on shares that have become of negligible value on your self-assessment tax return or by letter to your tax office.

Chapter 7

Investing in Property

*P*roperty investment generates income for millions of people in the UK. Homeowners benefit from increasing house prices, and home ownership remains an attractive investment for tax purposes. And a growing number of people are purchasing second homes and buy-to-let properties, taking in lodgers, or having a go at property developing. This chapter looks at the tax issues surrounding property, whether you're buying or selling, renovating or renting, living in or letting out.

Paying Taxes on Property

In the UK two specific property ownership taxes exist. When you buy a property you have to pay stamp duty, and when you own a property you pay council tax (or your tenant pays it for you).

Stumping up for stamp duty

Stamp duty land tax (stamp duty for short) is basically a tax that you pay on legal transactions. You pay stamp duty when you buy a property worth more than £125,000 and there's no escape from it. You have to pay it whether you buy the property to live in yourself or buy it as an investment.

The amount of duty payable depends on the purchase price of the property. Table 6-1 sets out the current rates.

Table 6-1	Stamp Duty Rates
Purchase Price	*Per Cent Due as Stamp Duty*
Up to £125,000	0
£125,001 to £250,000	1
£250,001 to £500,000	3
Over £500,000	4

Stamp duty is worked out on the price that you pay for the property, so you pay the rate for the purchase value on the whole sum, not just on the amount over each threshold.

Eric buys a house for £250,000. He pays stamp duty at 1 per cent, which equates to £2,500. Susan buys a house for £250,500. She pays stamp duty at 3 per cent, which is £7,515. You can see that even though the purchase price of Susan's house is only £500 more than Eric's, she has to pay an additional £5,015 in stamp duty because the next threshold has been exceeded.

One small variation to stamp duty exists: If you buy a property in one of the UK's most disadvantaged postcode areas, no stamp duty is due up to £150,000. Therefore, you can save up to £1,500. A full list of the areas where this increased threshold applies is on the HM Revenue & Customs' (HMRC) Web site at www.hmrc.gov.uk/so/dar/dar-search.htm.

If you're thinking of buying a property priced a few thousand pounds over one of the stamp duty thresholds, look to see whether you can purchase any items separately outside the main property deal so that the price of the house itself comes in below the threshold. Anything movable can fit into this category such as carpets, curtains, white appliances, and so on. You can't however, include things like fitted kitchens, bathrooms, and fitted wardrobes.

Naturally the taxman pays particular attention to property transactions that fall just below the various stamp duty thresholds and prevents arrangements being made between the buyer and the seller to hand over cash so that the purchase price looks lower. This type of practice is illegal and you should avoid getting involved with arrangements of this type.

Forking out for council tax

Council tax is an annual tax that the local authority charges to cover the cost of provisions such as schools, parks, libraries, local fire and police services, and refuse collection. Council tax rates vary according to where you live.

Council tax is based on the *rateable value* of your property, which determines a band under which your charge is calculated. These days the rateable value of a property often bares no resemblance to the actual value. The basic remit of the banding system is to ensure that those in smaller properties make a smaller contribution and those in larger properties pay a bigger slice. If you believe that your rateable value is widely inaccurate you can appeal against it, but note that few appeals are successful.

Under some conditions you may not have to pay council tax or may qualify for a reduction:

- ✔ The single adult rebate can reduce your annual bill by 25 per cent, if you're eligible. To qualify you must be living alone or live only with children under the age of 18. The rebate can also apply if the only other resident or residents are full-time students.

- ✔ Council tax benefit is a means-tested benefit that can pay up to 100 per cent of your annual bill. If you receive pension credit and a number of other benefits such as income support, you should also be assessed to see if you qualify for council tax benefit. You can't, however, receive any council tax benefit if you have savings of £16,000 or more.

Running a Property Income Business

More and more people are looking to property as a way of plumping up their bank balance. If you have a property (or properties) other than your main home, and you receive rent from letting it out, HMRC normally treats you as running a *property income business*. The following sections take you through the financial side of your property income business – from self assessment and defining rental income, through to deducting expenses, claiming capital allowances, and relieving losses.

Paying tax through self assessment

Renting property is a business and you must run it as such. You have to comply with the rules and regulations (including reporting your new business to HMRC within three months of starting), keep accounts, and pay tax on your income through self assessment.

Part V of this book takes you through starting and running a business, and Chapter 3 outlines self assessment.

The profits of a property business are normally charged to tax based on the tax year from 6 April one year to 5 April the next. If you receive income from renting out property, as well as completing the normal self-assessment tax return form, you need to complete the supplementary 'Land and Property' tax return pages each tax year. You can download these pages from the HMRC Web site at www.hmrc.gov.uk/forms/sa105.pdf. You can also download the HMRC notes, which help you complete the self-assessment pages from www.hmrc.gov.uk/worksheets/sa105notes.pdf.

Understanding rental income

Rental income from investment property is technically treated as investment income and not as earnings from a trade. In theory, therefore, you may not be able to claim as many deductions and reliefs that apply to traders in other business sectors, but in reality, little difference exists in tax treatment. One major bonus of this differing treatment though is that you don't have to pay national insurance contributions (NICs) on any profits you make from a property rental business.

HMRC classes the following income as part of your property business:

- Furnished and unfurnished lettings

- Furnished holiday lettings income (effectively treated as trading income for most tax purposes – see the later section 'Letting out a holiday home in the UK')

- Money received from a tenant or licensee for the use of furniture

- Rents for static caravans in the UK and for permanently moored houseboats

 Deposits charged to tenants don't count as income as long as they are refunded when the tenant leaves. If you keep all or part of the deposit, the cash retained is taxable in the same way as rental income.

Deducting expenses

To work out how much income tax you have to pay on your rental income each year, add up all the income you received and then take off all the costs you incurred in relation to the property. Here's a list of the main items you can deduct from the rent before arriving at a profit (or loss) for the year:

- ✔ **Advertising:** You can deduct costs of advertising for tenants.

- ✔ **Council tax:** You can deduct the council tax you pay relating to the property from your profits for income tax purposes.

- ✔ **Legal fees:** You can claim fees such as solicitor fees when you buy a property, the costs of chasing up outstanding rents, and any expenses you incur by taking tenants to court. You can't deduct fees for buying or selling the property.

- ✔ **Loan interest:** You can offset the mortgage interest (not the amount you borrowed and must repay) of a buy-to-let property against the rental income you receive (usually the biggest single item that you can set again rental income). You can also offset interest from a personal loan you raise wholly and exclusively for the property – for example, you may deduct the interest on a loan you raised to cover the 20 per cent deposit on your buy-to-let mortgage.

- ✔ **Management expenses:** You can deduct the costs of employing someone to manage your property, or if you use a management agent.

- ✔ **Professional fees:** You can deduct valuations for insurance purposes and accountancy fees for preparing the letting business accounts. But you can't claim for architects' and surveyors' fees for improving a property, or for planning applications (unless for permission to carry out repairs on a listed building).

- ✔ **Repairs, maintenance, and insurance:** You can claim for any costs you incur that relate to the property (or properties), from gardeners and window cleaners to plumbers and electricians. As well as the buildings and contents insurance, you can also include contracts for the maintenance of central-heating systems or drainage. Although you can't offset the costs of upgrades to the property (see the next section 'Claiming capital allowances'), you can claim for replacing single-glazed windows with double-glazing. And you can deduct the interest on any loan you take out to pay for upgrades.

You can deduct the expenses involved with your property income business only against the income you receive from it. If lettings dry up, you can't offset your losses against capital gains (see Chapter 6) or other income.

Claiming capital allowances

When you work out your property business income profits you can't deduct the cost of buying, altering, or improving a fixed asset (for example, furniture and other household equipment). You can, however, claim *capital allowances* on certain items of expenditure you incur in relation to running the property business (for example, tools for property maintenance and office equipment used in running the rental business). Generally, capital allowances allow the costs of equipment (known technically as 'plant and machinery') to be written off against a business's taxable profits. (Skip to Chapter 16 for more details on capital allowances and how to work out what you can claim.)

In addition to general capital allowances, some types of capital allowance are specifically available for investment property purposes: allowances for certain flat conversions and business premises renovations, and wear and tear allowances for furnished lettings.

Converting a flat

You can claim 100 per cent capital allowances for the cost of renovating or converting certain space above commercial properties into a flat or flats for short-term letting (referred to as *flat conversion allowances*). If the 100 per cent allowance isn't claimed in full in the first year, a writing-down allowance of 25 per cent a year (on the cost of the expenditure) can be claimed until the expenditure is fully relieved. A writing-down allowance means that you deduct 25 per cent of the expenditure in the first year, and then 25 per cent of the balance in the following year, and so on until you have deducted all the expenditure. Therefore, you may not have to pay any tax on your rental income from the flat for several years.

To qualify you must meet stringent conditions:

- ✔ Tenants' agreements must run from one to five years.

- ✔ The flat must not have more than four rooms (excluding hallway, kitchen and bathroom).

- ✔ The property must be directly accessible from the street and not via the downstairs business.

- ✔ You can't live there yourself and claim the allowances.

The rules cease to apply if the rental income is particularly high. HMRC publishes weekly rent limits for London and outside London (see www.hmrc.gov.uk/manuals/camanual/CA43250.htm), which are adjusted from time to time. You can find out more about flat conversion allowances on the HMRC Web site at www.hmrc.gov.uk/manuals/camanual/CA43000.htm.

Renovating business premises

From 11 April 2007 (for a period of five years) business premises renovation allowances (called BPRA) can be claimed for the costs of renovating or converting certain unused business property in any of the 2,000 or so areas of the UK that are designated as disadvantaged.

The allowances offer 100 per cent up-front tax relief and may be claimed by individuals or limited companies incurring capital expenditure on bringing qualifying business premises back into business use. The allowances are available both to landlords and to businesses occupying their own properties.

You can find out more about the BPRA on the HMRC Web site at www.hmrc.gov.uk/manuals/camanual/ca45100.htm.

Deducting for wear and tear

Although you can't claim capital allowances on furniture, furnishings, or fixtures (such as refrigerators and washing machines) within your rental property, you should be able to claim wear and tear allowance. The wear and tear allowance is equal to 10 per cent of the net rents from furnished lettings (that is, after deducting payments normally borne by the tenant, such as water rates).

In addition, you can claim a deduction for replacing fixtures that are an integral part of a building (for example, central heating systems), but excluding additional expenditure on improved versions of those items (for example, where a worn out but basic, cheap bathroom suite is replaced with an expensive, high-quality suite). However, replacing single-glazed windows with double-glazed units is treated as allowable repairs and not disallowable improvements.

As an alternative to the 10 per cent wear and tear allowance, a *renewals basis* may be claimed. No relief is allowed for the original cost of an asset, but a deduction is given for the cost of replacing it. The choice of which of these methods of deduction you apply is yours.

HMRC produces a help sheet (IR250), which explains all about capital allowances for rental business (www.hmrc.gov.uk/pdfs/1999_00/helpsheets/ir250.pdf).

Relieving your losses

The losses of a property business are worked out in the same way as profits. Rental business losses are generally carried forward and set off against future property business profits. Alternatively, if the loss has arisen because of a claim to capital allowances (see the preceding section), it may be possible to set it off against any other income you have in the same tax year (for example, earnings you receive from employment on which you've paid tax), or the following tax year.

Letting Your Spare Room

HMRC has different rules for those who rent out a room in their home as opposed to renting out a property, and it offers a special tax break. The rent-a-room scheme, which was introduced in 1992, is an optional exemption scheme that lets people receive £4,250 of tax-free *gross income* (income before expenses) from renting out spare rooms in their only or main home. You don't need to be a homeowner to take advantage of the scheme, but of course those who are renting need to check whether their lease allows them to take in a lodger.

The accommodation has to be furnished and a lodger can occupy a single room or an entire floor of the house. However, the scheme doesn't apply if the house is converted into separate flats that are rented out. Nor does the scheme apply to let unfurnished accommodation in your home.

You can't claim rent-a-room relief if you let part of your home as an office or other business premises. The relief only covers the circumstance where payments are made for the use of living accommodation. However, the relief isn't denied where a lodger living in the home is provided with a desk, or the use of a room with a desk, which he uses for work or study.

If you charge your lodger for additional services, for example, cleaning and laundry, you need to add the payments you receive to the rent, to work out your total income from the rental. If your income exceeds £4,250 a year in total, a liability to tax arises, even if the rent is less than that.

The £4,250 annual allowance equates to around £80 per week. Many lodgers nowadays pay more than this amount. If you're receiving more than £4,250 a year in rent, you have two options:

✔ Count the first £4,250 in rent as the tax-free allowance and pay income tax on the remaining income. In this case you have to keep a record just of the income you receive, because you don't make any claim for expenses.

✔ Treat renting the room as a normal rental business, working out a profit and loss account using the normal income and expenditure rules (Chapter 16 shows you how to keep business accounts for income tax purposes).

In most cases, the first option is more advantageous (known as the *alternative basis*), unless you're running a substantial room renting business with high-paying lodgers. In both cases, you have to keep proper records and complete a self-assessment return each year.

You have up to one year after the end of the tax year when your income from lodgers went over £4,250 to decide the best option to take, so take the time to work out which route produces the lowest tax bill. HMRC even allow you to change from year to year, as long as you let them know within the time limit.

Renting Out Holiday Homes and Overseas Properties

Buy an apartment in Barcelona or a mobile home in the New Forest and you not only have a perfect getaway destination, but also a potentially lucrative investment property. But before you decide to let out your UK holiday home or a property you own abroad, you need to understand the tax implications.

Letting out a holiday home in the UK

When you let out a furnished holiday home in the UK and you meet certain criteria, you qualify for special treatment by HMRC for income tax purposes.

Knowing whether your property qualifies

To qualify for the special treatment available for furnished holiday lettings, the property must be:

✔ Located in the UK

✔ Furnished

✔ Available for holiday letting to the public for at least 140 days
a year

✔ Let as a holiday let (which means commercial lets, not cheap
rates for friends and family) under the following conditions:

- You let the property for at least 70 days a year.

- The property isn't occupied for more than 31 days by
the same person in any period of seven months.

Your profit on UK holiday lettings is worked out in the same way as
for other rental income, except that you claim capital allowances
rather than the wear and tear allowance (see the earlier section
'Claiming capital allowances' for details of these allowances).

If your property doesn't qualify as a holiday let, you're taxed as
normal for residential property lettings (see the earlier section
'Running a Property Income Business').

Looking at the tax advantages of UK holiday lettings

If you qualify for the special treatment, the following tax advantages are available to you:

✔ Any loss can be offset against your other income, not just the
property income, which reduces your overall tax bill. Or you
can carry the loss forward and offset it against future letting
profits.

✔ When you sell the property, you may be able to take advantage of capital gains tax (CGT) reliefs, such as *business asset
roll-over relief* (check out Chapter 6 for more on CGT).
Business asset roll-over relief means that if you reinvest the
proceeds within three years in another UK holiday letting
property, or certain other assets costing the same as or more
than you received for the property you sold, you may be
able to defer payment of CGT until you dispose of those new
assets.

✔ You may also pay less CGT when you sell a property that
you've used for UK holiday letting, compared with other residential let property. This is because a UK holiday letting
property is treated as a business asset and so *entrepreneurs'
relief* may be available. Broadly, the first £1 million of profit
you make when you sell up may be charged to CGT at an
effective rate of 10 per cent, instead of the standard 18 per
cent capital gains tax rate. Chapter 6 has more on entrepreneurs' relief.

Receiving rent from property abroad

Rent and other income from properties outside the UK is taxed in much the same way as income from a UK residential property letting (see the earlier section 'Running a Property Income Business'). The profit or loss for an overseas rental business is worked out as a whole and not for each individual property. However, you need to make separate computations for tax credit relief purposes (that is, relief for any tax you pay in another country).

Normally, the tax authorities of the country where the let property is situated also charge tax on your letting profits. If you're a UK landlord (subject to UK income tax), you pay tax on the same profits both here and abroad. However, because the UK has double taxation treaties (an agreement between the UK and another country under which they agree to charge tax only in one country) with most other countries, you can avoid the double charge by deducting the overseas tax paid on the overseas property income from the UK tax due on the same income.

Excess expenditure on one overseas property is automatically set against surplus receipts from other overseas properties. Any overall overseas rental business loss can be carried forward and set against future overseas rental business profits; but such losses can't be set against UK rental business profits or against any other income.

William owns a house in Spain, which he let for five weeks in 2007–8. For that year he made a net loss (after allowable expenses on that property) of £2,500. He also owns a flat in London that was let for the whole year and generated a net profit of £5,000 for 2007–8. The loss from the Spanish property of £2,500 can't be set against the profit of £5,000 from the London flat because it arose on an overseas property and must be kept separate. The loss can, however, be carried forward to set against future letting profits from overseas properties.

When you rent out property abroad, you naturally need to travel occasionally to your foreign property and back. HMRC allows you to deduct your travel costs for tax purposes and any other type of property-income businesses. The catch is that you must be able to show that the travel was incurred wholly and exclusively for business purposes and you didn't also use the trip for some other purpose, such as a holiday. You need to keep records of business meetings and so forth to substantiate your claim.

Dabbling in Property Development

Property investment isn't just about rental income: You can also make money simply by buying property and selling it on for profit. Property development is a popular, if risky, pastime these days as all the current TV programmes set out to prove. At a basic level, property development usually involves buying a run-down property (cheaply!), renovating it (quickly!), and selling it on at a profit (hopefully!).

If you buy a house for £150,000, perhaps do a little decorating, and then sell it on a few years later for £165,000, the taxman has no claim on the £15,000 you gain, providing the property is your only or main home. However, if you aren't going to live in the property, and it's therefore not your main home, you're liable to CGT on any profits you make when you come to sell the property.

Because you're effectively running a business when you do up a house for profit that's not your main home, you need to keep records of all the expenditure you incur in connection with the renovations because you can deduct them from your profits when working out how much tax is due. You can also deduct the cost of legal and professional fees (for example, solicitors and accountants), and advertising (for example, estate agency fees).

After you work out your profits (basically the price you paid for the property, less costs) and deduct your expenses (including sale costs), you pay CGT on the balance at the rate of 18 per cent.

If you run, or are thinking about running, a property development business, seek the advice of an accountant or tax practitioner. The law surrounding property development can be complex (and outside the scope of this book), but an adviser should be able to keep you on the straight and narrow.

Flick to Chapters 15 and 16 for more on starting and running a business.

Selling Up

When you sell your only or main residence, you don't have to worry about any tax implications. So, if you bought your house 30 years ago for £10,000 and you sell it now for £500,000, no tax is payable on the £490,000 profit. However, other rules exist for second (or third or fourth) properties. This section helps you identify your main residence and understand when capital gains tax (CGT) may apply to a sale.

Deciding which is your main residence

In most cases, deciding on your main home is obvious – it's the one you live in! However, if any doubt exists, you have the right to elect which home is counted as your main residence and advise HMRC accordingly. You can generally change your election when-ever you want, but you must notify HMRC.

Where possible, designate the higher value property as your main residence. Because you don't pay tax on the sale of your main resi-dence, this home is more likely to produce the higher taxable gain.

Here are the main residence rules:

- ✔ Married couples and civil partners can only have one main residence between them, but unmarried couples (regardless of sex) can have one each.

- ✔ If you buy a new property before you complete the sale of your previous one, you don't have to worry about having two homes. The old one still counts as your main residence for tax purposes for 36 months.

- ✔ If you buy a new property but are delayed in moving in, you have a 12-month window when you can count it as your main residence. This window can be extended by a further 12 months in some cases, for example when you're having build-ing work done to make it habitable, making 24 months in total. This time can be useful when you're building your own new home. If you don't apply this rule, the taxman may think that you're building the new property for investment purposes rather than to live in yourself.

- ✔ Some people, such as vicars, priests, and those in the armed forces and police force often have to live where their job dic-tates. In these cases, you can still buy a house for your future security and nominate it as your main residence, and there-fore enjoy the same tax advantages on sale of the property even though you don't actually live in it.

If you leave your main residence and rent another property, a three-year window applies in which you can sell up tax-free.

You need to tell your HMRC office when you sell a property that's not your main residence; for example, if you sell a buy-to-let property, a holiday home, or a flat near your work that you use during the week. This is because you may have to pay tax on any profits you make. Contact details are on the HMRC Web site at www.hmrc.gov.uk.

Avoiding capital gains tax

If you sell your only or main residence, you don't have to pay any CGT on the profits. However, if you sell another property, whether in the UK or overseas, you may be liable to pay tax. If the property is held in your sole name, you should be able to deduct the annual CGT exemption from any gain you make (worth £9,600 in 2008–9), providing you haven't already used it up against other gains made in the same tax year. If the property is in joint names, you should each be entitled to two CGT exemptions, which may be worth £19,200 in 2008–9.

A couple of exemptions exist for CGT, but they probably aren't ideal tax-saving solutions for most people:

- ✔ If you have a large garden, you can sell off a *permitted area* of 0.5 hectares (about an acre) without selling the property itself, and not pay CGT on any profits.

- ✔ You may also be able to sell off part of your house for conversion into a smaller unit such as a granny flat without a tax charge. But you're still liable to CGT if you sell off a separate building such as a cottage or outbuilding in your grounds.

If you use part of your home exclusively for business purposes, when you sell the property, you may be charged CGT on any profit relating to that particular part. So, for example, if your house has seven rooms (excluding kitchens and bathrooms) and you use one room exclusively for business purposes, the taxman may seek to charge CGT on one-seventh of any profits made. This situation applies where a garage is used as storage or a workshop, or where an extension serves as an office. Don't forget though, that the room or garage has to be used 'exclusively' for business purposes, so doing your business accounts on your laptop in the dining room isn't a problem. A room that is used partly for business purposes and partly for residential purposes qualifies in full for relief and no CGT is charged.

Chapter 8

Passing On Your Wealth

● ●

In This Chapter

▶ Working out the value of your estate

▶ Thinking about gifts

▶ Forking out inheritance tax

▶ Organising your estate with a will

● ●

A s Benjamin Franklin observed in 1789: 'In this world nothing can be said to be certain, except death and taxes.' Unfortunately more than two centuries down the line this statement still holds true – everyone is destined to die and taxes are everywhere! To add insult to injury, if you add the two facts together and don't plan properly, a large slice of what you accumulate in your lifetime is destined to make its way back to the government in the form of inheritance tax after you die.

The good news is that inheritance tax is often referred to as a voluntary tax, because you can do so many things to reduce liability to it, or in the best case scenario, avoid it all together. HMRC figures show that only 35,000 estates paid inheritance tax last year. So although this chapter doesn't sound a very cheerful one, I show you how to maximise your *estate* (that's the total value of everything you leave behind and includes cash, your home, cars, savings and shares, and all you personal possessions) and protect it as much as possible from the taxman.

So read on to find out how to make the most of your money in your final years and from beyond the grave – whether you choose to leave the maximum to the younger generation or to grow old 'disgracefully', spending your hard-earned dosh unwisely and having fun before you go!

Adding Up What You're Worth

At a very basic level, working out inheritance tax is pretty straight-forward. When you die, your *executors* (the personal representa-tives who deal with your estate) add up the value of everything you owned, deduct anything that's exempt and report the total to HM Revenue & Customs (HMRC), who charges tax at 40 per cent on anything over a certain amount. The following sections take you through the stages of this process.

Understanding your estate

To work out the value of your estate, HMRC asks your executors to add up all your *assets*, including your home, your savings and investments (even Individual Savings Accounts and any other tax-free savings accounts), valuables (such as jewellery, artwork, and cars), certain life insurance policies, and the value of any debts other people owe to you when you die. (Anything that you leave to your spouse or civil partner can be ignored for this calculation; gifts between spouses and civil partners are totally exempt for inheritance tax purposes.)

But the process doesn't end there. HMRC also looks back to the previous seven years and to the value of your estate and add the amount of certain gifts you made to others during that period (see the section 'Making Gifts', later in this chapter, for further details on the types of gifts included).

For inheritance tax purposes all your assets are valued on the date you die or when you gave them away, not the date you bought or acquired them, or the date you included them in your will (assum-ing you have one). So if you bought your house for £60,000 in 1990 and the value is double on today's market, your executors list the value of the asset as £120,000.

Executors can deduct the following from the value of your estate:

✔ Any debts (such as credit cards, mortgages, and other loans and outstanding utilities bills)

✔ Money or property *bequeathed* (left in a will) to mainstream political parties (the party must have at least two MPs or one MP and at least 150,000 votes for its candidates at the most recent general election)

✔ Certain exemptions (such as donations to national galleries and museums, and gifts to housing associations)

> ✔ Charitable donations (left in a will)
>
> ✔ Costs of winding up your estate
>
> ✔ Funeral costs

The estates of UK military personnel are tax-exempt on death if the death is due to wounds or diseases resulting from active service. The death doesn't have to be immediate.

Discounting your business assets

The value of a business that you've owned for at least two years doesn't count for inheritance tax purposes. This exemption, known as *business property relief*, applies regardless of whether you ran the business as a sole trader, partnership, or limited company (flick to Chapter 15 for an explanation of the different types of business through which you can trade).

The exemption applies to any property that you operated as a business, including agricultural property such as farms and woodlands. Although this exception doesn't include buy-to-let properties, it does include holiday properties provided that you only let them short-term (usually up to one month at a time), you didn't use the property yourself, you didn't let friends and family stay there for free or for a token rent, and you advertised the property yourself or used a holiday letting agency.

In addition, *unquoted shares* (those not listed on the Stock Market), count as business assets, and so are also exempt from inheritance tax.

Knowing the tax rates

Once the executors have established the value of your estate, HMRC deducts the *nil-rate band* (£312,000 for 2008–9, rising to £325,000 in 2009–10 and £350,000 in 2010–11). The band is called nil rate because the tax rate on this slice of the estate is zero. Every estate is allowed to distribute assets – tax free – up to the threshold set by the nil-rate band. But if the value of the estate is more than the nil-rate band, inheritance tax is payable at the flat rate of 40 per cent.

Gifts that you made when you were alive (known as *lifetime gifts*) such as potentially exempt transfers (PETs; see 'Understanding the seven-year rule', later in this chapter) use up the nil-rate band before anything else that is given away on death. Therefore, when

HMRC gets the list of assets from your executors, it deducts life-time gifts first of all, before anything else.

In some cases, you pay inheritance tax on your estate during your lifetime. If you make an *immediately chargeable transfer* (such as a gift into certain types of trust), you pay inheritance tax on the amount exceeding the nil-rate band at the rate of 20 per cent in your lifetime and 40 per cent when you die. Every time you make an immediately chargeable transfer you have to look back seven years and identify any other immediately chargeable transfers made in that period. If any exist, you have to include them in determining how much of the nil-rate band is still available and how much tax is therefore due. If you make an immediately chargeable transfer and also agree to pay the tax on that transfer, the value of the gift is 'grossed-up' to determine the full value of the gift – that is, the amount given, plus the tax on that amount (see the example of Simon's gift, later in this section, for a practical explanation).

If you make an immediately chargeable transfer and die within seven years, and the chargeable value of the gift is above the nil-rate band at your date of death, tax is due at 40 per cent on the amount exceeding the taxable threshold. A credit is given for the tax previously paid at 20 per cent.

Simon made a gift of £300,000 cash to a discretionary trust (see Chapter 5 for a definition of this) on 6 April 2004. The taxable amount is £37,000 (£300,000 less the nil rate in force for 2004–5 of £263,000).

If Simon agreed to pay the tax due on the gift, instead of the tax being paid out of the trust fund, the value of the gift actually equals the gift plus the tax on the gift (the grossed-up amount), calculated as follows:

The 'grossed up' taxable amount is £37,000 x ¾ = £46,250

Tax due on grossed up amount @ 20 per cent (£46,250 x 20 per cent) = £9,250

The gift of £300,000 plus the tax due on the £300,000 is therefore equal to a gross gift of £309,250.

Making Gifts

The following sections show you how gifts (of cash or any other asset) you make during your lifetime and in your will relate to inheritance tax, and how a little generosity now reduces your estate's tax liability.

You should note that if you make a gift to a company or to certain types of trust, the gift is immediately chargeable for inheritance tax and you may have to pay some tax in your lifetime – if the total value of those gifts exceeds the inheritance tax threshold. See the earlier section 'Knowing the tax rates' for details on immediately chargeable transfers.

Understanding the seven-year rule

Any assets (cash or otherwise) that you give away during your life-time that don't fall under the exempt transfer rules, such as trans-fers between spouses and civil partners and gifts to charities, may escape inheritance tax as a *potentially exempt transfer* (PET). No limits exist on the amount of PETs you can make during your lifetime.

Basically, for a PET to escape inheritance tax completely you need to survive for seven years after making the gift. If you die within the seven-year period, the PET is partially chargeable depending on the number of years that have elapsed since you made the gift. The reduction is given in the form of *taper relief*, a sliding scale used to determine tax liabilities on gifts between three and seven years before death. Table 8-1 shows the current rates of taper relief.

Table 8-1	Rates of Taper Relief on PETs	
Period before Death in Which Gift Is Made	*Reduction (%)*	*Actual Tax Rate (%)*
0 to 3 years	0	40
3 to 4 years	20	32
4 to 5 years	40	24
5 to 6 years	60	16
6 to 7 years	80	8
More than 7 years	100	0

If you die within seven years of making a PET the value of that PET will be added in to the value of your estate to determine how much, if any, inheritance tax is due. The PET will therefore use up some or all of your available nil-rate band, potentially increasing or even creating an inheritance tax liability for your estate. Also, if the value of the PET exceeds the level of the nil-rate band in force for the year in which you die, then additional inheritance tax will be payable by the recipient of the gift.

Taper relief may reduce the amount of tax payable. But you must appreciate that taper relief can only reduce an inheritance tax liability resulting from a PET becoming chargeable on death. The relief doesn't reduce the value of the gift itself.

Susan gives her son David a gift of £374,000 on 1 March 2005. She dies on 16 July 2008. The inheritance tax nil-rate band for 2008–9 is £312,000, which means the gift exceeds the nil-rate band by £62,000. The full rate of inheritance tax due on the gift is £24,800 (£62,000 @ 40 per cent). The gift was made between three and four years prior to Susan's death, so taper relief of £4,960 is due (£24,800 @ 20 per cent). The revised inheritance tax charge is therefore £19,840 (£24,800 minus £4,960).

Taper relief is worthwhile for those with large estates. Giving away £1 million and living for seven years takes the money right out of the inheritance tax net. But even if you live for only six years, the £1 million less the nil-rate band is charged at just 8 per cent tax under taper relief (see Table 8-1), instead of the full 40 per cent. Obviously, anything transferred at death is chargeable at the full 40 per cent rate because you've used up all the nil-rate band.

You can take out a special life insurance policy to make sure that a potential liability to inheritance tax is covered if you don't live for the full seven years after making a PET. These types of policy are designed to fit in with the tax taper. You can stipulate that the proceeds of the policy pay into a trust when you die, so that they are outside your estate.

Using your exemptions

Sensible inheritance tax planning includes giving assets away that you can afford to dispose of *before* your death, without breaking the rules. Here are a few of the most common exemptions that people use to reduce the size of their estate (and in turn its liability to inheritance tax):

- ✔ **Annual exemption:** You can give away up to £3,000 (cash or assets) a year with no inheritance tax implications. Therefore, give your friend Bill £3,000 now, and you can save him £1,200 or 40 per cent in a future inheritance tax charge after your death. If you don't use the exemption in one year, you can carry it forward (or any unused part of it) to the next tax year.

But you can carry forward any unused amount for one year only – it's use it or lose it, and the exemption is lost after the following year. For example, a married couple, can give away £6,000 free of inheritance free every year, or £12,000 in one year if no gifts had been made in the previous year.

✓ **Charitable gifts:** Gifts made to a charity or other qualifying body are exempt from inheritance tax. Exemption from inheritance tax is also given for gifts and bequests to certain national institutions such as the National Gallery. A list of qualifying bodies and other information on this subject can be found in HMRC booklet IHT206A, page 4 (go to www.hmrc.gov.uk/cto/forms/iht206a.pdf).

✓ **Gifts of interest:** You can lend money interest free without having to account for inheritance tax on the interest you give up. This exemption means you can help family members get on the housing ladder for instance. No limits exist, but the money has to be returned to your estate on your death.

✓ **Gifts on marriage:** You can give up to £5,000 to your children when they marry, regardless of whether the child is legitimate, illegitimate, adopted, or a stepchild. Grandparents can give up to £2,500, whereas anyone else can give up to £1,000. Gifts can be made in cash or goods. The exemption is for each marriage. And if you have two children getting married in the same tax year, you can give each one the maximum. The allowance doesn't have to be shared.

✓ **Small gifts:** You can make any number of gifts worth up to £250 each without affecting any other allowance. But you can't give the same person more than one such gift in any tax year or give up to £250 to someone who has already gained from one of the other exemptions. Nor can you give £300 and count the first £250 as exempt. If the gift is over £250, it counts towards the annual exemption.

If you decide to leave all or part of your estate to your family, consider skipping a generation and leaving it to your grandchildren rather than your children. The advantage is that youngsters have far longer to live than their parents before they have to worry about inheritance tax issues.

Sharing with your spouse or civil partner

Gifts to spouses and civil partners are exempt from inheritance tax. The following rules apply:

✔ If the deceased (or donor) was domiciled in the UK, and their spouse or civil partner wasn't domiciled in the UK at the time of the transfer, the exemption is limited to £55,000.

✔ The legislation doesn't stretch to unmarried partners, no matter how long they have lived together or how many children they have together, or if one is wholly or largely dependent on the other.

✔ Transfers between spouses who are separated, but not divorced, qualify as exempt.

The estate left by someone who dies is entitled to the inheritance tax nil-rate band (see the earlier section 'Knowing the tax rates' for details). Someone who dies leaving some or all their assets to their spouse or civil partner may not have fully used up their nil-rate band. In this case, any nil-rate band unused on the first death may be used when the surviving spouse or civil partner dies. The amount of unused nil-rate band potentially available for transfer is based on the percentage of the band unused when the first spouse or civil partner dies.

George dies and leaves his entire estate to his wife Ruth. Because the assets transfer between spouses, none of the nil-rate band (£300,000 in that year) is used. When Ruth dies a month later, the nil-rate band for her estate increases by 100 per cent to £600,000, because George's unused nil-rate band carries forth to Ruth's estate. That means the government can charge inheritance tax only on anything over £600,000 in Ruth's estate.

When Kate dies, she leaves part of her estate to her civil partner Laura, but she also leaves assets to other relatives to the sum of £150,000. Laura's part of the estate is exempt from inheritance tax because she was Kate's civil partner, and HMRC deducts the £150,000 from the nil-rate band (£300,000 in that year), leaving 50 per cent of the original nil-rate band unused. When Laura dies several years later, the nil-rate band has risen to £350,000. HMRC increases the nil-tax rate for Laura's estate by the 50 per cent carried forth from Kate's estate, to leave a total nil-rate of £500,000.

The amount of additional nil-rate band that can be accumulated by any one surviving spouse or civil partner is limited to the value of the nil-rate band in force at the time of their death. This limit may be relevant when a person dies having survived more than one spouse or civil partner, or when a person dies having been married to, or the registered civil partner of, someone who had themselves survived one or more spouses or civil partners.

Inheriting an inheritance

Special rules reduce the inheritance tax payable on assets that the person who died inherited herself from someone else within the previous two to five years. This *quick succession relief* prevents HMRC from potentially getting inheritance tax twice on the same assets. The value of the quick succession relief is most valuable up to two years and tapers off over five years. It can be quite complicated to work out the figures, but keep it in mind and make sure that you apply for it if this situation arises. If the executors don't apply, the relief isn't given automatically because HMRC has no way of knowing where the assets originally came from.

Wherever possible, arrange matters to use the nil-rate band to make gifts to family members and beneficiaries other than your spouse or civil partner. That way, the nil-rate band isn't lost.

Giving with reservation

If you make a gift to someone but either attach certain conditions to it, or retain some of the benefit for yourself, HMRC treats the gift as a *gift with reservation of benefit*. For example, if you give your house to your son but you carry on living in it and specify that he can't sell it until you die, HMRC wouldn't accept that you had given the house to your son and it would be included in your estate for inheritance tax. Because you made no outright gift the seven-year limit doesn't apply (see the earlier section 'Understanding the seven-year rule').

If you give your house to your daughter but continue to live there rent free, that would be a gift with reservation. If after two years you start to pay a market rent for living in the house, the reservation ceases when you first pay the rent. The gift then becomes an outright gift at that point and the seven-year period runs from the date the reservation ceased.

Of course, a gift can start as an outright gift and then become a gift with reservation. If you give your house to your daughter and continue to live there but pay full market rent, no reservation applies. If over time you stop paying rent or the rent doesn't increase, so that it's no longer market rent, a reservation occurs at the time the rent stops or ceases to be market rent.

Turning Capital into an Income

One way to save on inheritance tax when you have substantial savings is to turn your *capital* (cash and assets) into a regular income through an *annuity* – an insurance company policy that pays a guaranteed income for life in return for foregoing the lump sum used to buy it. Buying an annuity reduces the value of your estate and so takes the original cost of the annuity out of the inheritance tax net. You can opt for a higher income (and a better standard of living) rather than leaving it all behind in your will to be taxed at 40 per cent. You can find more information on annuities in Chapters 6 and 9.

Annuities end on death but you can guarantee the income for a fixed period so that the annuity is paid for at least five or ten years irrespective of whether you die. This option may be worth considering if you expect your partner or dependant to outlive you.

Paying Inheritance Tax

Various rules exist for determining the time for payment of inheritance tax. You can sometimes negotiate with HMRC to pay in instalments, and you can even get the go ahead to pay by transferring ownership of assets to the Crown in settlement of a bill. For example, if you own a valuable painting, you may donate it to a national museum in lieu of an inheritance tax bill.

Unless it can be paid in instalments, inheritance tax is generally due for payment as follows:

- ✔ **Chargeable lifetime transfers:** Tax is due six months after the end of the month of the transfer. But if the transfer is made between 6 April and 1 October in any year, the tax is due at the end of April the following year.

- ✔ **Estates:** The personal representatives must pay the tax at the time that the inheritance tax account is sent to HMRC, and this depends on the length of time it takes to sort out the estate.

- ✔ **PETs:** Tax due on a PET that becomes chargeable because of the transferor's death within seven years needs to be paid six months after the end of the month in which the death occurs.

Inheritance tax is often due to be paid before the cash and assets left in a will are released to the beneficiaries. This means that the beneficiaries have to find the money to pay the tax elsewhere. The most obvious way to solve this problem is to take out a loan to pay the tax owed. You can then pay off the loan after you receive cash from the estate, or in the case of assets, you sell them to raise the funds needed.

Consider taking out a life insurance policy that will pay out on your death and so cover any inheritance tax due on your estate. Remember, though, that HMRC may consider your life insurance policy to form part of your estate, so the plan must be set up under a trust (see the later section 'Setting up trusts'). A fringe benefit of this is that all proceeds of the policy are paid free of tax.

Drawing Up a Will

If you care about who benefits from your estate after you die and you want to avoid causing unnecessary distress to friends and family, you need a *will*, which is a legal document that gives specific instructions on how your estate is to be administered, divided up, and distributed. If you don't leave a will, you may set the wheels in motion for the government to take a large chunk of money from your estate as inheritance tax. The following sections take you through the basics of wills.

Julian Knight's *Wills, Probate & Inheritance Tax For Dummies* (Wiley) is an excellent source of info on making a will.

Understanding the importance of a will

If you don't make a will strict rules determine who gets what, if anything, from your assets when you die. If no will exists, your spouse or civil partner doesn't necessarily inherit the whole of your estate when you die. Your friends, your favourite charities, even relatives may get nothing. Also, the inheritance tax law doesn't automatically recognise live-in partners, just married couples and civil partners. So even if you've lived together for many years your partner may get nothing if you haven't made a will, unless your property was in joint names before you died. And if you're separated from your spouse, even if you've begun divorce proceedings, the spouse is still entitled to your estate if you die before you get a *decree absolute*, which legally ends your marriage.

Making a will means that you get to make the decisions about your assets. You're in control and you can vary the assets going to your relatives and friends, set the conditions, and decide who you want to manage the process for you.

Setting up trusts

When you have children under 18, you need to consider how your estate is to be applied for their welfare and education if both you and your spouse/partner die. You can appoint trustees who administer the funds for them (usually the executors). If you think children (or grandchildren) wouldn't cope very well with inherited assets at the age of 18, you can raise the age at which they become entitled to 21 or even 25. Head to Chapter 5 for details on setting up a trust.

The proceeds of life insurance policies written in trust escape the inheritance tax net (because you don't legally own the policy any more; the trust owns it) and don't therefore use up the nil-rate band. The life insurance company can make arrangements for you even after you've taken out the policy if you ask them.

Although setting up a trust can save tax in one way, it can also cause tax charges from another direction. Tax charges apply when transferring assets into a trust, and income generated by a trust is taxed at 40 per cent, no matter what the personal tax rate of anyone involved. Seeking professional advice on such matters is always a good idea.

Making specific bequests

Make specific bequests in your will where possible, especially if you want to leave money to non-taxpayers such as children. A *specific bequest* is one in which you quote the source of the funds for the bequest. For example, you may say '£5,000 from my savings account with ABC Bank' or 'the entire balance of my savings account with ABC Bank', rather than a non-specific £5,000 gift.

When you die, your personal income tax allowances die, too. So even if you paid no tax on interest from savings, HMRC charges the 20 per cent savings tax on interest generated from the money you leave, even if all the money is due to go to non-taxpayers. This rate goes up to 40 per cent if the assets are not distributed within two years. Making specific bequests removes the designated money from your estate and gives it directly to your heirs. That way, they can claim back any tax paid on the interest after your death.

Changing your will

If all the beneficiaries agree, they can *vary* (or rewrite) a will, known as a *deed of variation*. A deed is often used to make better use of the inheritance tax nil-rate band or to pass assets on to a younger generation (*generation skipping*). This rewriting helps keep money out of the inheritance tax net for longer than if you give it to older relatives who may already be retired and facing their own inheritance tax planning issues.

Part III
Pensions and Benefits

'The Chancellor of the Exchequer was on TV again talking about pensions.'

In this part . . .

*N*obody wants to think about growing old, but unfortunately the reality is that one day everyone wakes up with grey hair (or no hair). You need to start thinking as early as possible about how you're going to cope financially when you retire. In this part, I tell you all about the tax benefits of paying into pensions — both works and personal plans — and how to make sure that you get the best state retirement pension deal.

I also take a look at state benefits. I help you get to grips with what your tax and national insurance contributions pay for, highlight which benefits you can claim, and explain how you can safeguard your entitlement to certain benefits.

Chapter 9

Understanding UK Pensions

· ·

In This Chapter

▶ Looking at types of pension

▶ Getting the low-down on state pensions

▶ Examining private and occupational pensions

▶ Knowing where to go with pension enquiries

· ·

*N*o one wants to get old. People prefer to use euphemisms such as 'senior citizens' when talking about the 'more mature section of our community'. But when you get older, you hopefully get wiser, and with a tax system as complicated as that in the UK, you need to be wise indeed.

Until your 60s, HM Revenue & Customs (HMRC) treats you just the same as everyone else, but once you hit retirement age a whole new world of tax laws and complexities opens up before you. In this chapter I introduce you to the world of *pensions* (regular income in retirement), so that you can prepare yourself in good time for your golden years. (For details on paying tax on your pension, flick to Chapter 10.)

Understanding the Basics

HMRC generally treats pensions as earnings and bases the tax on your pension on entitlement in the tax year. Here are a few examples of types of pensions:

✔ State retirement pensions

✔ Foreign pensions for services to the Crown or a government abroad

✔ Voluntary pensions paid by UK employers

✔ Other pensions (such as occupational pensions), other than tax-exempt pensions and pensions from abroad

Looking at State Pensions

If you've paid national insurance contributions (NICs) for enough qualifying years, you should receive a state retirement pension when you hit retirement age. This section takes you through the basics of the state pension, from working out how much you receive and when, to considering the benefits of deferring your pension.

Noting your entitlement

The amount of state pension you receive depends on how many years you have paid, are treated as having paid, or have been credited with NICs. If you build up enough qualifying years during your working life, when you reach state pension age you receive the full basic state pension (£90.70 per week from 7 April 2008 for a single person; £145.05 per week for a pensioner couple). *Qualifying years* are the years in which you've been paying or are treated as paying NICs. (For more details on NICs, state benefits, and qualifying years, take a look at Chapter 11.)

Before 6 April 2010, men need 44 qualifying years by the age of 65 to get a full basic state pension and women who are 60 before this date need 39 qualifying years. On or after 6 April 2010, anyone who reaches state pension age needs 30 qualifying years.

If you don't have the full number of qualifying years, you may still get a percentage of the full basic state pension, depending on the number of qualifying years you have. To get the minimum basic state pension (25 per cent) you normally need 10 (for women) or 11 (for men) qualifying years.

The state retirement pension is designed to give you a basic income when you retire, but you have the responsibility of deciding on the kind of lifestyle you want in retirement, and what you need to do to achieve it. If living on less than £400 a month during retirement sounds less than luxurious, you need to consider paying into a separate pension – see the later section 'Thinking about private and occupational pensions' for more details.

Figuring out when you reach retirement age

The earliest time you can receive a state pension is when you reach state pension age. This age is currently different for men and women, although women's state pension age is gradually going to increase between 2010 and 2020 to become the same as men's. At the moment, state pension age is as follows:

- ✔ Men: 65
- ✔ Women:
  - Born on or before 5 April 1950: 60
  - Born on or after 6 April 1955: 65
  - Born on or after 6 April 1950 but on or before 5 April 1955: 60 plus one month for each month (or part month) that the birth date fell on or after 6 April 1950

Obtaining a forecast

You can get a forecast that shows how much state pension (basic state pension, additional state pension, or both) you can expect to receive, reflecting today's position and given in today's values. The older you are (up until retirement), the more accurate this estimate is likely to be.

To get your forecast, go to the Pension Service Web site (www.thepensionservice.gov.uk).

Deferring your state pension

You can put off claiming your state retirement pension when you reach state pension age, or choose to stop claiming it after you've already claimed. This option is called pension *deferral*. Deferring your state pension allows you to build up extra income or a taxable lump-sum payment.

Extra state pension

To get extra state pension you have to put off claiming for at least five weeks. You build up extra pension at 1 per cent of your normal weekly state pension rate for every five weeks you put off claiming (equivalent to about 10.4 per cent extra for every full year you put off claiming). The amount of extra state pension you receive when you do claim is calculated by adding up all the extra state pension accrued. The amount isn't compounded and shouldn't be seen as interest.

Extra state pension is paid on top of your normal weekly state pension from when you start claiming it, and continues for as long as you're getting state pension. Also, extra state pension is increased each April in line with increases to your normal state pension.

Extra state pension is counted as earnings and is therefore liable to income tax, just like your normal state retirement pension.

Lump sum payment

To get a lump-sum payment you have to put off claiming for a continuous period of at least 12 months (which can't include any period before 6 April 2005).

The lump sum is a one-off, taxable payment based on the amount of normal weekly state pension you would have received, plus interest. You also get your state pension paid at the normal rate from when you start claiming it.

The interest rate is always 2 per cent above the Bank of England's base rate (so if the base rate is 4.5 per cent, the rate of interest would be 6.5 per cent). Because the Bank of England base rate may change from time to time, the rate of interest used to calculate the lump sum can also change.

Alfred decides to defer his weekly state pension entitlement of £105 for three years. When he finally claims it and chooses a lump sum, Alfred gets a lump sum of around £18,000 (before tax) as well as his normal weekly state pension entitlement. (Note that this example doesn't take any annual increases in state pension into account.)

You can find out more about deferring your state retirement pension online at www.thepensionservice.gov.uk, or telephone the Pension Forecasting Team on 0845 3000 168. If you're already over state pension age and you want to find out how much you can get if you stop claiming your state pension for a while (or if you haven't yet claimed it), phone the Pension Service on 0845 60 60 265.

If you aren't receiving the full state pension (£90.70 per week for a single person and £145.05 for a pensioner couple from 7 April 2008), because you chose to defer part of it until a later date or you don't qualify, check with your HMRC tax office that you aren't being taxed on amounts you're not receiving (contact details are on the HMRC Web site at www.hmrc.gov.uk).

Applying for Pension Credit

Pension Credit is a non-taxable income-related benefit for people aged 60 or over living in Great Britain that provides, or contributes to, a guaranteed level of income of £124.05 per week for a single person or £189.35 for a couple (2008–9). These amounts may be more for people who have caring responsibilities, are severely disabled, or have certain housing costs.

People aged 65 and over can also be rewarded for some of the savings and income they have for their retirement. This benefit gives pensioners a cash addition of 60p for every £1 of income they have above the level of basic state pension, up to a maximum of £24.05 a week (£32.91 a week for couples). After this, the maximum reward reduces by 40p for every £1 of income above the income guarantee, so that pensioners with incomes up to around £172 a week (£250 a week for couples) can still be entitled.

To apply for Pension Credit you must be aged at least 60 or within four months of your 60th birthday, and you can claim even if your partner is under 60. From 2010 the age from which you can get Pension Credit is gradually going to increase in line with the state pension age, becoming 65 for women as well as men by 2020.

If you apply for Pension Credit and are eligible, you may receive a payment backdated (for up to 12 months from the day you were first entitled to the date you first applied).

You can get further information about Pension Credit, including details on how to apply, online at www.thepensionservice.gov.uk. Alternatively, you can apply by calling the Pension Credit helpline on 0800 99 1234.

Thinking About Private and Occupational Pensions

If you dream of a secure retirement that doesn't involve fretting over heating bills and the price of bread, you need to supplement your state retirement pension. This section introduces you to paying into a pension scheme, which can help you enjoy a more comfortable retirement.

Paying into a pension

Following the recent pension crisis, the Government is keen to encourage people to plan ahead for their retirement. Consequently, HMRC's rules allow more flexibility than ever, and provide good opportunities to save tax.

Knowing the tax perks

Tax advantages of paying into a pension scheme or policy during your working life include:

- ✔ Your contributions (up to certain limits) attract tax relief at your top rate of income tax. This means that if you pay tax at 40 per cent on your income, you get tax relief at 40 per cent on payments you make to your pension.

- ✔ Your employer can contribute to your company pension scheme or your personal pension scheme and, in doing so, the company reduces its taxable business profits (because the contributions are treated as a business expense when the company works out its taxable profits). And the contributions aren't treated as a taxable perk so you won't have to pay tax on them.

- ✔ You can get a tax-free lump sum (within permitted limits) from your pension scheme when you retire.

- ✔ Non-taxpayers can obtain basic rate tax relief on personal pension contributions of up to £3,600 per tax year (see the following section for more).

Understanding the new laws

On 6 April 2006 a single set of simplified rules came into effect that govern how HMRC taxes pensions. The new rules are designed to make things simpler, and to make saving for your retirement more flexible. Here are some of the rules:

- ✔ You can save in more than one pension scheme at a time.

- ✔ You can get tax relief on contributions up to 100 per cent of your annual earnings up to an annual allowance set at £235,000 for 2008–9. When you exceed this annual allowance, you pay an annual allowance charge of 40 per cent on contributions or increases in excess of the annual allowance, but only where tax relief has been given on those contributions. This rule is subject to a limit of £3,600, which is the amount that everyone, even non-taxpayers, can pay into a pension each year.

- ✔ Non-taxpayers can invest up to £2,880 (from 2008–9 onwards) in any one tax year and receive tax relief of £720, so the total amount saved in their pension pot with tax relief is £3,600 gross per annum.

- ✔ You can pay as much as you like into your pension. However, you have a *lifetime allowance* (£1.65 million for 2008–9), which is the maximum amount on which you can get tax relief.

The pension tax simplification regime that came in from April 2006 abolished the complex rules regarding limits on annual contributions and instead set a lifetime allowance. So instead of a ceiling on what you can put in, the limit is now on how large your fund can grow. But most people can ignore this limit – only a few are ever going to hit the £1.65 million!

Understanding occupational pensions

Many firms offer *occupational pensions*, in which the employer pays in money to help build up your pension. This arrangement works out well for the employer because the contributions can be deducted from its own tax bill. Most occupational pension schemes ask the employee to pay something in, usually around 6 per cent of pre-tax pay. A minority of employers don't require employees to make contributions. These pension plans are known as *non-contributory*.

Two basic forms of occupational pension schemes are available and each comes with its own tax breaks:

- **Defined benefits schemes:** These schemes are often referred to as *final salary schemes*. In this type of scheme a formula is used to work out the amount of pension you receive when you retire. This amount is usually based on your final salary level and the number of years you've worked for your employer.

  The maximum pension you can receive from a final salary scheme is two-thirds of your final salary. However, only a small minority of people receive this much. Most people end up with less because they change jobs during their working life or miss out on past contributions.

- **Defined contributions schemes:** These schemes are also known as *money purchase schemes*. The amount of pension you receive under this type of scheme depends on how much your pension fund grows during the time you pay into it.

The amount of tax relief you get on pension contributions depends on the type of scheme you're in and how much you pay into it. Check out Chapter 10 for more on paying tax on occupational pensions.

Topping up with extra payments

The new simplified pensions tax regime that came into effect from April 2006 means that the complicated rules on annual limits and investments have been abolished. You can now put a wider range of assets into your pension through a self-invested personal pension (SIPP). These assets can include shares, bonds, cash, complicated futures, option-based plans, unit trusts, and commercial properties, to name but a few. You can also now pay even more contributions into your employer's or your own pension plan and enjoy the tax advantages.

Making additional voluntary payments

If you want to top up the required weekly or monthly amount you pay into your employer's pension scheme you can make *Additional Voluntary Contributions* (AVCs). Since the new pensions rules came into effect (April 2006), the only limit on contributions is your annual earnings – although you're unlikely to want to shovel your entire annual salary into your pension. If your employer puts a limit on the amount of AVCs you can make, you can go for a *stakeholder plan*, which has similar tax breaks.

Tax relief on AVCs works the same way as payments into your main pension fund; that is, your employer takes the contributions off your pre-tax pay. You shouldn't have to do anything to claim it.

When you decide to cash in your AVC plan, you can take up to 25 per cent of its value as a tax-free lump sum. This limit applies from April 2006, and you can cash in even if your AVC was paid under old rules that banned tax-free lump sums.

Claiming a stake in your future

A *stakeholder plan* is a low cost and flexible way of contributing to a personal pension. You can stop and start payments without being penalised. Minimum monthly contributions into stakeholder plans are usually £20 or less. You can get tax relief on the money you invest in a stakeholder plan, but here's the even better news – you can also get tax relief on money you invest for someone else. So non-working spouses, partners, students, and even babies can have a stakeholder plan and get tax relief on the money paid into it. The beneficiaries of the plan don't have to be related to you.

You can invest up to £3,600 a year into a stakeholder plan for any number of individuals provided you don't top the annual limit of your earnings. You get automatic tax relief at 20 per cent (from 2008–9) on your contributions, so each £1 invested only costs 80p. Non-taxpayers and those who pay tax at the 10 per cent rate also get relief at the 20 per cent rate. Higher rate taxpayers benefit the most because they get relief at 40 per cent, so a £1 contribution into a pension only costs 60p.

If you have an income from a second job or do freelance work, you can also pay into a pension based on these earnings.

Buying an annuity to save tax

You may want to consider purchasing an annuity in order to convert your pension pot (and any other savings) into an income that you then get for the rest of your life.

An *annuity* is often described as life insurance in reverse. Instead of paying in premiums each month and your family receiving a lump sum when you die, you pay over a lump sum and receive a monthly pension until you die. As you can see, you do a lot better out of this deal if you live longer!

Table 9-1 sets out the various types of annuity on offer.

Table 9-1	Types of Annuities and Their Benefits	
Annuity Type	*Definition*	*Tax Aspects*
Compulsory (pension)	A retirement income for life plan bought from a personal pension fund	The entire payment is taxed as income
Purchased	A retirement income for life plan bought from any other money	Only the investment element is taxed: The repayment of your lump sum savings is tax free

Most providers set a minimum lump sum of £20,000 (or even higher) for investment in a purchased annuity.

Purchased life annuities often work better for people with shorter life expectancies, perhaps when they are ill or very old, because the return of the capital element is greater in this type of plan.

Head over to Chapter 10 for more information on paying tax on your annuity.

Taking your pension

In the following three cases you can start collecting a pension at 50, even if you're still working:

- ✔ You retire early due to poor health.

- ✔ Your pension scheme gave you the right to retire before 50 at 6 April 2006.

- ✔ Your occupation is a professional footballer or model, which means you can collect a pension at 35 (not likely, I know, but you can dream!).

At the other end of the age range, the current maximum age to collect a regular pension is 75.

You don't have to stop working to draw your pension. You can carry on working for your employer and even pay into a second pension if you want to. Some people take this option to unlock the tax-free lump sum so they can spend it, but don't forget that this inevitably lowers your eventual retirement income.

Once you reach state pension age you no longer have to pay NICs. Ask HMRC for a 'certificate of exemption' to give to your employer if you're still working. Your employer carries on deducting income tax under the PAYE system (jump to Chapter 12 for information about PAYE) and carries on paying employer's NICs on your pay if appropriate.

But although you're exempt from NICs after state retirement age, you do still have to do a self-assessment tax return if you have spare-time earnings from self-employment. These earnings are added to your pension payments to produce an overall figure for taxation purposes.

Finding Further Help

Sometimes things can get unnecessarily complicated. Don't dig yourself in deeper. Plenty of people are ready and willing to help you – and plenty of that help is free.

For general advice on planning for your future, and more information on pensions, see Julian Knight's *Retiring Wealthy For Dummies* (Wiley).

Contacting HMRC

HMRC has a number of different contact points and runs a range of helplines (flick to the Appendix for a full list). If you want to arrange a face-to-face appointment at one of the HMRC Enquiry Centres, you can find your nearest one by logging on to www.hmrc.gov.uk/enq/index.htm.

Always give your National Insurance Number whether writing or telephoning. This number is unique to you and helps HMRC trace your records.

Talking about National Insurance

The National Insurance Enquiries for Individuals helpline deals with most general enquiries regarding national insurance for individual customers, including Age Exemption, Home Responsibilities Protection (HRP), Married Women's Reduced Rate Election (MWRRE), Statement requests, Class 3, Automated Refunds' and Deferment Renewals. You can call the helpline on 0845 302 1479 (Monday to Friday 8am to 5pm).

If you've received an NIC deficiency notice, or believe that you may have a shortfall in your contributions that may affect your entitlement to a state retirement pension, you can call the HMRC National Insurance Deficiency helpline on 0845 915 5995.

Seeking other support

Several organisations exist that specifically help pensioners and people on low incomes with tax matters. Here are details of a few:

- ✔ **Advicenow (www.advicenow.org.uk):** This independent, not-for-profit Web site provides accurate, up-to-date information on rights and legal issues.

- ✔ **Age Concern (www.ageconcern.org.uk):** Age Concern is a national charity that takes a proactive role towards influencing government policy particularly focusing on the needs of older people. They also offer a free helpline on 0800 00 99 66.

- ✔ **Citizens Advice Centres (NACAB; www.citizensadvice.org.uk):** NACAB offers free, confidential, impartial, and independent advice on a range of issues.

- ✔ **Department for Work and Pensions (DWP; www.dwp.gov.uk):** The DWP Web site has information on all benefits and State Pension. The Pensions and Retirement Section of the DWP Web site (www.dwp.gov.uk/lifeevent/penret) gives basic information on a number of benefit issues.

- ✔ **Low Incomes Tax Reform Group (LITRG; www.litrg.org.uk):** LITRG is run by a group of like-minded people who joined together with the support and encouragement of the Chartered Institute of Taxation (CIOT) to give a voice to those people on low incomes and pensioners who battle against the complexity of the tax/benefits systems.

✔ **TaxAid (www.taxaid.org.uk):** TaxAid is a UK charity providing free tax advice to people who can't afford to pay a professional adviser. The service is independent and confidential. The Web site contains a lot of useful information and is well worth a look. You can contact TaxAid on 0845 120 3779 and book a face-to-face appointment.

✔ **TaxHelp for Older People (TOP; www.taxvol.org.uk):** TOP is a charitable service providing free advice on personal tax to older people on low incomes who may otherwise not afford professional help. If this situation applies to you and you need help with your tax, you can phone their helpline on 0845 601 3321 or check the Web site for more information on TOP activities and for useful phone numbers.

Chapter 10

Paying Tax on Your Pension

• •

In This Chapter

▶ Determining which pensions you pay tax on

▶ Looking at age-related tax allowances

▶ Understanding pensions and PAYE

▶ Calculating the tax on your pension

• •

*E*ven though the government continues to close down opportunities to save tax in most areas, the Treasury remains pretty
generous with pensions. Good tax savings are to be had when you
pay into your pension and increased personal tax allowances are
on offer once you hit the age of 65. In this chapter I explain how
HM Revenue & Customs (HMRC) taxes your pension when you
eventually start to receive it, help you work out how much tax
you pay, and give you some guidance that may well slim down
your tax bill.

Knowing What's Taxable

Because your pension forms part of your income, the taxman
expects a share of most pensions payments. This section explains
the pensions on which you pay.

Understanding the basics

When you contribute to your pension, the money you pay in is
offset against your taxable income, using the Pay As You Earn
(PAYE) system if you're employed. This relief is at your highest
tax rate, and the pension payment comes off your salary before
anything else, other than national insurance contributions (NICs).
Everything appears to be rosy, doesn't it? But, as the saying goes,
there's no such thing as a free lunch and, when you retire, the
money you get back from your pension is taxable income.

When you retire, your pension pot provides a tax-free lump sum – all schemes now provide that 25 per cent of the pension pot can be paid as a lump sum, but some older plans that offered higher percentages can be protected. The rest of the pot is generally converted into an income for life, known as an *annuity*, on which you pay income tax. You pay tax only on the balance of your pension after tax allowances are taken off (see the later section 'Establishing Your Allowances').

Both your state retirement pension and your occupational pension (the annuity bit) are almost always taxable. Tax isn't taken off your state retirement pension before you get it, but your occupational pension is taxed (along with personal pension and retirement annuities, if appropriate), usually under the PAYE system, before receipt.

Looking at tax-exempt pensions

Some pensions are exempt from tax including:

- ✔ Armed forces compensation schemes
- ✔ Certain pensions paid to non-UK residents (for example, colonial and overseas service pensions)
- ✔ Early departure payments scheme
- ✔ Pensions awarded to employees who were disabled at work or suffer from a work-related illness
- ✔ Pensions for victims of Nazi persecution
- ✔ War widow's pension
- ✔ Wounds and Disability pensions for members of the Armed Forces

Certain lump sum payments (within permitted limits) received on retirement are also not taxable.

Receiving a foreign pension

If you're resident in the UK for tax purposes you generally have to pay UK income tax on your worldwide income in the tax year in which the income arises (referred to as the *arising basis*). Therefore, if you receive a pension from overseas but you're a UK resident, you're liable to pay UK tax on it. You are usually taxed on 90 per cent of the amount you receive.

If you're classed as not domiciled in the UK (refer to Chapter 2, which explains the meaning of domicile), you're liable to pay UK income tax on a foreign pension only to the extent that you bring the money into the country (referred to as the *remittance basis*).

Establishing Your Allowances

Ultimately, your aim is to take home as much of your pension as possible. The good news is that several tax allowances reduce the amount of income tax you pay:

- **Basic personal tax allowance:** Most people are entitled to the basic allowance (£5,435 for 2008–9). After you turn 65 the allowance increases, depending on your age and income level.

- **Age allowance:** Between 65 and 74 the age allowance (also called full or higher personal allowance) is £9,030 for 2008–9, rising to £9,180 for someone 75 and over. If your income, including your state pension, is too low to benefit from the age-related allowance, you can apply for a pension credit – Chapter 9 has more info on this credit.

- **Married couple's allowance:** This allowance doesn't come off your total income, but reduces your tax bill instead. Refer to Chapter 4 for the low-down on married couple's allowance.

However, if your total income (from pensions, employment, savings, and so on) before any allowances is more than £21,800 (in 2008–9) the situation gets more complicated. The following sections explain how the age-allowance trap increases your tax bill and how you can avoid getting caught in it.

Understanding the age-allowance trap

Age-related tax allowances at both the 65 and 75 year-old levels disappear for incomes that fall into the top tax rate of 40 per cent. This age-allowance trap hits those with a total income exceeding £21,800 a year (in 2008–9).

You can keep only some of the higher personal allowance if your income is below set levels. If your income for 2008–9 is over £28,990 for someone 65–74 (over £29,290 for someone 75 or over), your personal allowance is the basic allowance that everyone gets of £5,435. If your income falls between £21,800 and £28,990 or

£29,290 for 2008–9, your age allowance of £9,030 or £9,180 is reduced but never below the basic allowance of £5,435.

Once you top £21,800 a year in income, the age allowance goes down by £1 for every £2 of income you earn above that level until it falls back down to the same as the personal allowance for those aged under 65. So the gap is twice the number of pounds between the under-65 personal allowance and the age-related rate. For someone aged 65 to 74, the gap in 2008–9 is £7,190, and so the benefit stops entirely once your income reaches £28,990 (£21,800 plus £7,190). If you're 75 or more, the age trap disappears altogether at £29,290 (£21,800 plus £7,490). The £7,490 gap is twice the value of the 75-plus age allowance because you lose on a £1 for £2 basis.

Not just wealthy people lose out under the age allowance trap. Many basic-rate taxpayers with incomes of little more than half to two-thirds the top-rate starting level also lose out on their age allowance. Why? Because you pay a really high tax rate on each extra pound you earn once you hit the level where the age allowances starts to taper off.

Within the trap band, every extra £1 you earn costs a 30p tax deduction. This sum is made up of the standard rate of tax of 20p in every pound plus one half (10p) of the 20p in tax relief that's lost for each £2 you earn. So, for income caught in the trap, the result is just like having a special, ultra-high 30 per cent tax rate.

Escaping the tax trap

You can't do much if your income from employment and/or pensions means that you fall into the age-allowance trap. However, if you have other income from savings and investments, or other non-work sources, you may be able to find a partial or total escape route.

If you're married or have a civil partner, and are close to the level at which age-related allowances are reduced, consider transferring income-producing assets to the lower-earning spouse or partner.

Saving to save tax

By making clever investments you can receive income that HMRC doesn't count for age-related allowance purposes:

- ✔ **Capital profit investments:** Capital gains don't count for working out age-related tax allowances, so investments that produce little or no income but aim to give capital profits can be helpful here – although you have to give serious thought to the potential risks often involved with these types of investments. Chapter 6 gives details on capital gains and investments.

✔ **Insurance bonds:** Withdrawals from insurance bonds, such as with-profits bonds, are also exempt, provided they don't exceed 5 per cent of the original investment in any tax year. You can also add up any unused 5 per cent limits from previous years. So, if you missed 10 years, you can receive 50 per cent of your original investment back tax-free. And if you did nothing for 20 years or longer, you can take all your original cash.

✔ **Roll-up accounts:** A number of banks in places such as Jersey, Guernsey, and the Isle of Man offer these accounts. Instead of taking your interest every year and paying tax on it, you leave it there to grow (or roll up) and pay no tax until you bring it home to spend. That way, you can actually choose when to pay tax on it.

✔ **Tax-free investing:** Income from some types of savings and investments is tax-free, for example, interest earned on savings held in Individual Savings Accounts (ISAs) (Chapter 6 looks at tax-efficient savings and investments in detail). This type of income doesn't count against your total income for the age-related tax allowances purposes.

Giving it away

If you're feeling generous you may be able to reduce your income below the age-allowance trap limit by making a donation to charity using the Gift Aid scheme. You can make a donation to any registered charity and you take all that money away from the age-trap zone. Refer to Chapter 6 for more on Gift Aid.

Sidney's total income for the year is £22,800. He is therefore caught in the age-allowance trap for 2008–9 by £1,000. If he gives £1,000 to charity under the Gift Aid scheme, his total income for working out age allowances is reduced by that amount.

Paying Tax under PAYE

Paying tax on a pension is much the same as paying tax on your earnings from employment: Both types of income come under the PAYE scheme (Chapter 12 has further info on PAYE). The idea of PAYE is to try to make sure that you've paid the right amount of tax due on your income by the end of the tax year. The tax is collected from each weekly or monthly payment of pension that you receive so that if correctly operated, you should have no additional tax to pay at the end of the year. The following sections explain how PAYE works for collecting occupational, private, and state pensions.

After the end of the tax year you get a form P60 that shows your total pension and tax deducted. Keep this form safe in case you need it to fill in a tax return or repayment claim.

Paying tax on state pensions

If you only receive a state retirement pension and have no other income from earnings or savings, your income is below the personal tax allowance level each year and you won't have to pay any tax on it.

If you receive the state retirement pension, but no other pension, and have other income from savings and investments that puts your total income for the year above the level of personal tax allowances that you're entitled to (see Chapter 4 for details of personal allowances), you need to complete a self-assessment tax return and pay any tax you owe to HMRC (refer to Chapter 3 for more on self assessment).

Contact your local tax office if you need further help with paying tax on your state pension. You can find all the HMRC contact numbers online at www.hmrc.gov.uk, or contact the HMRC How to Pay helpline on 0845 366 7816.

Paying tax on occupational and private pensions

Under PAYE, HMRC issues your pension provider with a Notice of Coding, which contains your tax code. The tax code tells the pension provider what allowances it can set against your pension (see the previous section 'Establishing Your Allowances'). Chapter 12 explains tax codes in detail.

Tell HMRC when you start receiving a pension so that it can issue a new Notice of Coding to your pension payer.

Each time you're paid, your pension provider acts like an intermediary for the taxman – your pension provider deducts money for tax, and then pays this amount over to HMRC. You may receive a slip or other notice showing your total pension and the tax taken off but not all pension providers send a slip – some send out a payslip only when a change to the amount of tax you pay is involved.

Your pension provider deducts tax based on information given to it by HMRC, so that you receive only the net amount after this tax has been taken off. Tax is deducted at the following rates for 2008–9:

- ✔ Twenty per cent on the first £36,000
- ✔ Forty per cent on everything over £36,000

Remember that these rates apply to *taxable* income only, to that income over and above your personal allowance. For example, a pensioner aged 69 would need to have income of £45,030 before paying tax at 40 per cent.

In 2008–9, Teresa receives an occupational pension of £16,300 before any tax is taken off. HMRC sends Teresa's former employer a Notice of Coding that indicates she has a tax-free amount of allowances of £2,250.

	£
Pension	16,300
Less: tax-free allowances	2,250
Pension on which Teresa pays tax	14,050
Tax payable	
£14,050 × 20 per cent (basic rate)	2,810.00

Teresa's total tax liability for 2008–9 is £2,810. The tax she pays this year is £2,810, so she takes home a total of £13,490 over the course of the year.

Paying tax on both state and occupational or private pensions

If you're receiving a state retirement pension, HMRC collects the tax due on it at the same time as the tax due on the occupational or private pension. HMRC normally makes an adjustment to your PAYE tax code number to take into account the amount of state pension you receive. This means that your pension provider takes care of the tax due on both sources of income and you don't need to do anything else.

In 2008–9, Harry is 65 and starts to receive a state pension of £90.70 per week, so that's £4,716 a year. He also starts to receive a pension from his employer of £12,000 a year. He is entitled to the age-related personal tax allowance of £9,030. HMRC deduct the expected state pension from his personal allowance, leaving a balance of personal tax allowances to be used against his occupational pension of £4,314 (£9,030 – £4,716). A PAYE tax code is sent to Harry's former employer (now his pension provider) and they operate this code against his pension. His tax for year is calculated as follows:

	£
Pension	12,000
Less: Personal allowances	(4,314)
Taxable	7,686
Tax due:	
£7,686 × 20 per cent (basic rate)	
Total tax payable	1,537.20
Net pension (£12,000 – £1,537.20)	10,462.80

Harry's former employer pays the tax deducted over to HMRC and Harry receives a total of £15,178.80 (£10,462.80 + £4,716) in his pocket.

In the second year after retirement make sure that any adjustments made in your tax code, which were due in earlier years from your prior employment, aren't being simply carried forward (just because you had them last year).

Paying tax on your retirement annuity

Chapter 9 discusses buying an *annuity*, which means paying a lump sum now and receiving the money back later as a monthly pension. All retirement annuities are taxed under PAYE – just like a private or occupational pension – which makes it easier to work out how much tax you pay on your annuity. You receive a monthly payslip, or certificate at the end of each year, which sets it all out for you.

Jane, aged 67, paid into a retirement annuity policy at Global Investments for many years. She now receives an annuity of £5,000 a year and state pension of £5,700. Jane has tax-free personal allowances of £9,030 for 2008–9 so she pays tax on only £1,670 (5,700 + 5,000 – 9,030). At the 20 per cent basic rate of tax, therefore, her tax liability for 2008–9 is £334, which she pays under PAYE on her annuity.

Global Investments took 20 per cent tax of £1,000 off Jane's annuity before paying it to her, which is a lot more tax than the £334 Jane is due to pay for the year. Therefore, she needs to claim a repayment each tax year.

Chapter 11

Looking at State Benefits and Tax

. . . .

In This Chapter

▶ Checking eligibility to state benefits

▶ Identifying taxable and non-taxable state benefits

▶ Paying voluntary national insurance contributions

. . . .

*T*axation pays for the UK social security scheme, which exists to provide benefits to UK people. You pay your taxes, and in return you support a system that helps society – from giving a basic pension to older people through to supporting children and those who are disabled and infirm. And during your lifetime you no doubt benefit from the system yourself, which hopefully makes you feel marginally less inclined to complain about your tax bill.

In this chapter I run through which state benefits are taxable (liable to income tax) and which are exempt for tax purposes. Then I look at how you can make sure that you pay the right contributions in order to maximise your entitlement to state benefits.

Understanding State Benefits

The aim of the UK's national insurance scheme is to protect members of the population who retire or fall on hard times. You pay into the scheme through income tax and national insurance contributions (NICs) throughout your working life, with the hope that the State gives you support as and when you need it. The payments that the state provides, including state retirement pensions, are collectively known as *state benefits*. The following sections explore who's eligible for state benefits, and which benefits you pay tax on.

Looking at entitlement to state benefits

Some state benefits are paid to people who need them regardless of what they have paid into the national insurance scheme, for example Child Benefit, Income Support, and Council Tax Benefit. However, you are able to claim other state benefits only if you've paid enough into the national insurance scheme. Moreover, the amount that you're entitled to receive depends on the level of those contributions. Examples of contribution-based state benefits include Jobseeker's allowance, Maternity allowance, and state retirement pension.

Although some state benefits that you may be entitled to during your lifetime, such as state retirement pension, are linked to the total amount of NICs you've paid during your working life, entitlement to most benefits is based on whether you've paid at least the minimum NIC each week. If you've paid at least the minimum amount, that week should qualify for contributory state benefits. However, the actual amount you receive depends ultimately on how much you paid each week.

Here's a summary of some of the most common contribution-based state benefits and the NICs you must make to safeguard your entitlement:

- ✔ **Bereavement allowance:** Paid for one year to widows, widowers, and civil partners aged over 45 who were below pension age when their spouse died. The deceased spouse needs to have paid the equivalent of 25 minimum payments.

- ✔ **Contribution-based Jobseeker's allowance:** People who are available for and actively looking for (seeking) work can receive this allowance if they paid enough NICs in the past. To get benefit, you need to discuss, usually every two weeks, when you're available for work and what you're doing to find a job. If you don't qualify for contribution-based Jobseeker's allowance (because your NICs are insufficient), you may be able to claim income-based Jobseeker's allowance if your income and savings are below a certain level.

- ✔ **Incapacity benefit:** If you can't work because of ill health or a disability, you may be able to claim Incapacity Benefit, which is a contributions-based benefit paid at a set rate. It gives people of working age a replacement income when they can't work or look for work because of ill health or a disability. Incapacity benefit is paid at two rates (lower and higher) and for two periods (short-term and long-term).

✔ **State retirement pension:** Currently paid to men at age 65
and over and to women aged 60 and over. In very basic terms,
you, your late (or former) spouse, or your civil partner must
have paid 52 weekly payments (or the equivalent in monthly
or annual terms) of NICs each year for that year to qualify
towards your eventual state pension. You're allowed to miss
out one year in every ten. If you don't meet these minimum
requirements, you may get a percentage of the full amount,
depending on your shortfall.

✔ **Widowed parent's allowance:** Paid to widows and widowers,
and civil partners, with children usually aged under 19. The
contribution rules are similar to those for the state retirement
pension (see preceding bullet point).

Knowing which benefits are taxable

When you're entitled to a state benefit you receive it in full, without anything taken off for income tax. However, if you're a taxpayer
you may end up paying income tax later on some benefits, known
as *taxable state benefits*. The taxable state benefits are:

✔ Bereavement allowance

✔ Carer's allowance

✔ Incapacity benefit

✔ Industrial death benefit penalty

✔ Jobseeker's allowance

✔ State pension

✔ Widow's pension and widowed parent's allowance

You must keep a record of all taxable state benefits you receive
and include them as income on your self-assessment return (refer
to Chapter 3 for more on self assessment).

Some state benefits, known as *non-taxable state benefits*, are
exempt for income tax purposes, which means you never pay
any tax on your income from that benefit and you don't need to
declare the benefit on a self-assessment form. Here's a full list of
non-taxable state benefits:

✔ Attendance allowance

✔ Back to work bonus

✔ Bereavement payment

- ✔ Child benefit
- ✔ Child's special allowance
- ✔ Child tax credit
- ✔ Council tax benefit
- ✔ Disability living allowance
- ✔ Guardian's allowance
- ✔ Housing benefit
- ✔ Incapacity benefit (for the first 28 weeks only)
- ✔ Income support
- ✔ Industrial injuries benefit (a general term covering industrial injuries pension, reduced earnings allowance, retirement allowance, constant attendance allowance, and exceptionally severe disablement allowance)
- ✔ Invalidity benefit (replaced by Incapacity benefit from April 1995 but still payable where invalidity commenced before April 1995)
- ✔ Maternity allowance
- ✔ Pensioner's Christmas bonus
- ✔ Pension credit
- ✔ Severe disablement allowance
- ✔ Statutory redundancy payments
- ✔ Social fund payments – budgeting loan, cold weather payment, community care grant, crisis loan, funeral payment, winter fuel payments
- ✔ Vaccine damage
- ✔ War widow's pension
- ✔ Working tax credit

To find out the 2008–9 rates for some of the most common benefits, head to the Appendix of this book.

Paying Voluntary NICs

To work out your entitlement to contribution-based state benefits (see the earlier section 'Looking at entitlement to state benefits'), the government looks at how much you've paid under the various classes of national insurance. Employees pay Class 1, the self-employed pay Class 2 and Class 4, and Class 3 contributions are entirely voluntary contributions. 'Are you mad? Why does anyone pay tax voluntarily!' I hear you cry. Well, in this section I show you why you may need to pay voluntary contributions in order to safeguard your entitlement to benefits.

Working out who pays voluntary NICs

In order to safeguard your entitlement to the full state pension and other state benefits, such as widowed parent's allowance, bereavement payment, bereavement allowance, and child's special allowance, you can pay Class 3 NICs to help fill gaps in your NIC record. These gaps may exist because:

✔ Your earnings are low.

✔ You've been living abroad.

✔ You're unemployed and have not been claiming benefits.

You can pay voluntary contributions for any tax year in which you're aged over 16 and

✔ Employed but not liable to pay Class 1 and/or Class 2 contributions (because your earnings are too low to qualify for paying NICs)

✔ Excepted from paying Class 2 contributions (because your earnings from self-employment have not reached the level at which you're entitled to make payment)

✔ Not working

✔ Resident in the UK but living or working on secondment abroad

✔ Self-employed

You may be able to get national insurance credits if you're unable to work, entitled to certain benefits, or in other specific circumstances, for example being on an approved training course or attending jury service. And if you care for a child or a sick or disabled person, Home Responsibilities Protection (HRP) may cover gaps in your NIC record. To find out whether credits and HRP may apply to you, visit the Pension Service Web site at www.thepensionservice.gov.uk/atoz/atozdetailed/homeres.asp, or telephone their helpline on 0845 60 60 265.

Deciding whether to top up your NICS

So how do you know whether you need to make voluntary contributions? You can find out in one of two ways:

✔ You contact the HMRC National Insurance Contributions Office and ask it to check whether you owe any NICs (0845 302 1479; www.direct.gov.uk/en/Dll/Directories/DG_ 10011010). You can also request a state pension forecast from the Pension Service (0845 300 0168; www.thepensionservice. gov.uk).

✔ HMRC sends you a letter (between September and January) notifying you that your NICs are insufficient.

Class 3 NICs are voluntary, so however you discover a gap exists in your contributions, the choice to make voluntary contributions to make up the shortfall is entirely yours. However, if you want your full entitlement to benefits such as the state pension (and trust me, you really do), you must ensure that you top up your NICs in good time.

Paying for earlier years

If HMRC writes to you about gaps in your NIC record, the letter tells you how much you can pay if you want to fill the gaps and a payslip is enclosed. If you suspect that you owe NICs, contact the National Insurance Contributions Office, who can help you set up payments.

Voluntary contributions are payable at the rate of £8.10 per week for 2008–9. You have two main ways of paying your Class 3 NICs:

✔ **Monthly:** By direct debit – you can download a leaflet and a direct debit application form from the HMRC Web site at www. hmrc.gov.uk/pdfs/nico/ca04.pdf

✔ **Quarterly:** By having a bill sent to you every 13 weeks (if you live in the UK) – you can pay this bill at a bank, Post Office, or by Girobank

Usually, you have to make up the shortfall for unpaid NICs within six years. For example, you need to pay Class 3 contributions for the 2007–8 year by 5 April 2014. You don't have to pay anything until then, but the rate may increase so it may be cheaper if you do pay now.

However, for the 1996–7 to 2001–2 years only, special extended limits are in place, which mean that you can still pay Class 3 NICs for all those years provided that you pay by:

  ✔ 5 April 2009, if you reach pension age on or after 24 October 2004

  ✔ 5 April 2010, if you reach pension age before 24 October 2004

The rate of Class 3 NICs paid within these extended limits is the rate that was in force during the year to which it relates. So, if the payment relates to 2001–2 but is paid in June 2009, the contributions are based on the rate in force for 2001–2, not 2009–10.

If you're self-employed but exempt from paying Class 2 contributions, you can pay voluntary Class 2 contributions to maintain your NIC record. These amounts are considerably cheaper than Class 3 contributions (the rate for 2008–9 is £2.30 per week) and they protect your entitlement to more benefits.

Part IV
Working for Someone Else

'And to keep our sales executives fit and healthy and also in keeping with our company's green policy, we've decided to dispense with company cars.'

In this part . . .

Most people who have a job work for someone else. The Pay As You Earn (PAYE) system makes life simpler for most employees because the employer is responsible for taking off the right amount for tax and national insurance before giving out the pay packets each week or month. Therefore, most employees have nothing more to do tax-wise and, in most cases, the employer has to pick up the tab if something goes wrong, even if the employee profits from the mistake — thumbs up for PAYE!

In this part, I guide you through the basics of the PAYE system so that you can check your own payslip, and I tell you what to expect when you start or leave a job. If you receive any perks or expenses from your employer you may have to pay tax on them, so I show you which ones you pay tax on and help you work out how much you pay. And if you're lucky enough to be offered a stake in your employer's company by way of a share incentive scheme, this part helps you navigate your way around the tax and national insurance issues that may arise.

Chapter 12

PAYEing Tax in Employment

*I*f you're in employment, which means you work for someone else, you pay tax through Pay as You Earn (PAYE). PAYE is the name of the tax-collecting system used in the UK, under which your employer deducts income tax and national insurance contributions (NICs) on a weekly or monthly basis from your wage.

Over the years, PAYE has become increasingly sophisticated, but you can still pay too much tax under the system, especially when you change jobs. You do get overpayments back – eventually – but taking a look at the mechanics of the system is a good idea, so you know what's going on and can ensure that you pay the correct tax under PAYE.

Walking you through the PAYE scheme, this chapter aims to help you understand whether you are indeed employed (as opposed to self-employed), how you pay income tax and NICs, your employer's responsibilities, how to decipher your tax code, and how moving jobs affects your tax bill.

Considering Your Employment Status

Knowing whether you're employed or self-employed is important, because of all the differences that exist in the way you're taxed. Employed and self-employed people pay tax in different ways and are liable for different types of national insurance. Generally, employees are taxed under the PAYE system with income tax and Class 1 NICs being deducted from payments made to them. Class 1

NICs are also payable by employers. In contrast, the self-employed pay income tax and Class 4 NICs direct to HMRC and are also liable to Class 2 NICs (see Part V for more on self-employment).

Here are some more important differences in terms of paying tax:

- Self-employed people have a much lower liability to NICs than employees (especially when taking into account the employer's liability).

- Self-employed people benefit from a cash-flow advantage in the timing of tax payments under self assessment, compared with employees taxed under the PAYE system.

- Self-employed people benefit from more relaxed rules concerning tax relief for expenses, compared with employees.

- Employers who incorrectly treat an employee as self-employed are in some circumstances liable for the income tax and NICs that they should have deducted under PAYE.

No single fact is decisive in deciding employment status. First, the terms and conditions of the engagement need to be established – normally from the contract between the worker and client/employer, whether written, oral, implied, or a mixture of all three. Second, any surrounding facts that may be relevant need to be considered – for example, whether the worker has other clients and a business organisation.

Factors indicating employment include:

- Being paid by the hour, week, or month, and eligibility for overtime pay

- Being part and parcel of the organisation

- Being told what to do, and how and when to do it

- Having mutual obligations (to provide work on the one hand, and to carry out that work on the other)

- Having right of dismissal

- Having to carry out the work personally

- Receiving employee benefits such as holiday pay, sick pay, or a company car

- Working at the other party's premises, or at a location of the other party's choice

- Working for one party for long periods

- Working set hours, or a given number of hours per week or month

Chapter 15 lists the criteria you need to fulfil to qualify for self-employed status. You can also take a look at HMRC leaflet IR56: 'Are your workers employed or self-employed – advice for contractors' (available at www.hmrc.gov.uk/new-cis/cis349.pdf).

No legislation exists to distinguish between employment and self-employment, but many important tax cases have been decided in the courts and HM Revenue & Customs (HMRC) often uses these to help it decide in borderline cases.

Knowing What You Pay Income Tax On

Income from employment is treated as earnings and therefore charged to income tax, regardless of whether the income is paid in cash (such as wages or salary) or benefits-in-kind (such as company cars, medical insurance, and so on). Taxable earnings include:

- ✔ Benefits-in-kind

- ✔ Bonuses

- ✔ Commissions

- ✔ Holiday pay, sick pay, maternity pay, and paternity pay

- ✔ Incentive payments enticing you to join a firm, and some termination payments

- ✔ Redundancy payments (subject to possible relief up to £30,000)

- ✔ Reimbursement of expenses

- ✔ Tips and service charges

- ✔ Travelling-time payments

- ✔ Wages and salaries, fees, and overtime

Employment earnings are treated as being paid, and therefore chargeable to tax, when the payment is actually made or on the date that the employee becomes entitled to them, whichever is the earliest. These rules don't apply to benefits-in-kind, which are treated as received in the tax year in which they are provided. (Chapter 13 takes you through paying tax on benefits-in-kind.)

Paying Class 1 NICs

Unless specifically exempted (for example, because you're over state retirement age), all employees and employers must pay Class 1 NICs on the employee's earnings. Contributions that employees pay are called *primary contributions* and those that employers pay are known as *secondary contributions*. The following sections explain the basics of paying Class 1 NICs.

Your employer should deduct NICs when she calculates your take-home pay each week or month. She can't normally chase you later if she forgets.

Knowing who pays Class 1 NICs

Anyone aged between 16 and state pension age – currently 60 for a woman and 65 for a man – may have a liability to pay NICs. But if you're under 16 or over state pension age, you don't have to pay Class 1 NICs.

After you retire, you must pay any outstanding Class 1 NICs on earnings you received before you reached state pension age. Then, if you decide to continue working, you pay no further Class 1 NICs, but your employer continues to pay secondary Class 1 NICs until you stop work.

When you continue working past state pension age, you need to apply for an exemption certificate, which you give to your employer. The certificate is called a CA4140/CF384: Certificate Of Age Exception, and you can get one by contacting HM Revenue & Customs, National Insurance Contributions Office, Contributor Caseworker, Longbenton, Newcastle upon Tyne, NE98 1ZZ.

If you aren't liable to pay NICs, you may still be able to pay certain contributions on a voluntary basis (normally Class 3 NICs). Paying these contributions may help safeguard or improve your future entitlement to basic state pension and bereavement benefits. (Refer to Chapter 11, which explores voluntary NICs.)

Looking at how much you pay

For 2008–9, employees pay NICs from the *primary threshold* of £105 per week up to the *upper earnings limit* of £770 per week, at a rate of 11 per cent. You also pay 1 per cent on any earnings over the £770 per week limit. Employers pay contributions at the rate of 12.8 per cent on all earnings over £105 per week. No upper earnings limit applies for employers.

When you earn between £90 and £105 per week, contributions are paid at the zero rate. The £90 threshold is known as the *lower earnings limit*. Although neither the employee nor employer actually pay NICs, your entitlement to certain benefits is maintained and earnings count for the purposes of calculating statutory sick pay and statutory maternity pay.

Contracting out

Employees and employers pay a lower amount of NICs when the employee is 'contracted out' of the State Second Pension (S2P; formerly known as the State Earnings Related Pension Scheme or SERPS). If you're contracted out of S2P you get a reduction (known as a *rebate*) of 1.6 per cent on contributions between the lower earnings limit (£90 per week in 2008–9) and the primary threshold (£105 per week in 2008–9). The rebate for 2008–9 is therefore 24p per week.

Many people contract out of S2P when they join their employer's occupational pension scheme. If you're considering contracting out, you should seek independent advice from a financial adviser (your employer may be able to recommend one, or you can find one in the Yellow Pages). The rules are complicated and you may end up with less state retirement pension than you imagined when you come to retire.

Reducing contributions for married women

In the past, married women were permitted to pay reduced rate contributions on their earnings. They were also able to continue paying reduced rate contributions if they were widowed. These contributions don't count towards benefits or qualify for a retirement pension. This option was withdrawn in 1977. However, women who were already paying reduced rate contributions were allowed to opt to continue paying them. Married women paying reduced rate contributions pay NICs at 4.85 per cent on earnings between £105 and £770 per week for 2008–9 and at 1 per cent above £770.

Paying Class 1A and 1B NICs

Class 1A NICs are payable on most benefits-in-kind liable to income tax (for example, private medical insurance contracted by the employer, and certain beneficial loans). Only employers pay the Class 1A NICs charge, so you don't need to worry about paying it yourself.

PAYE settlement agreements (PSAs) allow employers to account for any tax liability in respect of their employees on payments that are minor or irregular, or that are shared benefits on which it would be impractical to determine individual liability, in one lump sum (for example, if your employer paid for all the staff to go to Paris for the weekend, all expenses paid, and she agreed to pay the income tax liability on providing this benefit). Employers can deal with NICs on items included in PSAs in the same manner as the tax, by paying Class 1B contributions – that is, in a lump sum after the end of the tax year. Only employers pay Class 1B NICs, and payment doesn't provide any benefit entitlement for individuals.

Collecting NICs directly

Some people don't work for an employer in the UK, and aren't attached to another UK business responsible for operating national insurance on their behalf. These people have to account for their own Class 1 contributions through a NI-only Direct Collection scheme. If this situation applies to you, contact your local HMRC office to set up a scheme.

Deferring payment of NICs

If you have more than one job with different employers, each employer has to deduct NICs when your gross pay (that is, before tax and national insurance) with one or both of them is above the earnings threshold (£105 per week in 2008–9). If you have more than one job with the same employer, your earnings may be added together for NIC purposes. If your total gross pay is above the earnings threshold, your employer has to deduct NICs.

 In any one week you should pay *total* NICs at the rate of 11 per cent on earnings between £105 per week and £770 per week (for 2008–9) and at 1 per cent on earnings above that. If you have two jobs, *each* employer may deduct NICs at 11 per cent each week up to the £770 limit, and means that you may overpay your contributions. To stop this overpayment happening, HMRC may instruct one of your employers to deduct NICs at a straight rate of 1 per cent on all your earnings, so that you pay the maximum rate at 11 per cent with one employer and just 1 per cent on everything else. This is known as *deferment*, but that's just the fancy term HMRC uses when it issues your employer with instructions on how much NIC she should deduct.

HMRC only defers your liability for one tax year at a time, though the HMRC Deferment Group contact you annually to check your current situation, and you normally can't defer for the tax year in which you reach state pension age (currently 60 for women and 65 for men). If HMRC agrees to your application for deferment, you're still required to pay Class 1 NICs at the rate of 1 per cent on all earnings above the earnings threshold (£105 per week for 2008–9) in all your deferred employments.

If you don't apply for deferment and all your contributions under the various classes (Classes 1, 2, and 4) come to more than the annual maximum, you can apply for a refund. Working out the maximum annual NICs you should pay can be tricky (and involves a nasty formula) – so if you've paid Classes 1, 2, and 4 it may be worthwhile asking HMRC to check whether you've overpaid. You can contact HMRC, National Insurance Contributions Office, Refunds Group, Longbenton, Newcastle upon Tyne, NE98 1ZZ for help.

To apply for deferment from Class 1 NICs, complete the application form CA72A – Application for deferment of payment of Class 1 National Insurance contributions (NICs) from 6 April 2008 to 5 April 2009, or contact HMRC, National Insurance Contributions Office, Deferment Services, Longbenton, Newcastle upon Tyne, NE98 1ZZ.

Understanding Your Employer's Responsibilities

Your employer is responsible for operating PAYE and the total amount deducted from employees each month must be paid to HMRC within 14 working days of the end of each month. In addition to employees and directors, the PAYE system applies to the following workers (although special rules apply in some cases): agency workers, part-time and casual workers, domestic workers and nannies, foreign workers, students, and young people in training schemes. Your employer has two key roles: to deduct tax according to your personal tax code, and to issue certification of the tax you pay.

Deducting tax using your PAYE code

Your employer uses a PAYE code number to work out how much tax to deduct from your pay each week or month. (Your pension provider applies the same process when the time comes to pay out your pension – refer to Chapter 10 for details of pensions and tax.)

The number part of the code is generally the tax-free income allowed with the last digit removed. The personal income tax allowance for 2008–9 is £5,435, so most people have a PAYE tax code number of 543 followed by a letter. Someone over 65, but under 75, has a £9,030 personal allowance, giving her a 903 code number followed by a letter, if she has a full personal allowance.

The letter helps the people paying your wages, telling them the type of taxpayer you are. The main codes are:

- **BR:** This code means that basic rate tax (20 per cent from April 2008; 22 per cent for 2007–8 and earlier years) is deducted from all your income from that source.

- **DO:** This code means that the operator has to deduct tax at the higher rate (40 per cent) from all your income. DO is usually used for high earners with income from other sources.

- **K:** This code indicates that total allowances are less than total deductions (for example, where benefits exceed personal allowances) and that tax must be deducted at more than the normal rate to take into account the tax due on untaxed income (the maximum rate at which tax may be deducted is 50 per cent). The code starts with a K, for example, K460. So if you have this particular K code you pay tax on an extra £460 × 10 or £4,600 of income on top of your earnings or pension.

- **L:** This code is used when you have only the basic personal allowance, for example, 543L.

- **P:** This code is used when you receive a full personal allowance and you're aged between 65–74 at some point in the tax year, for example, 903P.

- **T:** This code is used in several situations. For example, if you don't want your employer to know your tax status, you can ask HMRC to use this letter. This code is also used if your personal allowances have been reduced because your income exceeds the income limits (your code is therefore 0T), and the code is also used where no tax is to be deducted from your income (your code is therefore NT).

- **V:** This code is used when all the following apply:
    - You receive full age allowance (for those aged 65–74).
    - You receive full married couple's allowance because one or both of you were born before 6 April 1935 and both of you are aged under 75.
    - You're a basic rate taxpayer, for example, 550V.

- **Y:** This code is used where you receive a full personal allowance because you become 75 at some point in the tax year or are already more than 75 years old, for example, 918Y.

HMRC usually issues a Notice of Coding in January or February for the following tax year, allowing employers to use this code from 6 April (the start of the new tax year). An amended notice is then issued in the following May or June to correct any allowances for the tax year that have been announced in the Budget (which usually takes place in March). So for 2008–9, an initial notice is issued in January or February 2008, followed by an updated notice in May 2008, following the Budget in March 2008. HMRC may issue further notices amending your tax code number during the tax year if any changes in circumstance apply (for example, you start using a company car).

At the end of each tax year, your employer has to complete certain end-of-year return forms and send them to HMRC. These returns have to tally with amounts of tax and national insurance she has paid over on your behalf – if they don't, HMRC wants to know why.

Issuing tax certificates

Your employer must also give you certain forms that certify your tax position:

- ✔ **P45:** When you leave a job, your employer must give you a form P45, which shows your PAYE code and the cumulative pay and tax up to the date of leaving. You then give the P45 to your next employer to enable her to continue the cumulative system of tax deduction. You also retain a copy of the form, which may be needed if you have to file a self-assessment tax return. (Refer to Chapter 3 for more on self assessment.)

- ✔ **P46:** If you start a job and don't have a P45 (because you had no previous employment, lost the form, never received one, or don't want your new employer to know your previous pay), ask your new employer for a form P46. This form gives HMRC the necessary information to trace your tax records and issue the correct PAYE tax code to your employer. Depending on which statement or statements you make on the form P46, your employer may use an *emergency code* to deduct tax allowing for a personal allowance or code BR to deduct tax at the basic rate. This code is used until HMRC issues your employer with the appropriate tax code.

- ✔ **P60:** After the end of each tax year, and by 31 May, your employer is required to give you a certificate form P60. This certificate shows the total amount of pay you received during the year along with the total amounts of tax and NICs (including the employer's contributions) that have been deducted. A former employer doesn't have to give you a P60 if you left her employment some time during the tax year.

Checking Your Pay

All tax and NICs deducted by your employer should be accurate to the last penny. You should be able to check your payslip and agree that the money taken off is correct. Doing so is particularly important when you start a new job or receive a pay rise (or reduction). The following sections help you to verify your employer's deductions.

Payments of expenses and perks (technically known as benefits-in-kind) are not subject to PAYE even if tax is payable on them. Chapter 13 deals with tax issues relating to expenses and benefits.

Working out your take-home pay

To check that your employer deducts the correct amount of tax, you need an idea of how much money you should receive after deductions. The following steps give you an estimate of how much money you take home each month. The formula is designed to work across tax years because it pays no attention to minor changes in personal allowances. It also ignores pensions, the 10 per cent income tax starting rate, which applied up to the end of the 2007–8 tax year, charitable donations made through the payroll, and other deductions. But the formula works surprisingly well for people earning up to around £34,000 a year, which is more than 80 per cent of people in work. Chapter 4 shows you how to work out the exact figure for each year. This formula should, however, agree roughly with your monthly payslip.

1. **Subtract £5,400 from your gross annual salary.**

   For example, if you earn £25,000 a year gross and deduct £5,400, you're left with £19,600.

2. **Divide this figure by 12 to give you a monthly figure of taxable pay.**

   Dividing £19,600 by 12 gives £1,633.

3. **Deduct 31 per cent of this new figure – 20 per cent for income tax and 11 per cent for NICs.**

   31 per cent of £1,633 is £506 (£1,633 × 31/100), so that leaves £1,127.

4. **Add back the £5,400 you took off at the start but divide it by 12 to turn it into a monthly figure (£450). The result roughly equals your take-home pay, known as *net pay*.**

   £5,400 divided by 12 gives you £450. Adding that to the £1,127 in Step 3 gives you £1,577, which is roughly the amount your employer should pay you each month.

Paying the national minimum wage

When checking your pay, make sure that your employer is paying you at least the legal minimum. Most workers who are working legally in the UK, who aren't genuinely self-employed, and who have a written, oral, or implied contract are entitled to be paid at least the national minimum wage (NMW).

Three levels of minimum wage exist, and the rates from 1 October 2008 are:

✔ £5.73 per hour for workers aged 22 years and older

✔ £4.70 per hour (called a development rate) for workers aged 18–21 inclusive

✔ £3.53 per hour for all workers under the age of 18, who are no longer of compulsory school age

HMRC is responsible for enforcing the NMW. It does so by dealing with complaints it receives about employers suspected of not paying the minimum wage. A network of 16 HMRC compliance teams also work across the country, making random checks on all employers to make sure that they are meeting their legal obligations.

If you want to make a complaint about the NMW, you can download a complaint form from the HMRC Web site at www.hmrc.gov.uk/nmw/nmw_complaint_form.pdf, telephone the NMW helpline on 0845 6000 678, or make a complaint online at www.hmrc.gov.uk/nmw/complaint.htm.

Repaying a student loan

If you have a student loan, your employer is responsible for making deductions from your pay and paying the money to the Student Loans Company, so check your payslip to ensure that you make repayments.

Your employer makes deductions of 9 per cent from your pay on any earnings that exceed £15,000 a year (equating to £1,250 a month or £288 per week). Each pay day is looked at separately, and repayments may vary according to how much you've been paid in that week or month. If your income falls below the starting limits for that week/month, your employer shouldn't make a deduction.

Sanjay leaves university in June 2007 and starts work in August 2007, earning £1,500 per month (£18,000 per year). His student loan repayments start in April 2008. Sanjay earns £250 above the £1,250 threshold, and so Sanjay's employer deducts £22 a month from Sanjay's salary (9 per cent of £250).

Noticing when your employer gets it wrong

Your employer has a duty to verify your PAYE deductions for tax and national insurance, and to check on any expenses she pays you without making any deductions for tax and national insurance (skip to Chapter 13 for details of expenses). Unless your employer can show that a PAYE error was made in good faith (usually the polite way for saying that the employee or someone else tried to pull a fast one), the employer has to pay for the tax liabilities due.

Very few circumstances apply in which an employer is allowed to go back and ask an employee for extra tax money that she failed to deduct through the payroll. Always check with an accountant, tax adviser, Citizens Advice Bureau, or trade union before agreeing to such a deduction from your pay packet. Bankrupt bosses have been known to raid employees' pay packets before disappearing!

Pleading confusion or ignorance is no defence for a boss. Employers who fail to pass on PAYE deductions to HMRC face interest charges, penalties, and even criminal prosecution.

Looking at Special PAYE Situations

Certain people have slightly different PAYE obligations. If you work in the information technology (IT) or construction industry, or are employed by an agency that supplies temporary workers, your PAYE situation is slightly different from the norm:

- ✔ **Agency workers:** The agency that you work through is normally responsible for operating PAYE on your pay unless the firm or organisation for which you work has the same control over you, and your hours of work, as it does over its permanent employees.

- ✔ **Construction industry workers:** Many of those who work in the construction industry are referred to as 'labour-only subcontractors'. Contractors making payments to subcontractors are required to operate the construction industry scheme (CIS). The CIS is a simple PAYE system specifically designed to stop tax evasion in the construction industry. Chapter 16 tells you all about the scheme and how it works.

Working and lodging at a farm

Part-time casual and contract workers have to pay tax and NICs under the PAYE system in just the same way as those on normal full-time contracts. The government sees no difference.

However, HMRC does make a special allowance for farming and harvest casual workers. If the general rules for taxing income were to be applied, a tax liability would arise on the value of free board and lodging supplied to employees who, under the *Agricultural Wages Acts*, would be entitled to take a higher cash wage instead. HMRC, however, makes a concession that allows farmers to provide free board and lodging without any tax consequences for their employees and for casual employees taken on for harvest work, if all the following conditions are satisfied:

✔ The employee is a manual farmworker (that is, not a director, clerk, book-keeper, and so on).

✔ The farmworker doesn't earn at a rate of £8,500 or more in the year.

✔ The contract between the farmer and the employee provides for a net cash wage with free board and lodgings.

✔ The board and lodgings are provided in the farmhouse or by a third party whom the farmer pays direct under a contract the third party has with the farmer to provide the employee with board and lodging.

Employees on the Government's Seasonal Agricultural Workers Scheme (SAWS) are not eligible for the special PAYE and NICs concessions for harvest casuals.

✔ **IT contractors:** Many information technology contractors form one-man band limited companies, called *personal service companies*. Strict rules apply to the operation of PAYE on this type of company – known as the IR35 rules. See Chapter 17 for a summary of these special rules.

Receiving Payments for Losing or Leaving Your Job

When you leave a job you want to ensure that you pay the minimum tax on any payments from your existing employer for redundancy or in lieu of notice, and from your new employer as an incentive. The following sections explain how to deal with the tax issues of employment transitions.

If you're coming up to retirement age, make sure that any redundancy package, golden handshake, or pay in lieu of notice payment, is structured so that the taxman can't claim that the payment is effectively an early retirement sum. The money is taxable if it's treated as an early retirement payoff. Early retirement can include people near their normal retirement age leaving work to take care of elderly relatives.

Being made redundant

The first £30,000 of any redundancy payment is tax-free. This includes any statutory amount you receive under the Employment Protection (Consolidation) Act 1978, which is tax-free anyway.

 To calculate the statutory amount of redundancy payment your employer owes you if you're between the ages of 20 and 63, multiply your weekly pay up to £270 by one-and-a-half times the number of years you've worked for your employer. So, if you worked for ten years and earned £250 per week, you would be entitled to 15 times (1.5 × 10) the £250, giving you £3,750 in redundancy pay.

The statutory payments aren't that high and can't reach the £30,000 tax-free limit. Many employees manage to negotiate a better redundancy package than just the statutory minimum amount. Additional amounts should normally be paid tax-free, providing:

✔ You have been in the job for at least two years.

✔ Payments are made to all employees on equal terms.

✔ Payments are not excessively high in relation to levels of salaries and length of service.

If your redundancy package goes over the £30,000 limit, the excess is taxed as income under PAYE in the normal way. But if you have to leave your job because of ill-health, disability, or injury, any payoff you receive is normally paid tax-free.

 Don't forget to claim Jobseeker's allowance if you're out of work and trying to find a new job. You pay for this benefit through your tax and NICs, so don't ignore it. Someone over 25 is currently entitled to £59.15 a week (2008 rates) for six months. The payment isn't a fortune, but it helps to pay for stamps for sending off application forms and expenses in going to interviews.

Receiving pay in lieu of notice

If your contract obliges your employer to make a payment when she doesn't give you notice that your employment contract is to be terminated (often referred to as a PILON – Pay In Lieu Of Notice), HMRC treats the payment as arising under the terms of your employment contract and taxes the payment as part of your income under PAYE.

If your employment contract provides only for notice to be given by your employer, failure to give that notice is a breach of the contract. The payment you receive is therefore treated as compensation for that breach rather than arising under the contract. Such termination payments are generally paid tax- and NIC-free, provided that your employer's normal practice is not to make such payments and no understanding is in place that the payment would be made.

Emily earns £60,000 per annum and her employment is to be terminated. Her contract specifies a six-month notice period, with a discretionary PILON clause. Emily works out three months of her notice period. Her employer makes a payment of £45,000 at the end of this period. The following treatment is likely to apply for tax purposes: £15,000 is taxed as a contractual payment in lieu of the three months' salary that Emily would have received if she had worked out her notice period; and £30,000 is treated as a termination payment and paid to Emily tax free.

But if Emily's employer gives her notice and she chooses not to work it, Emily has to pay tax on the full payment. If a payment is made where notice has been given but not worked, the employee continues to be employed until the end of the period and the payment is taxable under the normal PAYE rules.

When you leave an employer, for whatever reason, you receive a form P45 to take to your next job. The P45 is a certificate that provides your next employer with all the information she needs to set you up on her payroll. The certificate usually shows your earnings to date in the current tax year. Check your P45 to make sure that the amount of any termination payment made to you tax-free isn't included on the P45 – if it is, you may be in for a big shock when you get your first pay packet from your new boss!

Going to a new employer

Payments made to an individual as an incentive to take up an employment, often known as 'golden hellos' or 'golden handcuffs',

are generally treated as advance pay for future services of employment and are therefore taxable as employment income. Certain
types of payment can escape income tax in certain circumstances,
including:

- ✔ Payments that wouldn't have to be returned if the new
  employee failed to take up the offer of employment, or didn't
  work for the new company for long

- ✔ Payments not linked to future earnings

- ✔ Payments made to someone who had to abandon a partnership (typically accountants, lawyers, and architects) or give
  up self-employment to join the new company

- ✔ Payments made to recompense someone for tuition fees for a
  course or qualification that is useful to the new employer

Generally, a payment can escape the tax net where it relates to
compensation for the loss or restriction of a right on taking up
employment, but this case is unusual and often difficult to prove.

Chapter 13

Receiving Expenses and Benefits

*Y*our employer may provide you with extra benefits, and when added to your normal salary, the total makes up your employment package. Extras often include things such as private medical insurance, company cars, and, of course, the annual Christmas bash.

All these extra non-cash items – anything that comes direct from your employer and not through your pay packet – are technically referred to as *benefits-in-kind*, although many people just call them perks. Some benefits are taxable, which means you have to pay income tax on them, whereas some are tax-free (plus some are even liable to national insurance contributions or NICs and some are not), so things can get complicated. This chapter looks at a wide variety of benefits that employers often pay. But persuading your boss to give them to you is up to you!

Taxing Expenses and Benefits

Many people receive perks from an employer – often a company car or private medical insurance. Some benefits are yours to enjoy tax-free – such as your office party – but others attract the interest of the taxman. This section takes you through the tax implications of expenses and benefits.

Explaining expenses and benefits

If you receive benefits-in-kind from your employer, you're likely to have to pay tax on their value. This value is added to your normal salary. So, if your annual salary is £23,000 and you receive £6,000 in benefits-in-kind, the taxman treats you as having earnings of £29,000.

Benefits-in-kind are split into three categories: Those that are taxed, those that are tax-free, and those that are essential for carrying out your job. Essential expenses are tax-free because, as HM Revenue & Customs (HMRC) puts it, they are 'wholly, exclusively, and necessarily incurred in the performance of your duties'.

HMRC often refers to 'taxable charges'. These charges aren't as big as they sound. The *taxable charge* is not what you pay but the value of the benefit that is added to your other income and then taxed at your highest tax rate. So, someone paying 40 per cent tax on his income, who has a benefit-in-kind with an annual taxable charge of £5,000, actually pays tax at 40 per cent on that charge – £2,000 (£5,000 × 40/100).

If you add up everything that makes up your employment package – that is, your salary and the value of all the perks you receive – the total amount is known as your total *emoluments*. The value of your total annual emoluments can push you from being a basic-rate taxpayer into the higher 40 per cent tax band (which applies when your income is higher than £36,000 for 2008–9). For example, if you earn £40,000 in salary, but also receive £5,000 in benefits, your total emoluments for the year are £45,000. Even after you take off personal tax allowances of £5,435, your taxable income will still be £39,565, and that's high enough to make the top slice of your income liable to tax at 40 per cent.

Your employer has to give HMRC details of all taxable benefits and expenses (on a form P11D) he has paid you each year. He is required to give you a copy of this information by 6 July following the end of each tax year. So for 2007–8, he must give you the information by 6 July 2008. You need to keep this information safe, because you need it to complete your self-assessment tax return.

If you have to pay tax on any benefits you receive, you do pay it in one of two ways: through the self-assessment system or by making an election to pay for them through PAYE (Pay As You Earn) deductions from your regular salary, providing the amount owing is less than £2,000. If the tax tops this amount, you've no choice other than to pay direct through the self-assessment system. Generally, this means that you pay a lump sum on 31 January following the year to which the due tax relates. If you fall into this category, make sure that you keep enough money aside to pay your tax bill. (You can find out more about self assessment in Chapter 3, and Chapter 12 outlines PAYE.)

Examining the general tax rules

This section outlines HMRC's rules for taxing expenses and benefits, from who escapes paying income tax to which benefits you pay tax on.

Looking at who's exempt from tax

Some benefits and expenses payments are taxable for all employees, regardless of their level of earnings. However, other benefits aren't taxable in 'lower-paid employments', in which an employee's rate of earnings is less than £8,500 per annum (which in practice means you only work part-time). To work out whether you earn more than £8,500 per annum, all expenses payments and the cash equivalent of all benefits must be added to your normal salary. Allowable expenses aren't taken into account for these purposes, although certain deductions (for example, contributions to your employer's pension scheme) may be taken into account.

In addition, some company directors may be exempt from paying tax if they:

- ✔ Earn at a rate of less than £8,500 per annum

- ✔ Alone, or together with associates and relatives, own not more than 5 per cent of the company's ordinary share capital or right to assets

- ✔ Work full-time or part-time for a charitable or non-profit-making body

Knowing which benefits you pay tax on

All employees and directors are liable to tax on the provision of certain benefits irrespective of their level of earnings, including:

- ✔ Assets your employer transfers to you at below market value

- ✔ Certain payments made by employer credit card

- ✔ Certain relocation expenses

- ✔ Gifts (if new, at cost, or for 'lower paid' employees at second-hand value)

- ✔ Living accommodation

- ✔ Loans your employer writes off

✔ Non-exempt vouchers, for example, travel season tickets or gift vouchers

✔ Payments made on your behalf and expenses payments other than those wholly for business purposes (for example, travel between home and work)

For employees earning at a rate of less than £8,500 per annum, and where the total expenses payments and benefits exceed £25 in a tax year, these benefits must be reported on form P9D. In addition to these benefits for P9D employees, other benefits also have to be reported on forms P11D for directors and employees earning at a rate of more than £8,500 per annum, including the following:

✔ Car fuel supplied for private motoring

✔ Cars your employer makes available for private use

✔ Certain scholarships

✔ Goods or services supplied at less than their full cost

✔ Interest-free or low-interest loans

✔ Private medical insurance (unless for treatment while working abroad)

✔ Taxable mileage allowances and passenger payments

✔ Use of employer's assets (other than cars or vans)

HMRC guide CWG2 contains a comprehensive list of benefits and expenses and whether they are reportable to HMRC for P9D or P11D purposes (www.hmrc.gov.uk/guidance/cwg2.htm).

For details of tax-free benefits, flick to the later section 'Receiving Other Benefits'.

Travelling to and for Work

For many people one of the biggest costs of working is getting to the workplace in the morning and coming home at night (or vice versa if you work the night shift). Your employer may offer help with some of these expenses. This section looks at a few of the ways in which travel expenses are paid.

Your employer can provide tax-free help, including the cost of hiring cars and hotel bills, if your normal travel arrangements are impossible due to an unusual event such as a rail strike. And you can have a tax-free taxi to take you home after 9pm as long as no public transport exists or it would be unreasonable for you to use it (for example, if you had to walk a mile down an unlit street to catch a bus). This concession doesn't apply if you have to work regularly or frequently past 9pm. (no more than 60 times a year).

Counting the cost of a company car

Although the financial benefits have eroded over recent years, being provided with a company car is still one of the most popular and potent status symbols.

Working out how much tax you pay on the car

To work out the taxable value of the car, you must first establish the car's full manufacturer's published UK list price including the full value of any accessories (excluding a mobile phone and anything to help drivers with disabilities). Any discounts, or extras such as air-conditioning, metallic paint, and so on that a private buyer can obtain, are ignored. So the taxable value is likely to be more than the cost would be to you as an individual, but under the present rules, the maximum value of any car for these calculations is £80,000.

If you make a contribution towards the cost of the company car (for example, you want a better one than your employer was prepared to provide), you can take off the amount you paid, up to a maximum of £5,000, from the list price calculation.

 Special pricing rules apply for classic cars (those over 15 years old at the end of the tax year with a market value more than the list price and worth at least £15,000). HMRC helpsheet IR203 has further information on classic cars (available at www.hmrc.gov.uk/helpsheets/ir203.pdf).

Next, you need to find out the car's carbon dioxide (CO_2) emissions. The greener the car, the less tax you pay. You can find the approved CO_2 emissions figure as follows:

✔ From the Vehicle Registration Document (V5), for cars first registered on or after 1 March 2001

✔ From www.vcacarfueldata.org.uk (download the data after the car was first registered), for cars first registered from 1 January 1998 to 28 February 2001

✔ From the manufacturer (or importer, where appropriate). The manufacturer holds the type approval certificate for each type of car, including the approved CO_2 emissions figure for the type to which the vehicle conforms. The manufacturer should provide this information when requested, normally by providing a certificate of conformity. Although manufacturers are entitled to charge a small fee, some manufacturers are happy to provide this information free of charge.

HMRC taxes a proportion of the car's original cost according to its carbon emissions. The taxable amount can range from 10 per cent of cost for the cleanest cars up to 35 per cent for those pumping out the dirtiest fumes. You can find the appropriate percentage for your company car in the HMRC helpsheet IR203 (www.hmrc.gov.uk/helpsheets/ir203.pdf).

You then multiply the list price by the appropriate percentage and this figure gives you the taxable value. If you only had use of the car for part of the year, you time-apportion this figure accordingly. So, if you only had the car for four months of the tax year, you take four-twelfths of the taxable value figure. You then pay income tax at 20 per cent or 40 per cent on the final figure, depending on whether you're a basic rate or higher rate taxpayer.

HMRC provides an online company car and car fuel benefit calculator, which allows you to work out the taxable value and gives an indication of the income tax you're likely to pay. Check it out at www.hmrc.gov.uk/calcs/cars.htm.

Fuelling concerns

In addition to the company car benefit, you have to pay tax on any fuel your employer provides that you use for private mileage. For 2008–9 you calculate this amount by multiplying the car's CO_2 percentage (see the preceding section 'Working out how much tax you pay on the car') by £16,900 (£14,400 before 6 April 2008). So, if the percentage is 20, the tax charge for petrol is £3,380. For a basic rate taxpayer (taxed 20 per cent), the after-tax cash equivalent is £676 and for a higher rate taxpayer (taxed at 40 per cent) £1,352. The charge is the same regardless of whether you use 2 litres or 2,000 litres of fuel.

You can avoid this tax charge if you pay all the private fuel costs back to your employer. You need to keep accurate records (mileage logs and fuel receipts) to support such a claim to HMRC.

Your employer can give you a tax-free fuel allowance if you pay for fuel used for business travel in your company car. This ranges from 11p per mile for smaller diesel and petrol cars (under 1400cc) to 19p per mile for larger petrol cars (over 2000cc). Lower rates apply for cars using cheaper liquid petroleum gas (LPG), ranging from 7p to 11p a mile. For a full list of current mileage rates, log on to www.hmrc.gov.uk/cars/advisory_fuel_current.htm.

Making the most of mileage

In many cases, you may be better off negotiating a pay rise and giving up the company car benefit. Employers can pay you a tax-free and national insurance-free amount for every mile you drive on workplace duties, currently:

- 40p per mile for the first 10,000 miles

- 25p per mile for each subsequent mile

- 24p per mile for motorcycles

- 20p per mile for bicycles

- 5p per mile extra for each passenger carried on work-related journeys

 If your employer reimburses your mileage as less than these rates, you can claim the balance (but not the 5p per mile passenger extra) against your taxable income. For instance, if your employer gives you 30p per mile for 1,000 miles, you have a 10p per mile shortfall and can claim £100 against your taxable income.

The big exception to business mileage is the daily commute from home to work and back again. HMRC defines regular commuting as travel to a location you report to on 40 per cent or more of your working days.

If you have to go for work purposes to a location that is not your normal place of work, you may be able to claim business mileage on this travel. For example, living in Reading and regularly commuting to your workplace in Heathrow is not business travel. But if you're asked to go to Brighton for the day, this mileage counts.

You can also claim the costs involved with site travel, in which you have to go to and from a location that isn't your official place of work. You may also be able to claim tax relief on *subsistence* costs, such as buying yourself a midday meal when you aren't at your normal workplace. You can't do this forever though – after 24 months, HMRC says that the site is now your normal workplace.

Driving the work's van

Driving a van can potentially save you loads of tax, but only on the right sort of journey and the right sort of van. In the past, anyone who was allowed to use the company van for private use was given an automatic £500 tax charge (reduced to £350 for older vans), so the actual cash cost was only £110 to a basic-rate taxpayer (22 per cent of £500) and £200 to a higher-rate taxpayer (40 per cent of £500).

That tax charge no longer applies if the van is only used for business journeys to and from work, and other insignificant usage. Insignificant usage means making a slight detour every morning on the journey to work to buy a newspaper or sandwich, going to the doctor for medical reasons, and using the van once or twice a year to take rubbish to the local tip. Insignificant usage doesn't mean going to the supermarket for the weekly shop or using the van for holidays, parties, and other social events.

For 2007–8 onwards, when you use the van for private purposes (other than insignificant usage), you're charged a straight £3,000. This amount equates to a cash cost of £600 for a basic rate tax-payer for 2008–9 onwards (£660 for 2007–8) and £1,200 for a higher rate taxpayer. The amount is reduced if you don't have the van for the whole tax year, if someone else also uses it for private travel, or if you pay something for using it privately.

If your employer lets you have free or subsidised fuel for private use, you have to pay an extra tax charge of £500 from 2007–8 onwards, which for a basic rate taxpayer is tax of around £100 (for 2008–9); £200 for higher rate taxpayers.

Some firms offer double-cab vans to staff as an alternative to a company car. These vans are often luxurious inside and out, with leather trim and all the kit. From April 2007, however, such vehicles are treated as cars for tax purposes, which means you pay a higher tax on them.

Going green and saving tax

The government is keen to encourage employers to set up green *Travel Plans* for their employees. A Travel Plan is a package of practical measures to reduce car use for journeys to and from work and for business travel. Where an employer helps employees to get to and from work, such as providing petrol or season tickets, these benefits are normally taxable. But no tax or NICs are payable if an employer offers the following:

- ✔ **Cycles and safety equipment for employees:** Employees can use cycles and safety equipment for leisure as long as the main use is for commuting.

- ✔ **Free or subsidised work buses:** Any number of employers can join together and provide a works bus or minibus service for their joint workforces. The bus has to seat at least nine passengers and must be used mainly for commuting or travel between workplaces, but employees and their families can use it occasionally for other trips.

- ✔ **Low-interest or free season ticket loan:** Employers can offer their employees a loan up to £5,000 per year to cover a season ticket for public transport. No tax or NICs are payable pro-vided the full amount of the loan is repaid to the employer and total loans outstanding don't exceed £5,000 at any time.

✔ **Subsidies for public bus services:** Some employers pay subsidies to finance a public transport service that is useful to the employer, for example one that stops outside the factory gate. As long as the service is available to all employees, no tax or NICs are payable.

✔ **Workplace parking for cycles and motorcycles:** Employers can provide parking facilities for employees' own vehicles at or near the workplace tax-free.

Receiving Other Benefits

A huge variety of benefits exist that employers can give as part of an overall remuneration package. The following sections look at a few of them.

Claiming relocation expenses

When you relocate, your employer may help you finance your move. The limit for qualifying expenses is £8,000. Expenses must be incurred during the period from the date of the job change to the end of the next following tax year, although this period may be extended with the agreement of HMRC. Qualifying expenses include:

✔ **Acquisition benefits and expenses:** You can claim legal expenses in connection with the acquisition of a new main residence, loan fees and mortgage insurance costs, survey and land registry fees, stamp duty, and connection of public utilities. Abortive costs in connection with an acquisition that doesn't proceed are also allowed.

✔ **Bridging loan expenses and beneficial bridging loans:** You can claim relief for any interest or expense you incur in connection with selling your old property and buying your new one. For example, if you complete on the purchase of your new home, but haven't completed on the sale of your old one, you may have to take out a loan to bridge the gap (known as a bridging loan).

✔ **Disposal expenses and benefits:** You may be able to claim expenses for legal and advertising costs in connection with the disposal of an accommodation, any penalty for redeeming a mortgage, auctioneers' and estate agents' fees, disconnection of public utilities, rent, maintenance, and insurance costs while the property is unoccupied.

✔ **Duplicate expenses and benefits in respect of the new residence:** For example, you can claim replacement domestic items but not new school uniforms.

✔ **Transportation of domestic belongings:** You can claim for your removals costs, including insurance.

✔ **Travelling and subsistence expenses and benefits:** You can claim for expenditure on temporary visits to the new residence before relocation, travel from the old residence to new place of work, or travel from the new residence to old place of work where the date of move and relocation of work don't coincide. You can also claim travelling and subsistence costs for children aged under 19, who relocate before or after parents for educational reasons.

Paying for childcare

Employers can provide childcare (such as a nursery, crèche, or after-school club) free of income tax and NICs, providing the childcare isn't in a private home, meets with local authority guidelines, and is concerned with care rather than education (that is, it must be a nursery not a school).

Alternatively, employers can pay employees up to £55 per week free of tax and NICs towards the cost of other childcare arrangements that are registered and approved, such as registered childminders. The money is normally in the form of vouchers or goes directly to the childcare provider. This scheme must be made available to all employees or all employees at a particular location.

Lots of information on getting help with childcare is available on the HMRC Web site at www.hmrc.gov.uk/childcare.

Realising other tax-free perks

The self-employed have considerable freedom in deciding the expenses they can set against earnings, and so remove them from the tax net. This freedom doesn't apply to employees. They have to convince the taxman that any expenses they receive from their employers are 'wholly, exclusively, and necessarily incurred in the performance of their duties'. These guidelines are strict and often difficult to pass. You can't, for instance, claim the cost of a new suit just because your employer asks you to wear one to work – HMRC wouldn't accept that a suit was 'exclusively' for work (you can wear it to your cousin's wedding, for instance).

Some benefits are, however, exempt for tax purposes:

✓ **Business trips:** Personal expenses when you're away from home on business of up to £5 per night in the UK and £10 a night abroad. This covers the cost of incidental living expenses such as newspapers, telephone calls home, and so on. You can also claim the cost of meals when you're away from home on business, and for any medical treatment you require when overseas on business.

✓ **Entertaining:** The taxman has no claim on most costs of valid entertaining expenses, such as entertaining customers, contacts, and clients.

✓ **Eye tests:** Health and safety regulations demand that employers offer regular eye checks to staff who use computer screens. This benefit is tax free, as is any fixed amount you're given towards buying glasses.

✓ **Financial and pensions advice:** Advice worth up to £150 per year is tax free.

✓ **Long service awards:** These awards qualify for tax exemption as long as the recipient has at least 20 years with the same employer and no similar gift has been given in the past ten years. The gift can be worth as much as £50 for each year of service but can't be in the form of cash.

✓ **Luncheon vouchers:** You're entitled to up to a 15p per day tax-free.

✓ **Travel expenses:** When your employer orders you to make a journey, or travel to a temporary workplace for up to 24 months, you can claim the travel expenses. You can also claim the cost of two return journeys a year for your spouse and children to a location outside the UK if you have to work overseas for a continuous period of at least 60 days.

✓ **Working from home:** Your employer can pay you up to £2 per week towards household costs if you're required under the terms of your employment contract to work at home.

Special deals for special jobs

HMRC allows you to deduct the cost of subscriptions to various professional bodies that are essential if you're to continue with your work. In some cases, only part of the amount is allowable because the balance covers non-essential items such as lobbying.

Many flat-rate deductions exist that people in various manual jobs requiring special clothing or tools can claim. Although these amounts are quite small they're still worth having, and so if you think you qualify, have a look at the list on the HMRC Web site at www.hmrc.gov.uk/manuals/eimanual/eim32712.htm. If you qualify, contact your HMRC office. The expense is normally given via an increase in your PAYE tax code number. (Refer to Chapter 12 for more on PAYE.)

Chapter 14

Sharing Your Employer's Fortunes

· ·

· ·

*M*ore and more firms are offering their employees a share stake in the company, giving them the chance to participate in the success and growth of the organisation. And the government offers tax incentives to encourage employees to invest in their employer's business through a share scheme.

In a *share scheme*, the company's owners (usually the directors) offer employees the opportunity to invest in the company by buying shares in the firm or by offering options to buy shares at some time in the future. An *option* is a sort of one-way promise: If the shares go up in value, you can take up the option but if they go down, or you can't afford them, you can tear up the option and not suffer any penalty.

Different share schemes have differing rules on how much you can put in, what your employer can add, when you can cash in your investment, and how much (if any) tax you pay on any profits you make. This chapter looks at the various share schemes on offer and the tax breaks that go with them.

Introducing Share Schemes

If you're considering joining your employer's share scheme, you need as much info as possible about how the different schemes work. In this section I run through the basics of share schemes to get you started.

Working out what's on offer to whom

Employers don't have to offer a share scheme but companies that offer their staff share plans often reckon it's well worth the cost of issuing shares – employees tend to be more motivated, work harder, take more interest in the business, and are more loyal when given the chance to share in the firm's future success.

Schemes are more common in large *quoted companies* (those listed on the stock exchange) and rarer in smaller companies in which the shareholder list is likely to be restricted to members of the family that owns the firm. No bar exists against overseas companies offering access to their foreign-quoted shares to their UK employees.

With the exception of free share incentive plans (SIPs), share schemes must be available to all employees on similar terms. Therefore, the scheme must be offered to full-time and part-time employees, and must not take into account salary levels or job status. An employer can't set up a share scheme and only offer it to, say, her team of sales people – she must offer it to staff right across the company. In a Save As You Earn (SAYE) scheme and some SIPs, the company can impose a qualifying period of up to five years' work for the firm, providing it applies equally to everyone. (Check out the later sections on SIPs and SAYE for more details.)

Adding up the tax savings

Company share schemes can be worth over £1,000 per year in tax savings. Most of these incentive plans include tax saving opportunities. The exact amount of tax savings depends on how much you go in for and what happens to the shares. You get the tax savings at the end of the scheme period. And, of course, the shares have to go up in value for you to make any tax savings at all.

To benefit from the tax advantages, share schemes have to be set up and run properly. A straight gift of shares from your employer counts as a taxable benefit-in-kind. (Refer to Chapter 13 regarding tax on benefits.) You have to pay tax based on the market value of the shares on the day you received them. If you pay part of their worth, you're taxed on the gap between what you paid and their open market value.

Listing the types of schemes

To get the tax savings on offer, the shares have to be issued through one of a number of HM Revenue & Customs (HMRC)-approved schemes. A scheme doesn't have to be an approved scheme, but if it isn't, you can't claim the tax savings – flick to the later section 'Going beyond Approval' for more on unapproved schemes. The great advantage of approval is that your employer can just slot a scheme into a pre-existing blueprint, which makes it easy and cheap to set up.

You can take three main routes into employee shareholding:

- ✔ Free shares, where your employer gives you a handout.

- ✔ Option plans, where your employer gives you the right to buy a certain number of shares at an agreed price (known as the 'strike price'), at a set future date or dates. You don't have to buy the shares, you just have an option to buy, and you can walk away without any penalty.

- ✔ Schemes where you buy shares at their current market value, or at an 'undervalue' (that is, less than market value), in the expectation that they go up in value over time.

Saving with a SAYE Scheme

Save As You Earn (SAYE) is the most common share incentive scheme currently on offer. You save a set amount for a set period of time, and at the end of the savings period you have the option to use the savings and the tax-free bonus you receive to buy company shares.

Think carefully before you commit to paying into a SAYE scheme. You can't increase or decrease the amount you agree to pay during the term of the plan. Decreasing or permanently stopping payments ends the plan.

Understanding how SAYE works

The SAYE scheme enables employees to save a set amount each week or month of between £10 and £250 out of their pay packets for a set period of time – usually three or five years. Another option is to leave the money in the account for a further two years after the fifth year to earn a bigger bonus. Employers can offer (and many do) a choice of these periods or you may have only one option.

You are allowed to delay up to six monthly payments during your SAYE plan, which extends your contract by the number of missed months. After you go beyond six missed payments, the plan is terminated.

Under the SAYE scheme, you don't acquire any shares yourself with each monthly payment. Instead, you're entitled to buy the share at the end of the plan. When you start a SAYE plan, the company sets the share value anywhere in a range between the current stock market value or 20 per cent lower: This is your starting price. You compare the price at the end of the scheme with this starting price to see if you've made money on the shares. If the shares have increased in value, you can buy them at the end of the plan with the proceeds of your SAYE account at the pre-agreed option price. If the price is lower, you can opt not to buy the shares and walk away from the plan with your SAYE proceeds. You pay no income tax or national insurance on these undervalued shares.

You can have more than one SAYE scheme with your employer providing that your total monthly contributions don't exceed £250. Firms usually have regular offers, each with a different option price, to reflect the ups and downs in the stock market.

Growing your money in a SAYE scheme

The money that you save in the plan each month goes into a special SAYE account with a bank or building society, chosen by your employer. The money earns tax-free interest and a tax-free interest-related bonus. The interest you earn is set at the time you sign up for the plan.

Jeff opts for the three-year plan, which means that his money is refunded on maturity plus a bonus equal to 2.4 monthly contributions. Jeff pays in £100 per month, so he receives £3,600 (36 months) plus £240, which becomes £3,840. Sally opts for the five-year plan, which gives a bigger bonus equal to 7.2 monthly payments. So Sally's £100 a month investment yields a repayment of £6,000 (60 months) plus £720 to give a tax-free amount of £6,720. Nicolae opts for seven years, which means he pays no more after five years. Nicolae receives 13.3 times his monthly payment at the end, so his £100 per month contributions yield a tax-free £1,330 bonus.

You get no interest at all if you stop within the first 12 months of starting a scheme. If you withdraw your money after 12 months but before the third anniversary of the plan, you receive interest on your investment at the current rate of just 3 per cent (known as the 'early leaver rate').

SAYE plan rates and bonuses rise and fall with the Bank of England base rates, but they are fixed for the life of the contract at the time you sign up.

Cashing in your SAYE fund

SAYE share schemes are pretty much win-win for participating employees. If the shares go up in value, the employees gain. If the shares drop in value, your fallback is that you gain tax-free interest in the bank or building society account.

Your monthly savings and their tax-free growth belong to you no matter what happens to the share price. If the shares go up, you can keep them or sell them. If they go down, you can get your money back, plus the interest (see the preceding section 'Growing your money in a SAYE scheme' for information on interest). Either way, you pay no income tax or national insurance on the profits.

At the end of the plan, if you decide to buy the shares, your employer issues you with the paperwork to prove that you own them. You choose what you do with the shares. You can keep them and hope they go up in value, or sell them through a stockbroker. Some companies have in-house schemes to help you find a broker, and your bank can help as well. Chapter 6 can help you decipher capital gains tax (CGT) issues that may apply when you sell shares.

Leaving the scheme early

SAYE schemes end when you leave the company before the end of the contracted period of the scheme for which you signed up, whether three, five, or seven years. You get a refund of your savings with any interest, but you don't get the attractive interest-rate bonus, which is automatically paid at the end of three years on all plans.

An exception applies, however: If you have to leave your job before the scheme finishes due to retirement, illness, injury, or redundancy, you can still exercise your options if they are worthwhile. You have a six-month window to do so. If you die within this timeframe then your family can exercise your options on your behalf if they want, and in this case the period of taking the option is extended to 12 months. Special rules also apply if the company (or the part where you work) is taken over.

Making money from SAYE

Suppose the shares of your company were valued at 100p each when you start. At that time your employer gives you an option to buy shares under an SAYE scheme at 80p each, the maximum 20 per cent discount.

You save £100 per month for five years, which, including the tax-free interest, gives you a fund of £6,720. This buys you 8,400 shares no matter what has happened to the share price over the period of the plan.

If the price of the shares when you buy them is over 80p, you can make a profit by exercising the option with the money in the SAYE account and then selling the shares straight away. This profit is liable to capital gains tax (CGT) on the amount between the present value and the option price. But don't forget that you have an annual zero allowance for CGT (£9,600 for 2008–9). Of course you don't have to sell your shares straightaway. You can keep them all and sell them in the future or just sell some of them to make the best use of your CGT exemption – Chapter 6 has more on this aspect.

Participating in Share Incentive Plans

Share Incentive Plans (SIPs) offer more in the way of tax-saving benefits than SAYE schemes (see the earlier section 'Saving with a SAYE Scheme'), but they do come with higher risks. You buy actual shares from the start instead of accumulating options to buy sometime in the future. The shares you buy aren't like options that you can abandon when the stock market price falls; if the share price goes down, you take a loss. You don't receive the shares when awarded them. Instead, trustees hold them on your behalf in a plan for three to five years, depending on the terms of the scheme.

 If you leave the firm, other than for disability or death, you may forfeit your tax-saving arrangement. Keep full records of all SIP shares transactions for five years. You can face an income tax charge if you withdraw your shares from the plan within five years of joining it.

 Share prices in your company may fall along with share prices generally in the stock market, no matter how hard you and your colleagues work. No tax compensation exists if you have to sell out at a loss.

You can obtain shares under a SIP scheme in three different ways: free shares, partnership shares, and matching shares. The type you receive is up to your employer. In the following sections I examine each type, and look at receiving dividends from the shares.

Getting free shares

Getting free shares is obviously the best deal because, as the name suggests, they cost you nothing. Unlike most other work-related benefits, you pay no income tax or national insurance when you're given the shares.

Under an HMRC-approved SIP, your employer can give you up to £3,000 a year of shares free from income tax and national insurance. A gift of £3,000 in shares is worth up to £930 in tax benefits for basic-rate taxpayers and up to £1,230 for top-rate payers.

Some or all these shares may be awarded in recognition of your individual achievements, or they can be given in relation to team or divisional performance targets. You can receive free shares according to performance measures, salary, or length of service. These targets must be published at the start of the scheme and can't be changed once the scheme is under way, and the highest performance-linked handout can't be greater than four times the non-performance figure.

An important feature of SIPs is the 'all-employee' rule. The plan must be available to everyone in the company, including part-timers. However, firms can set a qualifying limit of up to 18 months' employment before letting an employee join.

The shares are held on your behalf in a trust. If you leave the company within three years of starting the scheme, you generally lose your rights to the tax benefits on free shares. If you take your investment out of the plan between the three- and five-year period, you may face a tax charge on the difference between the value of the shares on the day you acquired them and the day you took them out of the plan. The exact rules depend on the company and the way it sets up the trust. You don't lose your tax benefits if you have to leave because of illness, injury, disability, retirement, or redundancy. If you die, your family can make use of the tax savings.

Going into partnership with your employer

Partnership shares is the second share category that you may acquire under a SIP. Partnership shares give you the chance to invest in the company using your own cash. You buy shares at market value with money that's free from income tax and national insurance deductions. The annual limit on buying partnership shares is currently £1,500 (or 10 per cent of your gross – before deductions – pay but after pension plan contributions, and any workplace charitable donations if this amount is lower). The £1,500 is worth up to around £450 for basic-rate taxpayers and up to £615 for higher-rate taxpayers.

If you take partnership shares from the trust within three years of joining the plan, you pay tax based on the market value of the shares at the time you take the shares, not the original value, which may of course be lower or higher. After five years, you can take them out of the plan and sell them without any income tax worries. As long as you keep the shares in the plan, they also grow free of CGT.

Matching shares with your employer

Your company can give you up to two matching shares for each partnership share you buy in a SIP (see the preceding section 'Going into partnership with your employer'). So, although you can't be forced to buy shares, the fact that your employer may give you another two shares for every one you buy may make it hard to resist. This arrangement gives a maximum of £3,000 a year in matching shares, which are all income tax and national insurance free.

Matching shares have to be given to all employees on the same basis. So, if the senior managers get a two-for-one offer, most junior staff must also be offered the same deal.

Divvying up the dividends

Dividends (distribution payments that a company makes to its shareholders) from SIPs are taxable. However, most employers offer a dividend reinvestment scheme so that you can buy even more shares instead of receiving cash dividends. (Chapter 6 deals with the tax aspects of receiving cash dividends.) Dividends that are reinvested are tax-free. You can reinvest up to £1,500 a year in this way.

HMRC produces a booklet called Share Incentive Plans and your entitlement to benefits (IR177), which you can download from www.hmrc.gov.uk/shareschemes/ir177.pdf. The booklet explains what may happen to your entitlement to certain state benefits if you buy shares through a SIP.

Sharing Out the Options

Some employers want to give only certain members of staff the opportunity to hold shares in the company. For this reason, a SAYE or SIP scheme would not be suitable because these schemes must offer shares to all employees equally. However, Company Share Option Plan (CSOP) and Enterprise Management Incentive (EMI) schemes allow an employer to choose which employees he wants to reward.

Opting for a Company Share Option Plan

A Company Share Option Plan (CSOP) can give selected employees the right to buy shares worth up to £30,000 on the day the option is awarded to them. Provided the options are held for at least three years, the only tax due is income tax on the gain, if any, between the option price and the value of the shares on the market on the day the option is exercised.

Employees who leave the scheme due to retirement, illness, injury, or redundancy can exercise their options within three years of being given them, provided they do so within six months of leaving.

Enterprising investments

Enterprise Management Incentive (EMI) schemes are designed to help small, higher-risk companies recruit and retain employees who have the skills to help them grow and succeed. They are also a way of rewarding employees for taking a risk by investing their time and skills to help small companies achieve their potential.

Firms with fewer than 250 full-time employees and assets worth up to £30 million can give share options worth up to £120,000 per employee (from 6 April 2008) under the scheme. This amount is subject to an overall total share value of £3 million under EMI options to all employees.

Under the scheme, employees are given the promise that they can buy a set number of shares at a set price on a future date. The grant of the option is tax-free and normally the employee pays no tax or national insurance when the option is exercised.

The options can be issued at or below market value. Most are issued at market value because this allows the recipient to cash in the options without paying income tax or national insurance on their value.

Capital gains tax (CGT) is payable on any gains made when the shares are sold, on the difference between the sale proceeds and the market value of the shares when they were first acquired. CGT liability can often be successfully managed by selling shares over a number of years, so making use of several annual exemptions. Refer to Chapter 6 for further explanation of how CGT is worked out.

Going beyond Approval

A number of employee shares incentive schemes are treated as 'unapproved' by HMRC. This status doesn't mean that they are illegal, but does often mean that the scheme is complicated and may be intended to boost the earnings of senior staff members rather than being available more generally to employees. Being *unapproved* means that, unlike approved schemes in which all the rules are laid out, precise details aren't checked out by HMRC.

Although they don't have the same tax advantages associated with the approved schemes (SAYE, SIPs, and CSOPs), unapproved schemes are useful because they're more flexible in their application and can be better tailored to suit the needs of the organisation. For example, individual employees can be rewarded on an ad hoc basis for good performance.

No income tax or national insurance is due on the grant of an option under an unapproved scheme, but when that option is exercised (that is, the shares are purchased) income tax is payable on the difference between the option price and the market value of the shares at the date of the exercise.

These schemes are generally offered by small companies and are usually intended to help retain key members of staff.

Part V
Working for Yourself

'Good heavens – this tax investigation must be really serious – You're the third tax inspector to visit my little taxidermist business this month.'

In this part . . .

*M*ore and more people are making a break from employment and stepping out on their own into the business world. Not only does working for yourself bring independence and the chance to increase your earnings, but you can also organise your finances to benefit from some big tax advantages.

In this part, I guide you through setting up and maintaining business records, registering with HMRC, working out your tax bill, and paying over what you owe. I also give you the low-down on the pros and cons of setting up a limited company and show you the most tax-efficient (but perfectly legal) methods of taking money out of the company.

Chapter 15

Starting a Business

● ●

In This Chapter

▶ Looking at sole traders, partnerships, and limited companies

▶ Making sure that you really are self-employed

▶ Registering your new business

▶ Thinking about national insurance and VAT

▶ Getting more info

● ●

*I*n the UK today around four million people work for themselves, each of whom is responsible for setting up and maintaining business records, registering with HM Revenue & Customs (HMRC) for tax and national insurance contributions (NICs) (and possibly even Value Added Tax – VAT), and paying over the necessary amounts as and when due. This chapter guides you through setting up your business and keeping HMRC happy. Doing your administration properly right from the beginning helps put your new business firmly on the road to success.

 For a more comprehensive look at how to set up and run your own business, take a look at *Starting and Running a Business For Dummies* by Liz Barclay *et al.* (Wiley).

Understanding the Terms

To put your business on a proper footing with HMRC and other authorities (for example, your bank and the council for business rates), you need to make sure that the right legal structure is in place. Spend a bit of time thinking about which structure best suits your business needs because it affects the following:

▸ The tax and NICs that you pay

▸ The records and accounts that you have to keep

▸ The financial liability if the business runs into difficulties

✔ The ways in which your business can raise money

✔ How you make future management decisions

The following sections lead you through the various legal structures you can choose between, and help you to fathom whether you are, indeed, self-employed and trading as such.

Sole traders

Most people who set up in business on their own account start up as *sole traders*, the technical term for people who work for themselves, and who are often referred to as *self-employed*.

Being a sole trader is generally the simplest way to run a business and doesn't involve paying any registration fees for tax purposes. Keeping records and accounts is usually quite straightforward, and you pay NICs and income tax on your profits.

The great thing about being a sole trader is that you get to keep all your profits. However, for every up side you find a down side. As a sole trader, you're personally liable for any debts that your business incurs and this liability can make it a risky option for businesses that require a lot of investment.

Sole traders must register with HMRC within three months of starting work – the later section 'Registering your new business' explains how to register.

Partnerships

Where two or more people get together and start a business they often form a *partnership*. Often, a solicitor helps the partners draw up a *formal partnership deed* – a legal document that sets out what each partner is responsible for and what he can expect from the business.

In a partnership situation, each partner is self-employed and takes a share of the profits. Usually, the partners share the decision-making and management of the business. Each partner is person-ally responsible for any (and potentially all) debts that the partnership incurs, and each person pays income tax and NICs on his share of the partnership profits.

As well as an active partner (or partners), your partnership may include a *sleeping partner*. No, not someone who takes naps in the office: The sleeping partner contributes money to the business but doesn't get involved in running it. This partner usually receives a smaller annual share of the partnership profits.

A partnership can be a simple and extremely flexible way for two or more people to own and run a business together. However, bear in mind that partners don't have any protection if the partnership fails. Unlike a limited company (see the later section 'Limited liability company'), a partnership has no legal existence separate from the partners themselves. If one of the partners resigns, dies, or goes bankrupt, the partnership has to be dissolved, even though the business itself may not need to cease.

You can ask a solicitor to help you draw up an agreement or you can draw up your own. Plenty of free advice is available on the Internet to help you (www.startups.co.uk is one such place among many others).

Although you can go into partnership with anyone you choose, if a member of a partnership is under the age of 18, he can't be legally bound by the terms of a partnership agreement.

The partnership needs to appoint one of its officers (the *nominated officer*) to fill in the partnership tax return each year and send it to HMRC. This return includes a Partnership Statement, which shows how profits or losses have been divided amongst the partners. The nominated partner also has to give each partner a copy of the Partnership Statement to help them complete their own personal tax return correctly.

Limited liability partnership

A *limited liability partnership* (LLP) is similar to an ordinary partnership in that a number of people or limited companies join together and share the costs, risks, and responsibilities of the business. They also take a share of the profits, and pay income tax and NICs on their share of the partnership profits.

An LLP differs from an ordinary partnership in that debt is limited to the amount of money each partner invested in the business and to any personal guarantees given to raise business finance. Therefore, members have some protection if the business runs into difficulties because their liability is restricted in general terms to the level of their investment.

No restriction exists on the number of partners, but at least two partners must be *designated members* who have additional legal responsibilities. If the LLP reduces in number and fewer than two designated members remain, every member is treated as a designated member.

Limited liability company

You can start a business by forming a *limited liability company*. The technical term for this is *incorporation* (flick to Chapter 17 for more details on incorporating). When a business incorporates, shares are issued in the new company. The *shareholders* are the owners of the company. The shareholders are usually, but not necessarily, also the *company directors*. Currently, a limited company must have at least one company director and a company secretary, both of whom may also be shareholders. But from October 2008, private limited companies don't need a company secretary.

The important thing to understand about a limited company is that it exists in its own right, which means that the company's finances are separate from the personal finances of the company owners. Strict laws mean that you can't simply take money out of the company whenever you feel like it.

Companies are formed by issuing shares. Shareholders can be individuals or other companies. They aren't responsible for the company's debts but directors may be asked to give personal guarantees of loans to the company. Shareholders may lose the money they invest in the company if it fails.

Finance for the company comes from shareholders, borrowing, and profits that the business retains. Profits are usually distributed to the shareholders in the form of *dividends*, apart from profits retained in the business as working capital. Directors and employees of the company are often paid a mixture of salary, bonuses, and/or dividends.

Companies pay corporation tax and must make annual returns to HMRC. Company directors are employees of the company and usually pay Class 1 NICs as well as income tax on their salaries.

Qualifying for self-employed status

You can't simply decide that you're self-employed. HMRC applies various basic tests to determine whether you're really in business on your own account and therefore self-employed, or whether someone else actually employs you. If you do qualify for self-employment, you can claim considerable business expenses against your income tax liability and this in turn means that you pay less tax (which is why the taxman wants to be sure that you qualify).

If you can answer 'yes' to most of the following statements, the tax authorities are likely to treat you as self-employed:

- ✔ You have more than one customer – preferably many.

- ✔ You have your own business premises or, if you don't have actual premises, you work in several locations. For example, if you're an electrician, you work at your customers' premises.

- ✔ You have a business address – often your home – from which you carry out some business functions, even if these functions are only message taking.

- ✔ You decide when and where you work. You set your own prices and can turn down work if you want.

- ✔ You agree on a set price for a job regardless of how long the job may take.

- ✔ You aren't entitled to overtime, bonuses, or holiday and sick pay.

- ✔ You buy and maintain your own tools, vehicles, and any other items you need to do your job.

- ✔ You have to provide your own insurance cover.

- ✔ You're responsible for correcting unsatisfactory work in your own time and at your own expense.

Some people who provide labour-only services believe that they're in business on their own account and can be treated as self-employed. Consider computer consultants who work only for one company, subcontracted builders who work for others on site, and hairdressers who rent a chair and basin space in a hair salon owned by someone else. The tax authorities make big, and often successful, efforts to deny such people self-employed status and the tax savings that can go with it. If you're in any doubt as to your employment status, ask the tax authorities or a tax adviser to help you clarify things right from the start. You can find information on finding professional help in Chapter 20.

Establishing whether you're trading

You need to establish whether you're actually *trading*, which means you're in business on your own account, or whether you're simply carrying out a one-off or irregular task such as selling something or doing a casual job for someone in your spare time.

For example, if you have a clear out at home and take some items to sell at the local car boot sale, you're not trading in the eyes of the tax authorities. If, however, you regularly buy t-shirts from a local wholesaler and sell them every Sunday morning at the same car boot sale, you're trading and you need to notify HMRC accordingly.

 If you buy goods from a wholesaler, from auctions, or even from charity shops with the intention of selling them on at a profit, the tax authorities treat you as a trader and you're liable to pay income tax and NICs accordingly.

Formalising the Business

After you establish that you are in fact in business on your own account, and you decide which legal structure to adopt – sole trader, partnership, or limited company – you need to spend a bit of time doing the paperwork to make sure that you set everything up correctly. The following sections guide you through the nitty gritty of setting up your business.

Registering your new business

How you register your business depends on the legal structure you choose. Sole traders and ordinary partnerships register as self-employed, and LLPs and limited companies register the business with Companies House.

Sole traders and partnerships

When you start a business as a sole trader or in a partnership, you need to register with the tax authorities within three months of the last day of the month in which the business begins. If you don't register, HMRC charges a penalty of £100. In some cases, the business's exact start date may be debatable, so I recommend that you register as soon as you can to avoid a fine – the process is quick and painless.

 You register as self-employed by

- ✔ **Calling a special helpline:** Ring the Newly Self-Employed Helpline on 0845 915 4515.

- ✔ **Filling in form CWF1.** You download this form from the HMRC Web site at www.hmrc.gov.uk/forms/cwf1.pdf, and then post the completed form to HM Revenue & Customs, National Insurance Contributions Office, CAAT, Longbenton, Newcastle upon Tyne, NE98 1ZZ.

- ✔ **Registering online:** Go to www.workingforyourself.co.uk/selfemployed/form.asp.

HMRC also offers some useful support for new sole traders and members of partnerships:

- ✔ **'Working for yourself: The Guide':** This HMRC guide informs you about what you need to do when you set up a business. You can download the guide from the HMRC Web site at www.hmrc.gov.uk/startingup/working-for-yourself.pdf, or call 0845 915 4515 and request a copy.

- ✔ **Free workshops:** The Revenue and Customs Business Support Teams run workshops that give you practical advice on things like record-keeping, filling in your tax return, and what to do if you take someone on. Best of all, these useful sessions don't cost you a penny. To arrange a workshop call 0845 915 4515 or book online at www.hmrc.gov.uk/bst/index.htm.

LLPs and limited companies

When you set up an LLP or a limited company, you must register your business with Companies House (www.companieshouse.gov.uk).

When you apply to register an LLP, you pay a registration fee of £20 (£50 for Same Day registration). You also pay £20 to register a limited company (£15 if you apply electronically). For both LLPs and limited companies, you file an annual return that costs you £30 (£15 when you file electronically).

Paying national insurance contributions

Anyone who is aged between 16 and state pension age – currently 60 for a woman and 65 for a man – may be liable to pay NICs. If you run your own business as a sole trader, or in partnership, you usually pay Class 2 and Class 4 NICs and you need to register with HMRC accordingly. If you trade through a limited company, you're usually treated as an employee and pay Class 1 NICs (usually called *primary contributions*). The company also has to pay Class 1 NICs on your earnings (called *secondary contributions*).

Chapter 16 explores paying Class 2 and 4 NICs in detail, and Chapter 12 covers Class 1 NICs.

You must notify HMRC of your liability to pay Class 2 contributions within three months from the last day of the month in which your new self-employment commenced. If you fail to tell HMRC, you're charged a fixed penalty of £100. (This penalty may be reduced at HMRC's discretion, and can be avoided if you have a 'reasonable excuse' for late notification or if self-employment earnings for the period were below the small earnings exception limit.)

Registering for VAT

When your sales reach a certain threshold, the government expects you to register to pay and to charge Value Added Tax (VAT) – a tax charged by registered businesses on most business transactions. The following sections lead you through when you register and how much you charge.

Knowing when to register

All traders – whether sole traders, partnerships, or limited companies – have to register to charge and pay VAT once annual sales reach a certain threshold (£67,000 for 2008–9). The threshold tends to rise each year roughly in line with inflation.

The annual VAT threshold is determined by *total sales* and is not the same as *total profits* (which is generally sales minus expenses). You can make a loss and still need to register for VAT.

The threshold operates on a month-by-month basis, so you need to check at the end of each month to make sure you haven't gone over the limit in the previous 12 months. You also need to think about whether you're going to go over that limit in the following 12 months. If you think your total sales may exceed the VAT threshold, you need to register.

You must register with HMRC within 30 days of being aware that you're going to exceed the threshold. If you fail to register you're charged a penalty, which can eventually be up to 15 per cent of the VAT owed and is in addition to the actual VAT due. So make sure that you register on time and avoid incurring costly penalties.

Outlining the VAT rates

VAT has three rates:

- ✔ Standard rate (currently 17.5 per cent)
- ✔ Reduced rate (currently 5 per cent)
- ✔ Zero rate

Some items and supplies (generally goods and services) are exempt from VAT, which means that no VAT is payable on them. Also, supplies are outside the scope of VAT completely if they are made outside the UK (and the Isle of Man), and not made for business purposes.

Most goods and services are charged at the standard rate of VAT. However, gas and electricity supplies to your home, for example, are charged at the reduced rate. Many everyday items, such as fresh food, books, magazines, newspapers, and children's clothes are charged at the zero rate (called *zero rating*). You must register for VAT even if all the goods and services you supply are zero rated if your total sales exceed the annual VAT registration threshold.

When you've registered for VAT, you must charge VAT on all the work or goods you supply to customers (other than on items or supplies that are exempt). On the plus side, you can also claim back the VAT on goods and services you have to buy in for your business.

Registering voluntarily

You can register for VAT even if your *turnover* (total sales) is below the threshold and you may actually save tax by doing so, particularly if your main clients or customers are organisations that can reclaim VAT themselves.

Say you buy a new office printer for your business, which is not VAT registered. The printer costs £100 and you pay VAT on it, so you pay £117.50 (£100 plus VAT at 17.5 per cent). You set £117.50 against your profits for income tax purposes. If you're a basic rate taxpayer paying tax at 20 per cent, you save £23.50 on your tax bill (20 per cent of £117.50), so the printer actually costs the business £94. However, if you're registered for VAT, you reclaim the £17.50 VAT you paid on the item (called *input tax*) and set £100 against your profits for income tax. Your tax reduction is therefore £20 (20 per cent of £100) and the printer costs your business just £80 – so you save £14 by being VAT registered.

VAT-registered businesses supplying goods and services to private individuals often feel disadvantaged compared to their non-registered counterparts because they have to charge an additional 17.5 per cent on every bill issued. If you don't want to have to register for VAT, you may be able to stay below the annual VAT registration threshold by supplying labour-only services and getting your customers to buy any goods needed themselves. For example, a plumber can ask his customer to buy taps and hoses directly from the DIY shop. Despite still paying VAT on these items, the customer doesn't have to pay on the non-VAT registered plumber's labour charge for fitting them, thus reducing the plumber's turnover.

Charging VAT

When your business is VAT-registered you need to obtain, issue, and keep various documents – including receipts and suppliers' invoices.

As soon as your business is registered for VAT you must

- ✔ Raise a VAT invoice whenever you supply standard-rate (at 17.5 per cent) or reduced-rate (at 5 per cent) goods or services to a VAT registered customer.
- ✔ Keep copies of all invoices you send or receive.
- ✔ Keep a note of all the VAT you pay and charge.
- ✔ Keep a summary of VAT for each tax period covered by your VAT returns.

Whenever you supply goods or services on which VAT is chargeable to another VAT-registered person or business, you must provide a document showing certain information about what you're supplying. This document is called a *VAT invoice*. Normally, you must issue a VAT invoice within 30 days of the date you make the supply and it must show the following:

- ✔ An invoice identifying number
- ✔ Your name, address, and VAT registration number
- ✔ The date of issue of the invoice
- ✔ The time of supply (called the *tax point*) – if different from date of issue of the invoice
- ✔ Your customer's name (or trading name) and address
- ✔ A description identifying the goods or services supplied
- ✔ The unit price or goods supplied
- ✔ The rate of any cash discount offered
- ✔ The total amount of VAT charged, shown in pounds sterling
- ✔ The gross total amount payable, excluding VAT

For each description of goods and services, you must show the following:

- ✔ Amount payable, excluding VAT
- ✔ Quantity of goods or extent of the services
- ✔ Rate of VAT

Figure 15-1 gives you an idea of what a completed VAT invoice looks like.

Invoice Number   1569

VAT registration number   867 4536 26

To: ABC Limited, 45 Pound Street, London, WIC 4XX

From: Widgits Abound Ltd, 23 Euro Lane, Brighton, Sussex, BH34 2RG

Quantity	Description and Price per Unit	Amount (exc. VAT)	VAT Rate	VAT Payable
12	Door handles @ £10.00	£120.00		
7	Door hinges @ £5.00	£35.00		
24	Letter box covers @ £17.00	£408.00		
	Total	£563.00	17.5%	93.60*
	*Cash discount of 5% if paid within 30 days	£28.15		
	VAT	£93.60		
	Total	£656.60		

Figure 15-1: Example of a completed VAT invoice.

Paying VAT

Generally, if you register for VAT you make a quarterly return to HMRC. The return form asks for two figures in particular:

- ✔ Your *output tax*: The amount you receive for selling goods or supplying services shown on your invoices to customers
- ✔ Your *input tax*: The value of goods or services you buy in to help carry out your business shown on invoices you receive from suppliers

Some businesses like the discipline of quarterly VAT returns, which help them keep on top of their paperwork, but others really feel the administrative burden of making such frequent returns. For such businesses you may be able pay your VAT via different schemes, which I explore in the following sections.

Cash accounting

Under the normal method of accounting for VAT, you account for the output tax on your sales as they take place or as soon as you issue a VAT invoice, even if your customer hasn't paid you. Then you can reclaim input tax on purchases you make as soon as you receive a VAT invoice, even if you haven't paid your supplier. This method can cause cash flow problems if you have to pay a VAT bill before your customer pays you.

The cash accounting scheme turns this normal method upside down. In cash accounting, you account for the output tax when you receive payment for the sale, rather than when the customer received the goods or service. So this way, you have the money from your customer to pay the VAT you charged on his bill. However, this scheme cuts both ways because you can only reclaim the input tax once you pay your supplier, which means that when your VAT bill is due you can't offset the VAT you owe suppliers against your total bill.

The cash accounting scheme can help your cash flow because in general you don't have to pay VAT until your customers have paid you. The scheme is especially helpful if you give your customers extended credit or suffer a lot of bad debts. However, the scheme may not give you any benefit if you

✔ Are usually paid as soon as you make a sale

✔ Regularly reclaim more VAT than you pay

✔ Make continuous supplies of services

The cash accounting scheme is available to most businesses with an annual taxable turnover up to £1.35 million. Once in the scheme, businesses can continue to use it until their annual taxable turnover exceeds £1.6 million. You can choose to use the cash accounting scheme as soon as you register for VAT if you think it may be beneficial for you to do so. If you find the scheme of no benefit, you can leave the scheme voluntarily at the end of a VAT accounting period and return to the normal method of accounting for VAT.

Annual accounting

The annual accounting scheme allows you to complete just one VAT return each year, instead of the usual four. You pay three (quarterly) or nine (monthly) instalments of the VAT that you expect to owe, to avoid a large VAT bill at the end of the year.

These instalments must be paid by Direct Debit, Standing Order, or other electronic means. When you join the scheme, HMRC calculates and notifies you of the instalment amounts and dates the instalments are due. If you think the payments are wrong, or your business changes, you can ask for the instalments to be amended.

Using the annual accounting scheme may help you for the following reasons:

- ✔ You can smooth out your cash flow by paying a set amount in manageable instalments.

- ✔ You can make additional payments as and when you can afford to.

- ✔ You need to fill in only one VAT return each year, instead of four.

- ✔ You get two months to complete and send in your annual VAT return and balancing payment, instead of one.

- ✔ You can align your VAT year with the end of your business tax year, to simplify your end-of-year routines.

The scheme is available to most businesses with turnovers of up to £1.35 million, but you have to leave the scheme if your turnover goes over £1.6 million a year.

Flat rate scheme for small businesses

This scheme is designed to help small businesses with a turnover of no more than £150,000 a year, excluding VAT, by taking some of the work out of recording VAT sales and purchases. If you use the scheme, you pay HMRC a single percentage of your turnover in a VAT period.

The percentages applicable to this scheme vary from 2 per cent for food and children's clothing retailers up to 13.5 per cent for builders and contractors who supply labour-only services. Full details of the scheme are included in the HMRC 'VAT Notice 733: Flat rate scheme for small businesses', which you can download from the HMRC Web site at www.hmrc.gov.uk.

In your first year of VAT registration you get a 1 per cent reduction in flat rate, which means that you can take 1 per cent off the flat rate you apply to your turnover, until the day before your first anniversary of becoming VAT registered.

The scheme works well for some but not others. On the positive side, the scheme may save you some admin because you don't have to work out every item of input and output tax, but if your customers are VAT registered, you do have to calculate the VAT and issue VAT invoices in the normal way. Financially, the flat rates averages may work out cheaper for you than normal accounting or you may find this scheme more expensive – use HMRC's ready reckoner to check.

Under the scheme, you pay the VAT quarterly and you can swap back to the normal VAT scheme at any time if your inputs rise – making the flat rate scheme a bad deal. You can also claim VAT on any capital expenditure of more than £2,000 excluding VAT.

To join the scheme, submit form VAT 600 (FRS) to HMRC. You can download the form from the HMRC Web site (www.hmrc.gov.uk).

Other VAT schemes

If you sell direct to the public, you may find it difficult to issue a VAT invoice for each sale. HMRC has several retail schemes available that may help. If you make a mixture of retail and non-retail sales you can use a retail scheme to calculate the tax due on your retail sales only. You must account for non-retail sales by using the normal method of accounting.

Choosing an Accountant

Unless you're setting up a simple sole trading activity, such as providing a service on a freelance basis from home, and you've a good idea about book-keeping and tax matters, you should think about appointing an accountant to help you with your business as soon as you can, and definitely by the time you're trading. A good accountant can help not only with your paperwork for tax purposes, but also with business plans and strategy for future development and growth.

Other people can help you as well – for example your bank or a specialist small business consultancy – but in terms of tax and VAT advice on setting up your business as a sole trader, partnership, or limited company, you probably need an accountant.

If any of the following activities are required in the running of your business, your accountant can help with them:

✓ Managing and administering your payroll system, calculating Pay as You Earn tax (refer to Chapter 12 for more about PAYE), and generating payslips for you and your staff

✓ Calculating the NICs that you're required to pay

✓ Helping you to administer VAT and Customs & Excise duties

✓ Advising on budgeting, invoicing, credit control, and cash flow

✓ Advising on record-keeping systems (including computerised records)

As a sole trader, partner, or director, you're responsible for calculating and paying your own income tax. An advantage of having an accountant dealing with your business finances is that he's also well placed to manage your personal tax matters.

Getting Other Help

One of the best places to start looking for help and advice is the Internet, and many organisations offer free advice to new businesses. Here are some of the main ones:

- **Business Link** (www.startupanswers.co.uk) is funded by the government and aims to make starting-up as easy as possible, as well as help small businesses reach their potential and flourish. It runs a programme of user-friendly 'Starting your own business' workshops, free of charge, to anyone with a clear business idea. If you don't have access to the Web site, you can call Business Link on 0845 600 9 006 and request a starter pack.

- **HM Revenue & Customs** (www.hmrc.gov.uk/businesses) offer free information, help, and a range of seminars and workshops. If you don't have access to the Internet, you can call the HMRC Newly Self-Employed helpline on 0845 915 4515.

- **SmallBusiness.co.uk** (www.smallbusiness.co.uk) provides useful resources, products, and services for small business owners and start-ups. It offers free online advice in the form of news articles, guides, tips, and features that can point you in the right direction to start and run your own small business. You can also use a Q&A Forum to ask questions to a panel of experts, leave comments, and discuss the listed topics.

- **Startups.co.uk** (www.startups.co.uk) offers an extensive range of 'how-to' guides. Topics include raising finance, drafting business plans, finding premises, when to buy and sell, marketing, doing business online, wholesaling, insurance, technology, hiring and firing, health and safety, and complying with legal issues. The site also features a forum where visitors share their ideas on how to start a business.

- **TaxationWeb** (www.taxationweb.co.uk) is a great information directory and tax community Web site offering tax news, articles, details of tax courses and conferences, book reviews, a book shop, and a useful tax calendar. It also runs a Tax Tips Forum, where you can post your tax questions for discussion with others.

Chapter 16

Running a Business

*R*unning your own business can be exciting, rewarding, and fun. It can also be incredibly hard work, extremely frustrating, and hugely stressful. However, at the end of the day, most people who work for themselves agree that no other feeling comes close to it.

In this chapter I look at the tax and national insurance contributions (NICs) aspects of running your business, including what records you need to keep, how to choose your accounting date, items you can claim tax relief on (and those you can't), paying NICs, and the special Construction Industry Scheme (CIS). I also look at taking on employees to expand your business. Finally I give you pointers on what happens when you want to wind the business up and move on.

Keeping Business Accounts

To give your business the best chance of success, you need to set up an organised and efficient accounts procedure. You need to get to grips with what records you must keep and how, and which scraps of paper belong neatly filed away as opposed to lost or binned. Then you can sit down and decide the most convenient and tax-efficient financial year dates for your business.

Paul Barrow and Lita Epstein's *Bookkeeping For Dummies* (Wiley) contains plenty of useful guidance to help you set up and manage your business accounts.

Getting to grips with record-keeping

You must do certain things when you run your own business and keeping proper records for tax purposes is probably one of the most important. Nobody relishes a visit from the taxman, so set up an organised record-keeping system from the outset to keep everything in order and stress to a minimum.

You're legally required to keep certain records for income tax purposes, and if you're a VAT-registered trader, for VAT purposes. The basic requirement is that records must be retained for five years from the 31 January following the tax year for which the tax return is made. For example, for the 2007–8 tax return sent to you on or shortly after 6 April 2008, to complete and send back by 31 January 2009, records must be retained until at least 31 January 2014. HM Revenue & Customs (HMRC) may charge a penalty of up to £3,000 if you fail to keep adequate records to back up your tax return.

HMRC normally expects you to record all money coming into the business and every penny that goes out. Your records must include:

- ✔ All purchases and expenses as they arise. Retain invoices or receipts for your expenses. If you can't get a receipt (for example, you pay £5 to get into a business exhibition and no receipt is available), record the amount you spent, when you spent it, and what it was for.

- ✔ All sales of products, services, and business assets. Keep back-up records to show where your income came from – for example, invoices, bank statements, paying-in slips, and till receipt rolls.

- ✔ Any money you pay into the business from personal funds.

- ✔ Any money you take out of the business bank account for you or your family's personal use.

- ✔ Money you pay into the business when taking goods for personal use (if you take goods without paying for them you still owe the business for them and have to add the retail cost of the items to your overall pre-tax profit figure).

Ticking off the benefits of good record-keeping

Although keeping good records when you're starting up a new business may seem like a challenge, it brings real benefits. Just look at a few of the advantages of keeping good records:

✔ Enables HMRC to check your tax position accurately, which helps you avoid paying too much tax

✔ Gives you the information you need to manage your business and help it grow

✔ Keeps you organised, so you pay the right tax at the right time and avoid interest and penalty charges

✔ Makes filling in your tax return easier and quicker

✔ Provides the details you need in order to budget for your tax payments

✔ Reduces your accountant's fees if you use one – well-organised information saves them time, too

✔ Supports your claims to certain reliefs or capital allowances

✔ A little organisation never hurt anybody, and in terms of tax it can actually save you money. Get a proper record-keeping system in place and make sure that you update the information regularly.

Choosing your accounting date

The tax year runs from 6 April to 5 April and most businesses use this system for their accounting year too, although you may find it convenient to use 31 March as the end date for your business year. Using 31 March or 5 April as the last day of your year is called opting for *fiscal accounting*, so-called because your business year is the same as the tax, or fiscal, year.

You can use any other date for your business year-end. Choosing a different date can give you longer to file your tax return and longer to pay the tax due, which means that money can stay earning interest in your bank account a little longer.

However, choosing a different year-end date has one big drawback: You pay tax twice on the same profits in the first two years of trading, because if you don't use the 5 April as your business year-end, HMRC handles your tax bills for your first two years of trading a little differently:

- ✔ **First year of trading:** Your tax bill is based on your profits (assuming you have some!) from the date you started your business to the following 5 April – even if this isn't your chosen business year-end. Therefore, your first tax bill can cover just a few days (if you started to trade on, say, 25 March), or nearly a full year (if you started on say, 20 April).

- ✔ **Second year of trading:** Your tax bill is usually based on the 12 months of trading that ends on your chosen year-end date. However, if you choose a year-end date that is less than 12 months after the start of your business, your tax bill is based on your first 12 months of trading.

From the third year onwards, your tax bill is calculated using your accounts for the 12 months ending in the tax year to which the self-assessment return relates. So, if you draw your accounts up to 30 June each year, your tax bill for 2008–9 is based on your accounts for the 12 months ending on 30 June 2008.

James started his business on 1 August 2007 and produces his accounts to 5 April 2008, that is, to the end of the fiscal year, and annually thereafter. James's tax bill is based on the following profits:

Tax year	Accounting period	Taxable profits (£)
2007–8	1 August 2007 to 5 April 2008	8,000
2008–9	6 April 2008 to 5 April 2009	18,000
2009–10	6 April 2009 to 5 April 2010	24,000
2010–11	6 April 2010 to 5 April 2011	30,000

Jill also started a business on 1 August 2007 but she produces accounts to 31 July 2008, that is, for a period of 12 months, and annually thereafter. Jill's tax bill is based on the following profits:

Tax year	Accounting period	Taxable profits (£)
2007–8	1 August 2007 to 5 April 2008	9,512 (248/ 365 days × 14,000)
2008–9	1 August 2007 to 31 July 2008	14,000
2009–10	1 August 2008 to 31 July 2009	20,000
2010–11	1 August 2009 to 31 July 2010	26,000

The period from the date Jill started trading on 1 August 2007 to 5 April 2008 is taxed both for 2007–8 and 2008–9. This period is called the *overlap period*, and the amount that has been taxed twice (£9,512) is called the *overlap profit*. Effectively, Jill pays tax on profits she hasn't yet made. When Jill stops trading, she can deduct the whole amount of overlap profit from her taxable profit figure for her last year of trading. Although this deduction helps reduce her tax bill for her final year of trading, it may be many years before she can claim it, and when she does her overpayments aren't adjusted for inflation or changing tax rates.

If your costs in your first few years of trading are likely to be greater than your income, the overlap rules don't affect you, because you make no profits on which to pay tax. But for most small businesses, overlap is something to avoided, and you can do so by aligning your business year-end with the tax year.

You can change your accounting year-end during the life of your business to lessen the effect of the overlap rules if you need to, although you should be aware that some restrictions apply. You can elect for a year-end change by notifying HMRC in writing in a letter or on a self-assessment form.

If you have to borrow money because paying tax on overlap profits means you have to take cash out of your business, you can claim tax relief on any loan interest you pay against future tax bills.

Working Out Your Business's Income Tax Bill

When you're self-employed you have to calculate your business's tax bill and file a self-assessment tax return that notifies HMRC of your accounts. (Chapter 3 explains self assessment in detail.) To start, you calculate your *annual profit*, which is your business's total income minus all the tax-deductible expenditure (often referred to as a *profit and loss account*). If you make a profit, you pay income tax and NICs on this amount. If, however, the picture's less than rosy and you make a loss, you can claim tax relief. Read on to find out more.

Adding up your income

Taxable business profits are usually worked out on amounts earned during your business year (the *earnings basis*), as opposed to amounts received (the *cash basis*). Business income falls into two categories for profit and loss reporting: sales and other income. The total sales of products and/or services in a trading year is referred to as your *turnover*, the starting point for your profit and loss account. But as well as reporting sales income, you also need to tell HMRC about income from any other sources, such as bank and/or building society interest, sales of any equipment no longer needed for the business, and any rental income received.

Offsetting business expenses

Those who work for someone else under PAYE can only claim business expenses for tax if they are incurred 'wholly, exclusively, and necessarily' in carrying out their employment duties. That definition is really hard to meet. Being self-employed, however, means that money you spend 'wholly and exclusively' for business purposes can be set against your earnings for tax purposes. The 'necessarily' part of the rule doesn't apply to business. The reason is because it would be impossible for an outsider to define the 'necessity' of an expense to a business (for example, is your computer over-specified and do you need one at all? Do you need a new car when the old one is still working?). This rule applies equally to big companies and small businesses.

 Although you can claim for a wide range of business expenditure, remember that HMRC isn't stupid and is on the look out for exaggerated expenses. Don't try claiming that the cost of running your Rolls-Royce is wholly and exclusively for business purposes, unless of course you run a wedding car hire business.

Looking at the categories of business expenses

HMRC divides business expenses into different categories. Legitimate business expenses that you can offset against your business income for tax purposes include:

- ✔ **Advertising/promotions:** Costs directly associated with advertising and promoting your business, for example, newspaper adverts.

✔ **Costs associated with your business premises:** Includes rent, heating, and lighting. Check out the later section 'Claiming expenses when you work from home' for important info on this category of expense.

✔ **Costs of hiring employees, including casuals:** Wages and salaries paid to employees, and any employer NICs you pay.

✔ **General administration:** All administrative costs of running your business. Don't underestimate how much the cost of paper, pens, postage stamps, mobile and fixed telephone charges, and so on can add up to. Set up a ledger and make sure that you keep a record of everything you spend.

✔ **Interest on business loans:** The interest on a loan used for both business and private purposes (for example, a car that you use for both business and pleasure) can be apportioned according to the amount of time you use it in your business.

✔ **Legal or professional fees:** Subscriptions to any professional body of which you need to be a member for your business count. So do legal fees you incur trying to collect a customer debt. You can't claim for any legal costs incurred in settling tax disputes, or costs and fines imposed for breaking the law.

✔ **Motor expenses:** Cost of running your business vehicle(s). If you use vehicles for both business and private purposes, you can apportion the costs based on mileage or time used within the business.

✔ **Other finance charges:** Cost of overdrafts and so on.

✔ **Repairs to any equipment:** Cost of any repairs made to assets you use in your business.

✔ **Travel and subsistence:** Keep records of business travel costs. You should be able to claim reasonable costs for subsistence (food and drinks) if you have to work away from your normal business premises.

Where business expenses apply partly to business and partly to non-business or personal use, you need to record the whole expense on your tax return, and then separately record the amount that relates to non-business use. For example, if you buy a printer and use it half for business and half for personal use, include the full price of the printer as a business expenses on your self-assessment tax return, but later in the tax return add back in an amount for the half that relates to your private use.

Claiming expenses when you work from home

If you use part of your home for the business, you can claim part of your household bills as a business expense. No specific rules are in place for this claim and it's generally a question of common sense. For example, if you have a house with six rooms (excluding kitchens and bathrooms) and you use half of one room for your business, look at your domestic bills and claim half of one-sixth (one-twelfth) as a business expenditure.

Try not to use rooms in your house exclusively for business purposes, because you may run into capital gains tax (CGT) problems when you come to sell your home. (In general, no CGT is due on the sale of your private home, but a charge may apply on the sale of the part used as business premises – skip to Chapter 6 for more on this subject.) And don't claim mortgage interest or council tax for the part of your home used for business because your local council may charge you business rates, which can be far greater than the normal domestic rate charges.

Distinguishing between types of expenditure

When working out which business expenses you can deduct, you need to understand the difference between the two types of expenditure:

- **Revenue expenditure** generally covers the day-to-day running costs of your business. Examples of revenue expenditure include staff wages, stock purchase, and business premises rent. You can deduct revenue expenditure from your total income when working out your taxable profits.

- **Capital expenditure** brings about an 'enduring benefit of a trade', which means it's used to buy something used in day-to-day operation of your business. Examples of capital expenditure include the purchase of business premises, equipment, and machinery used in the business (for example, ladders if you're a window cleaner), and cars and other vehicles bought for business use. You can't deduct this type of expenditure as a business expense when working out your taxable profits, but you can usually claim capital allowances on this type of expenditure (see the following section 'Claiming capital allowances').

Claiming capital allowances

Any items of equipment you buy or lease for long-term use for your business are called *capital items* or *fixed assets*. HMRC classifies all capital items under the heading 'plant and machinery'. Capital items include:

- Business premises
- Cars or vans for business use

✔ Computer equipment (including printers, scanners, keyboards, and so on)

✔ Furniture

✔ Machinery

You can't deduct capital items from your turnover in the same way as business expenses. Instead, you may be able to claim capital allowances for the cost of the asset (but not costs for any bank loan or other financing that helped you purchase or lease the asset). In general, *capital allowances* mean that you spread the costs over several years and claim a bit of tax relief each year as you go along.

To complicate matters, a new system for claiming capital allowances is currently being introduced and you need to know about both systems if you have recently set up your own business. The following sections explain the old system and the new one, and look at the special rules that apply when you claim capital allowances on cars.

If the item you buy is partly for business use and partly for personal use, you can only claim capital allowances on the business element.

Understanding the old rules

You need to know about the old capital allowances system for your tax return for the 2007–8 tax year. Up to and including the 2007–8 tax year, if you qualify as a small or medium-sized business (generally, one that has fewer than 250 employees, an annual turnover of less than £22.8 million, and a balance sheet total of less than £11.4 million) on most items of plant and machinery you can claim a *first-year allowance* of 40 per cent of the value, and then *writing-down allowance* (WDA) of 25 per cent of the balance in each following year.

So an item costing £1,000 can be offset as follows:

Year 1	£400 (40 per cent of £1,000)
Year 2	£150 (25 per cent of £600)
Year 3	£112 (25 per cent of (£600 – £150))
Year 4	£84 (25 per cent of (£450 – £112))

and so on. . . .

If you run a small business you're entitled to a higher first-year allowance of 50 per cent, followed by the usual 25 per cent annual allowance. So an item costing £1,000 can be offset as follows:

Year 1	£500 (50 per cent of £1,000)
Year 2	£125 (25 per cent of £500)
Year 3	£94 (25 per cent of (£500 – £125))
Year 4	£70 (25 per cent of (£375 – £94))

and so on . . . .

Getting to grips with the new system

From the tax year 2008–9 onwards, HMRC is changing the capital allowances system. The 40 per cent and 50 per cent first year allowances are being replaced with a new allowance called the *annual investment allowance* (AIA). In general, all businesses can claim the AIA at 100 per cent on the first £50,000 of expenditure incurred on capital items, and WDAs at 20 per cent on the remainder. For example, to claim capital allowances for an asset costing £80,000, you first deduct the AIA of £50,000, which leaves a balance of £30,000 from which you deduct the WDA at 20 per cent (£6,000). You receive tax relief on a total of £56,000 (£50,000 plus £6,000).

A slightly different rule applies to claiming for the cost of fixtures that are integral to buildings, such as central heating, air conditioning systems, lifts, escalators, and moving walkways. From 2008–9, writing-down allowances may be claimed at a lower rate of 10 per cent per annum.

Plan the timing of any expenditure to make the most of capital allowances available. If you spend £100,000 in one tax year on capital items you get immediate relief for £55,000 (AIA of £50,000 plus WDA of £5,000), and you have to keep claiming the rest over future years, taking a long time to offset the full expenditure. But if the £100,000 investment straddles two years, you can claim the full relief immediately (two amounts of £50,000 AIA), and save yourself tax now rather than later.

You don't need to make a full claim for capital allowances when doing so isn't tax efficient, that is, where you can make better use of other available reliefs and personal allowances. If you make a reduced claim, the allowances are generally deferred to a future tax year so you don't miss out financially.

Remembering the rules for cars

For the years up to and including 2007–8, cars qualify for a 25 per cent capital allowance each year but a maximum value of £12,000 is used for each car. So, if your car is worth £24,000, for working out capital allowances, you have to take the value as being £12,000 in the first year you claim. The maximum allowance available each year is therefore restricted to £3,000 (25 per cent of £12,000), and then you can deduct 25 per cent of the remaining £9,000 (£2,250), and so on.

From 2008–9, cars qualify for 20 per cent capital allowances each year in line with other general business assets, which I explain in the preceding section.

Low-emission vehicles benefit from a 100 per cent allowance from the first year. To qualify as a low-emission car, a car must be first registered with the DVLA after 16 April 2002 and have CO_2 emissions not exceeding 110g/km.

Relieving your losses

You have to face it, even with the best will in the world, your business may make a loss. Although being in this position isn't great, at least some good news applies for tax purposes – you can claim tax relief for your losses. The following sections explore the options available to you when you make a loss during the course of your business, depending on your circumstances (skip to the section 'Claiming for losses on cessation' to find out how to relieve your losses when you stop trading).

Deducting the loss from other income

Providing you were carrying on your business on a commercial basis with a view to making a profit, you should be able to claim relief for a trading loss in one tax year against your other taxable income from the same year, or the one before. You can decide which year to claim the losses against. Other taxable income may be a PAYE job, a pension, dividends (paid on shares you hold in limited companies), and bank/building society interest.

This relief may be particularly beneficial if you're self-employed on a part-time basis. For example, if you receive £20,000 a year from a PAYE employment, and you make a £2,000 loss from your part-time business, your tax bill for the year is based on income of £18,000.

In addition, if you make a loss in any of the first four tax years of a new business, you can carry them back against your total income of the three previous tax years, starting with the earliest year. Therefore, if you've paid income tax in any of the previous three years, you should be entitled to a repayment of tax. You must offset the maximum you can for each year – you can't offset just a proportion of the loss in order to spread the loss across three years to take advantage of beneficial tax rates. Again, relief isn't available unless you were trading on a commercial basis with a view to making a profit within a reasonable timescale. In practice, this requirement may be difficult to prove in the case of a new business and you may need a viable business plan to support your claim.

To make a claim for loss relief, you need to inform HMRC within 12 months following 31 January after the end of your loss-making business year.

Carrying losses forward

If you make a loss and you can't offset it against any other income, you can carry it forward indefinitely and use it to reduce the first available profits of the same business in subsequent years.

If you're a sole trader or partnership and you *incorporate* your business (you transfer to a limited company), you can usually carry forward any unused losses of the business and set them off against your first available income derived from the company. Flick to Chapter 17 for more details.

Setting losses against capital gains

You can set any losses you make from your business against any capital gains you make (refer to Chapter 6 for an explanation of capital gains) for the tax year of the loss and/or the previous tax year. However, the trading loss first has to be used against any other income you may have for the year of the claim (for example, against earnings from employment) in priority to any capital gains.

Paying National Insurance on Your Self-Employment Income

As a self-employed person, taxable profits you make from your business are added to other earnings, pensions, dividends, and interest for income tax purposes. National insurance is calculated differently, with special rules applying for self-employed people and two types of payment you may have to make.

Clarifying the classes

Individuals pay four classes of NICs. Class 1 applies to employed people (see Chapter 12 for more) and Class 3 is voluntary – usually paid by people who don't work but want to keep up their entitlement to a state retirement pension and other benefits (refer to Chapter 11 for details). Self-employed people have to consider Classes 2 and 4. If you're a company director or an employee, you're not self-employed and pay NICs under PAYE (see Chapter 12).

Paying Class 2

Anyone who is self-employed must register for Class 2 NICs. Class 2 contributions are payable at a flat weekly rate. The rate for 2008–9 is £2.30. This contribution maintains your payment record and entitles you to a future state retirement pension and health-related benefits. It doesn't, however, entitle you to Jobseeker's allowance (Class 4 NICs entitles you to this benefit). You usually pay Class 2 NICs monthly by direct debit from your business bank account.

If your earnings from all self-employment are below the *small earnings exemption* limit (£4,825 for 2008–9) you can apply for exemption from Class 2 contributions. To obtain an exemption certificate you need to complete form CF10 and send it to HMRC, National Insurance Contributions Office, Self Employment Services, Benton Park View, Newcastle upon Tyne, NE98 1ZZ.

You can also be exempted from Class 2 contributions in any week that you are (for the whole week)

- ✔ In receipt of Sickness Benefit, Invalidity Benefit, or Incapacity Benefit

- ✔ Incapable of work

- ✔ Undergoing imprisonment or detention in legal custody

- ✔ A Volunteer Development Worker

- ✔ In receipt of Maternity Allowance

- ✔ In receipt of Invalid Care Allowance

Paying Class 4

Class 4 NICs is effectively an additional tax on self-employed people. It doesn't provide any extra benefits (except entitlement to Jobseeker's allowance) or go towards a future state retirement pension. If your profits are more than the annual lower earnings limit (£5,435 for 2008–9) you have to pay Class 4 NICs.

'Profits' for Class 4 purposes are generally calculated in the same way as for income tax (total income less costs and other allowable business expenditure). However, if you make a loss in your business, which you offset against other income or gains you have in the same tax year, you can still carry forward the loss and deduct it from future taxable business profits, but only for the purposes of calculating Class 4 NICs. Therefore, your NIC liability for a future year when you make a taxable profit is reduced. If you have more than one self-employment, the profits of each of your businesses are added together to calculate the Class 4 liability. Individual business partners are each liable to Class 4 NICs on their profit shares.

Class 4 NIC is currently charged at 8 per cent of your taxable profits between £5,435 and £40,040 (2008–9). If your profits are over £40,040 (the upper earnings limit), you pay at 1 per cent on everything over that limit. So, if your profits for the year are £45,000, your liability to Class 4 NICs is:

(£40,040 – £5,435) × 8 per cent =	2,768.40
(£45,000 – £40,040) × 1 per cent =	49.60
Total payable	2,818.00

You're automatically exempted from paying Class 4 NICs if you

- ✔ Have reached or are over state pension age at the beginning of the tax year

- ✔ Are treated as not resident in the UK for income tax purposes

- ✔ Are a trustee of a trust, or executor or administrator of an estate (but only in some cases)

- ✔ Are a *sleeping partner* (someone who puts money into a business and takes a share of the profits, but doesn't take an active part in the day-to-day running of the business)

- ✔ Are a diver or diving supervisor (exemption only applies to certain divers/supervisors)

You can apply for special exemption from Class 4 NICs if you're under 16 at the start of the tax year. You only need to apply once, because your application covers all tax years up to and including the year of your 16th birthday. To apply for exception you need to complete form CA2835U and send it to HMRC, National Insurance Contributions Office, Deferment Services, Benton Park View, Newcastle upon Tyne, NE98 1ZZ.

Avoiding overpayment

Someone with a mix of self-employment and employment can be charged Class 1, Class 2, and Class 4 NICs. The bad news is that many people in this position end up paying more in NICs for the same amount of income if it comes from a variety of sources, such as employment and self-employment, than if it all came from one source. The good news is that ceilings apply, albeit partial ones, on payments:

- ✔ The overall maximum for someone who is self-employed and pays Class 2 and Class 4 NICs is £2,890 (2008–9).

- ✔ The overall maximum for someone who is both employed and self-employed and pays Class 1, Class 2, and Class 4 NICs is £3,876 (2008–9).

None of these limits include the 1 per cent additional surcharge on earnings over £40,040 (for 2008–9).

 If you have earnings from employment and self-employment, you may well have paid a lot more tax than you should have when you add up all the amounts from each source. You can claim a refund from HMRC (on form CA5610, which you can obtain from HMRC, National Insurance Contributions Office, Deferment Services, Longbenton, Newcastle upon Tyne, NE98 1ZZ) if you've overpaid by more than £38.50.

 If you know, or are reasonably sure, that your earnings are going to hit the overall national insurance limits outlined above, you can apply for Class 2 and/or Class 4 payments to be deferred until you know the outcome of the year's total income. You should apply before the start of the tax year, but HMRC, who administers the collection of national insurance, often allows later applications.

Contracting and Subcontracting in the Construction Industry

Businesses operating in the construction industry are known as contractors and subcontractors. A *contractor* pays a subcontractor for construction operations, and a *subcontractor* carries out building work for a contractor. Contractors and subcontractors may be self-employed individuals, partnerships, or companies; and contractors range from building firms to government departments and local authorities. Private householders, and non-construction related businesses spending less than £1 million a year on construction work, are not contractors.

The Construction Industry Scheme (CIS) affects all contractors and subcontractors in the construction industry. The CIS is a simple PAYE system designed to stop tax evasion in the construction industry. It means that in some circumstances a contractor has to deduct tax from any payments she makes to subcontractors working for her (known as making *net payments*). The tax deducted is then paid over to HMRC and the subcontractor receives a credit for it when she sends in her annual tax return form. If the subcontractor has registered for tax with HMRC, the contractor is usually authorised (by HMRC) to pay her without taking anything off for tax (known as making *gross payments*). The subcontractor then completes her self-assessment return at the end of the year and pays her yearly tax bill in the usual way. (See Chapter 3 for more on self assessment.)

The following sections explain the CIS from the perspectives of both contractors and subcontractors.

Examining contractors

A new set of rules for the CIS came into force from April 2007. Subcontractors in the construction industry have to register with HMRC if they want a contractor to pay them gross (that is, without taking anything off for tax). If a contractor hasn't worked with a particular subcontractor recently, she must check or *verify* the subcontractor with HMRC before she can pay her.

Verifying subcontractors

Verification is the process HMRC uses to make sure that subcontractors have the correct amount of tax taken off their pay. The rate at which tax is deducted (the *rate of deduction*) can be zero, 20, or 30 per cent, depending on the circumstances of the individual subcontractor (see later section 'Looking at subcontractors').

Knowing who you don't have to verify

Under the new CIS rules, a contractor doesn't have to verify a subcontractor if she included that subcontractor on her tax return in the current or previous two tax years. If you don't have to verify a subcontractor, you must pay the subcontractor on the same basis as the last payment made to them. Therefore, if last time you paid the subcontractor you deducted tax at a certain rate, you do the same again.

Understanding the process

If you're a contractor, you need to know the three main steps of the verification process:

1. **You contact HMRC with personal details of the subcontractor you're taking on (name, address, national insurance number, and so on).**

2. **HMRC checks that the subcontractor is registered with HMRC.**

3. **HMRC tells you the rate of tax (if any) you have to deduct from the subcontractor's payments.**

HMRC tells you to pay the subcontractor in one of the following ways:

✔ **Gross:** You pay the subcontractor her full pay without any deductions for tax.

✔ **Net:** You deduct tax at the standard rate (currently 20 per cent), or the higher rate (currently 30 per cent). The higher rate applies when HMRC has no record of that subcontractor's registration or is unable to verify the details for any other reason.

When HMRC verifies a subcontractor, it gives you a verification reference number. The verification reference number is the same for each subcontractor that it has verified at the same time. If verifying a subcontractor isn't possible, HMRC adds one or two letters to the end of the number so that the number is unique to that subcontractor.

Paying your workers

To work out the subcontractor's pay when HMRC indicates that you must deduct tax, calculate the gross amount from which a deduction is to be made by excluding VAT charged by the subcontractor if she is registered and any amount equal to the Construction Industry Training Board (CITB) levy (this levy is the CITB's annual fee; details are available at www.citb.org.uk). You need to include any travelling expenses (including fuel costs) and subsistence paid to the subcontractor in the gross amount of payment. Keep a record of the gross payment amounts so that you can enter these on your monthly returns (see the later section 'Making your returns').

To complete the sum, deduct from the gross payment the amount the subcontractor paid for the following items used in the construction operations, including VAT paid if the subcontractor isn't registered for VAT:

✔ Consumable stores

✔ Cost of manufacture or prefabrication of materials

✔ Fuel (except fuel for travelling)

✔ Materials

✔ Plant hire

You need to ask the subcontractor for evidence of the direct cost of materials, but if the subcontractor fails to give you this information, you have to make a fair estimate of the actual cost of materials. You must always check, as far as possible, that the part of the payment for materials supplied is not overstated. If the materials element looks to be excessive, HMRC may ask you to explain why.

Now you have the gross pay of the subcontractor, you deduct tax according to the rate HMRC gives you. You have to give a written statement to every subcontractor from whom you have deducted tax within 14 days of the end of each *tax month*. A tax month runs from the 6th of one month to the 5th of the next month, so the statement must be provided by the 19th of the month.

Figure 16-1 shows a sample payment and deduction statement to be given to subcontractors paid monthly with tax deducted at the rate of 20 per cent.

Any Contractors Ltd
56 High Street
Anytown
ABC 123

Contractor's Employer's Reference Number: 123/456789

Construction Industry Scheme
Statement of payment and deduction for month ending:
05 April 2008

Subcontractor Name Unique Taxpayer Reference Verification Number*	Mr A N Other 98765 43210

Gross amount paid (excl VAT) (A)	£5,450.36
Less cost of materials	£584.72
Amount liable to deduction @ 20%	£4,865.64
Amount deducted (B)	£973.12
Amount payable (A − B)	£3,892.53

* Verification number only to be entered where a deduction at the higher rate has been made.

Figure 16-1: Sample payment and deduction statement for subcontractor.

Making your returns

If you're a contractor, each month HMRC sends you a return form (CIS300), which you must complete with details of all payments made to your subcontractors in the preceding tax month. You need to complete this form regardless of whether the subcontractors were paid gross or net of the standard or higher deduction. Your monthly returns must reach HMRC within 14 days of the end of the tax month to which they apply. You can send in your returns online or manually through the post. Further details about online filing can be found at www.hmrc.gov.uk/contractors/iwtfile-cis-information-electronically.shtml.

If you don't get your monthly returns in on time, you're charged a penalty of £100. If you don't make any payments to subcontractors in a particular month you still have to send HMRC a 'nil' return, otherwise you pay the penalty.

To complete your monthly return, you must do the following:

1. Check the pre-printed names and unique taxpayer reference (UTR) numbers of all the subcontractors you have paid in the month (the subcontractor should have provided you with her UTR, given to people who register with HMRC, when she first started working for you).

2. Leave blank any pre-printed entries for subcontractors you haven't paid in the month.

3. Add the names and UTRs of any additional subcontractors to whom you have made payments in the month, including the verification numbers against those subcontractors from whom a deduction at the higher rate has been made.

4. Enter details of the amounts paid to each subcontractor and details of materials allowed and deductions made from those subcontractors not entitled to receive gross payments.

5. Sign (or confirm, if submitting electronically) the declarations about verification and the subcontractors' employment status.

6. If using the post, send the return to HMRC using the pre-addressed envelopes provided.

You also have to pay the tax that you deducted from your subcontractors to HMRC monthly, and you have to pay it within 14 days of the end of each month (or within 17 days where payment is made electronically).

Looking at subcontractors

If you're a subcontractor working in the construction industry and haven't registered for tax with HMRC, the contractor paying your wages takes off 30 per cent tax each time she pays you. If you do register for tax, but don't fit the criteria for the new CIS, the contractor deducts 20 per cent tax from your wages. If, however, you meet the criteria for the new CIS (see the later section 'Looking at the tests HMRC apply'), HMRC authorises the contractor to pay you without taking anything off for tax (gross payment).

Knowing who needs to register

If you've been a subcontractor in the construction industry for many years, and you were registered under the previous CIS (that is, before 6 April 2007) you don't need to need to register for the new CIS if you, or your business, had one of the following:

- ✔ A tax certificate CIS5, CIS5(Partner), or CIS6

- ✔ A permanent registration card CIS4(P)

- ✔ A temporary registration card CIS4(T) with an expiry date of 04/2007 or later

However, if you're a new subcontractor, starting working in the construction industry on a self-employed basis for the first time after 5 April 2007, or an existing subcontractor who last had a temporary registration card CIS4(T) that expired on or before 03/2007, you should register for the new CIS if you don't want tax deductions at the higher rate (30 per cent) made from your pay.

If you had a tax certificate CIS5, CIS5(Partner), or CIS6 at the start of the new CIS, you keep gross payment status only where your certificate was due to expire on or after April 2007. Otherwise, you're only registered for payment under deduction and a fresh application is needed if you want to be paid gross under new CIS.

Looking at the tests HMRC apply

HMRC only authorises a contractor to make gross payments (that is, without taking anything off for tax) to a subcontractor when she passes three tests: the business test, the turnover test, and the compliance test within the *qualifying period* (a period of 12 months that ends on the date of the subcontractor's application).

The business test

To pass this test you must provide evidence that proves the following:

- ✔ Your business consists of, or includes the carrying out of, construction operations or the furnishing or arranging for the furnishing of labour in carrying out construction operations.

- ✔ Your business is, to a substantial extent, run using a business bank account.

Evidence prescribed to satisfy the business test is as follows:

- ✔ Books and accounts of the business
- ✔ Business address
- ✔ Details of payments for construction work
- ✔ Details of the business bank account, including bank statements
- ✔ Invoices, contracts, or purchase orders for construction work you've carried out

The turnover test

To pass this test you have to be able to satisfy HMRC that in the year following your application you fit one of these criteria:

- ✔ As an individual, your net business turnover from construction work (that is, after the cost of any materials used to earn that income) is £30,000 a year or more.

- ✔ As a partnership or company, the net business turnover from construction work (that is, after deducting the cost of any materials) is £30,000 a year or more multiplied by the number of partners or directors.

In the case of 'close companies' (companies controlled by five or fewer individuals), the figure is multiplied by the number of individuals who are directors and/or shareholders. For a husband and wife team, for instance, the amount is £60,000. An alternative test for partnerships and companies is that the business has an annual net turnover from construction work (after deducting the cost of materials) of £200,000 or more.

The compliance test

To pass this test you must have kept all your tax affairs up-to-date during the qualifying period. Therefore, you must have paid all tax liabilities, including any PAYE and subcontractor deductions, and submitted all tax returns on time. HMRC don't accept an application from a subcontractor who brings her tax affairs up-to-date just prior to submitting it.

Paying tax under the CIS

A subcontractor in the construction industry is treated just like any other self-employed person, and you have to send HMRC a self-assessment tax return showing your total income each year. (Chapter 3 takes you through self assessment.) Your tax bill is based on that tax return.

You may already have paid tax by *payments on account* (payments you make on 31 January and 31 July each year towards your final tax bill for each year), or had deductions taken from your payments for construction work, as shown on the payment and deduction statements given to you by your contractors. If the amount already paid or deducted is greater than the amount due, HMRC refunds you the excess. If a shortfall exists, you need to make an extra payment (called a *balancing payment*) to cover the extra tax due.

Expanding Your Business

Being a sole trader is just a tax definition – it doesn't mean that you have to work on your own! Although many people start their own business as a sole trader, if things take off, a time usually comes when they need help on a part-time or full-time basis. You may only need someone to help you out every now and then when you get busy, or you may have family members who can chip in. The next sections tell you the tax rules for hiring employees, including members of your family.

Taking on employees

When someone begins working for you, you become her employer and certain responsibilities come with that role.

Working out whether you need to register with HMRC

As soon as you take someone on, you must check with HMRC whether you need to operate PAYE and register as an employer. You can check by:

- ✔ Telephoning the New Employer Helpline on 0845 607 0143
- ✔ Visiting the Web site at www.hmrc.gov.uk/employers/ iwtregister-as-an-employer.shtml

Setting up your payroll

After you register as an employer with HMRC, you're responsible for calculating and deducting PAYE tax and NICs from your employee's pay. You therefore need to decide how to keep and maintain your payroll records, and several different options are available. You can ask a bookkeeper or a payroll bureau to operate your payroll for you (although of course you have to pay for this service), you can use a payroll software package, or, if your payroll is very small, you can operate it yourself manually using a manual wages record (P11 deduction workings sheet provided by HMRC) and tax tables.

You must pay your workers at least the national minimum wage as defined by law. Refer to Chapter 12 for details of the national minimum wage.

Each time you pay your employee, you must calculate and deduct the correct amount of tax and NICs from her pay and provide her with a payslip. You must also calculate and pay an employer's NICs and pay these amounts to HMRC, normally on a monthly basis. (Chapter 12 deals with employee and employer NICs.) If your monthly payments are less than £1,500, you have the option of sending them to HMRC quarterly.

Once you have set up your payroll you may come across unfamiliar issues, for example, employee sickness or making student loan deductions. You can contact the HMRC New Employer Helpline (telephone: 0845 60 70 143) whenever you want help with any part of your payroll operation. The advisor can also put your mind at rest if you're feeling a little nervous about being an employer.

At the end of each tax year (5 April) you need to complete an employer end-of-year return form (P35) and send it to HMRC. If you have fewer than 50 employees, you can get money back tax-free from HMRC by submitting your employer annual return online. Details of the financial incentives on offer can be found online at www.hmrc.gov.uk/employers/onlineindex.htm.

Keeping and maintaining accurate records for both your business and your employees is essential. You must record each employee's personal details, how much you pay her, and what deductions you make. You must also keep records of any expenses and benefits, such as company cars or medical insurance, which you provide to your employees.

Employing your family

More than 60 per cent of UK businesses are family owned. You can employ any family members in your business and take advantage of the lower tax rates and personal allowances that may be available to your spouse, civil partner, or children. In turn, this arrangement helps reduce your household's overall tax bill. Employing a spouse or partner can be particular tax-efficient when you run a limited company – flick to Chapter 17 for details.

A few rules, however, do apply that you need to keep in mind:

- ✔ Your relative has to be hired to do real work at a proper commercial wages rate. HMRC is sure to query payments to your 5-year-old son of £100 per hour for taking telephone messages!

- ✔ Local authorities have rules on children working. The rules don't usually apply to a few hours working at home, say, stuffing envelopes for you. However, if you want to employ a child under 16 in other circumstances, best check with the council first.

- ✔ Family members (over 16 years of age) who earn more that the *lower earnings limit* of £105 (for 2008–9) in any week are liable for NICs. As the employer, you also have to pay NICs on their behalf.

- ✔ You do have to actually pay the money. The taxman can ask to see evidence that the money has gone from the business to the family member concerned.

If you employ your spouse or civil partner, you can pay him or her between £90 and £105 per week. Although neither the spouse or partner (as an employee), nor you (as the employer), have to pay NICs, the employee protects his or her entitlement to a future state pension and other state benefits by doing so.

You run a television repair business from a workshop at the bottom of your garden. Your 16-year-old son helps you out for five hours a week at £6.00 per hour, earning a total of £30 per week. This amount equates to £1,500 a year, allowing for school holidays and some overtime.

You can offset the £1,500 you pay your son against your profits for income tax purposes. If your son has no other income, he doesn't have to pay any tax on the money because he falls well below the annual tax-free personal allowance (£5,435 in 2008–9).

If you had done the work yourself and not employed your son, that £1,500 remains part of your taxable profits for the year and you would be due to pay tax on it. Imagine you paid tax on that £1,500 at the top rate of income tax of 40 per cent: The household would have received only £900 (£1,500 less 40 per cent) instead of the full £1,500.

Winding Up the Business

Sooner or later you're going to want to stop working. Luckily, stopping is usually much easier than starting, although you need to consider a few things in advance, such as when to stop and whether to close down or sell your business. In this section, I look at the tax aspects relevant to stopping work and give you guidance on notifying the relevant authorities.

Closing down a sole trader or partnership business is fairly straightforward, but things get a little trickier with limited companies. Head to Chapter 17 to find out the specifics of selling a limited company.

Choosing between closing down and selling up

The decision of how and when to sell a business is usually prompted by a combination of three main factors – market conditions, market forces, and life changes. You may have built up a highly profitable business over many years and be reluctant to pass it on to anyone. However, even if the business is not very profitable, you may still find hidden or potential value that may be attractive to potential investors.

Sometimes, however, closing down is the only option. You can be forced to close down by a change in regulations, an unforeseen series of events, market forces, or a hostile legal action. Only you can decide the right exit route for you.

Letting your employees know

If you have employees, you have obligations to safeguard their rights, finalise their pay and deductions, and issue forms P45 to them. (Refer to Chapter 12 for details on form P45.) You may also need to consider redundancy pay and help them find new employment elsewhere.

When your business ceases, you also have to complete an employer cessation return (form P35). You can do this online (www.hmrc.gov.uk/employers/tmapaye-online-for-employers. shtml) before the end of the financial year, so if your business stops part way through the tax year, you don't need to wait until the end of that tax year before sending it in.

If you're a small employer (generally one with less than 50 employees), you qualify for a tax-free incentive payment if you file your cessation return online, and HMRC sends you your payment as soon as it has processed your return. HMRC sends you a letter telling you how to claim your tax-free payment. You can find out more about these payments online at www.hmrc.gov.uk/manuals/pommanual/PAYE44020.htm. '

Calculating your final tax liability

After you stop trading, you tot up your final tax bill for HMRC. You add up all your income, and then deduct your expenses and any allowances and reliefs available (as the earlier section 'Working Out Your Business's Income Tax Bill' describes). The following sections detail other things to bear in mind as you do your sums.

When you decide to cease trading you must notify your suppliers and customers so that they can raise any outstanding invoices or pay you any money they owe you. You need to account for these amounts in your final accounts.

Identifying what period your final bill covers

The final tax year in which a business is taxed is the tax year in which it actually ceases to trade, so if you stop trading on 30 September 2008, your final tax bill is for 2008–9. Your tax bill for the year before that is based on the accounting year that ended in the tax year before you stopped trading (so if you made your accounts up to 30 June each year, your tax bill for 2007–8 is based on your profits for the year that ended on 30 June 2007). Your profits (if you have any) from the accounting date in the previous tax year (30 June 2007 in this example) to the date on which your business finally stopped (30 September 2008), are then charged to tax for the tax year in which the cessation occurs (2008–9). Therefore, that final period may be more or less than 12 months long (15 months in this example – 1 July 2007 to 30 September 2008). If this situation sounds a bit tricky, check out the following example.

Esam has been trading for many years and makes his accounts up to 30 September each year. He narrows his options to stop trading to one of two dates:

- 30 June 2007
- 31 December 2007

His annual tax bill is calculated as normal up to and including the 2006–7 tax year (based on accounts for the year ending on 30 September 2006). His final tax bill is for 2007–8 (because he stops the business in this year). So, depending on the date he chooses to stop trading, his final tax bill is based on profits for

- ✔ 9 months from 1 October 2006 to 30 June 2007, or
- ✔ 15 months from 1 October 2006 to 31 December 2007

Getting relief for overlap profits

The earlier section 'Choosing your accounting date' explains that sometimes you pay tax twice on the same profit, known as *overlap*. If Esam was caught by overlap profits when he started his business, and he hasn't used them during the lifetime of his business (for example, on a change of accounting date), he can claim relief for them against his final year's tax bill.

Claiming capital allowances on cessation

Your final accounts take care of what happens when you sell your assets. Generally, the cessation of a business brings to an end the annual cycle of writing-down allowances (WDAs) and, where relevant, first-year allowances on assets (see the earlier section 'Claiming capital allowances').

In your last year of trading you don't get any annual WDAs. Instead you're given *balancing allowances* or are taxed on *balancing charges*. To work out the allowance due (or chargeable amount), you deduct the proceeds from the sale of your assets from the brought-forward value of your capital allowances pool (see 'Claiming capital allowances' for an explanation of how capital allowances work). If this amount is a minus figure – referred to as a balancing allowance – you can deduct it from your taxable profits, helping to reduce your final tax bill. If the figure is positive – known as a balancing charge – too many capital allowances have been given in previous years and you now have to add back that amount to your taxable profits figure, which, of course, increases your tax bill. If you take any assets from the business for your own use after you stop trading you have to do exactly the same calculation, except that you use the market value of the asset instead of the sale proceeds.

Claiming for losses on cessation

The earlier section 'Relieving your losses' explains the rules for off-setting losses against your income. When you trade you can carry forward any losses and offset them against future profits of the same trade. But clearly this situation doesn't apply when you close your business, because you won't make any future profits.

The good news is that you can still offset your losses against your other income for the year or previous years. If you make a loss in your last 12 months of trading, you can offset it against your trading income of the tax year in which your business permanently ceases and the three previous years, starting with the latest year. This special relief is called *terminal loss relief.*

Terminal loss relief is given as far as possible against the profits of later years before earlier years, even if the result is that your personal tax allowances are wasted. (See Chapter 4 for details on personal allowances.) So, if you have a terminal loss in 2008–9, you set it first against income from any other sources in 2008–9 (for example, from employment or savings). If any loss is left over after you've set it against other income, you set the balance against any income you had in 2007–8, and then 2006–7, and finally against 2005–6. HMRC gives you a refund of tax overpaid or sets the refund against any outstanding tax bills.

The HMRC helpsheet IR222 (How to calculate your taxable profits) shows you how to work out how much terminal loss relief you can claim. You can download it from the HMRC Web site at `http://www.hmrc.gov.uk/helpsheets/ir222.pdf`.

The time limit for a claim is five years from 31 January following the tax year in which the loss arises.

Deregistering for taxes

When you cease your business you need to notify your HMRC office. You also need to deregister for Class 2 NICs and VAT: The following sections show you how.

Deregistering for Class 2 NICs

You don't need to worry about deregistering for Class 4 NICs because you only pay these contributions on your profits. However, because you pay Class 2 contributions as a flat fee each month, you don't want to keep paying those after you stop trading. All you need to do is notify the National Insurance Contributions Office, Self Employment Services, Longbenton, Newcastle upon Tyne, NE98 1ZZ, or call the self-employed contact centre on 0845 915 4655.

Deregistering for VAT

If you're VAT registered, you need deregister when you stop trading. You must let HMRC know within 30 days of 'ceasing to make supplies' – that is, when you stop trading – and you must specify the date of cessation. You need to complete form VAT 7 (included in the HMRC VAT Notice 700/11 – Cancelling your VAT registration) and send it to the HMRC Wolverhampton Registration and

Deregistration Unit, Deansgate, 62–70 Tettenhall Road, Wolverhampton, WV1 4TZ (telephone 0845 039 0129).

After HMRC is satisfied that your registration should be cancelled, it confirms the effective date and issues a final VAT return. You need to account for VAT on stock and certain assets on hand at the close of business on the day your registration is cancelled.

Instead of shutting down your business, someone else may take it over – called a *transfer of a going concern* for VAT purposes. You may want to transfer your business rather than shut it down if, for example, you're

- ✔ Retiring and someone else is taking over the assets of the business
- ✔ Selling your business and its assets to someone else
- ✔ Selling part of your business that can be operated separately to someone else

In certain situations the new owner of your business can apply to keep your VAT registration number. If she wants to do so, and you agree, don't fill in form VAT 7. Instead, you both need to complete and sign form VAT 68, which is included in the HMRC VAT Notice 700/11– Cancelling your VAT registration (look on the HMRC Web site www.hmrc.gov.uk under VAT Information and Guides).

When you deregister for VAT, HMRC treats you as having sold all your stock and other assets at market value on the day you stopped trading. You don't, however, have to account for VAT if the total VAT due on your stock and assets would be £1,000 or less. You ignore any assets you bought during the lifetime of your business on which you can't reclaim the VAT (for example, cars and goods used wholly for business entertaining).

When you sell your business you must retain all your VAT records. When a buyer obtains permission to keep your VAT number, you must pass the records to the new owner unless you obtain permission from HMRC to keep the records yourself. However, you still have to make sure that the buyer of your business has all the information she needs to complete his VAT returns.

Chapter 17

Incorporating Your Business

- -

In This Chapter

▶ Looking at the pros and cons of incorporation

▶ Examining the implications for your accounts

▶ Setting up a limited company

▶ Paying yourself and others

▶ Selling up

- -

*W*hen the rate of corporation tax was cut to zero in 2002 for the smallest businesses (those with profits of less than £10,000), sole traders and partnerships rushed to turn themselves into limited liability companies (I use the word 'company' throughout this chapter to mean an incorporated, limited liability company, as distinct from self-employed sole traders or partnerships). Unfortunately, the government caught onto the fact that so many small businesses were incorporating just to reduce their tax bill and the then Chancellor Gordon Brown realised that the Treasury coffers weren't going to be as full as he wanted. As a result, he axed the zero rate of corporation tax from April 2006 and increased the rate payable by small companies from 19 per cent to 20 per cent from April 2007 and 21 per cent from April 2008.

Despite these minor setbacks, the current rates of corporation tax that companies pay are still pretty favourable and are indeed generally lower than those paid by individuals. In addition, many other ways exist to use a company to save tax. Although the costs and regulations involved with running a company are usually greater than trading as a sole trader or partnership, and more administration is generally needed, using a company as a vehicle through which to trade is still popular.

Chapter 15 gives you the basics on limited companies. In this chapter I examine the pros and cons of *incorporating* (the fancy word for starting a limited company) and help you work out how to set up and structure the company. At the end of the chapter I look at selling a company and give you pre-sale guidance.

Evaluating Incorporation

When you consider incorporating your business, the crucial point to understand is that a limited company exists in its own right: The company's finances are distinct from the personal finances of its owners (the company directors and shareholders). If you run your business through a limited company, HM Revenue & Customs (HMRC) treats you as an employee (even though you probably call yourself a director). You pay tax and national insurance contributions (NICs) through PAYE (covered in Chapter 12), and your company pays corporation tax and makes annual returns to HMRC. The tax and national insurance rules relating to self-employed people (covered in Chapter 16) don't apply.

Incorporating your business is most likely to become essential when things really take off – you often need the limited liability status that the company gives you to start winning contracts with bigger companies. However, incorporating may not be such a good deal for you in the early days of trading, or if you don't intend to grow beyond the status of a one-man or one-woman band. The following sections help you weigh up the pros and cons of incorporating.

Looking at the disadvantages of the company route

Incorporation can be a really bad option for many small businesses, especially in the early years of trading. The following list sets out the main disadvantages that incorporation can bring. If two or more of these items concern you, you may be better off not incorporating and carrying on trading as self-employed.

- ✔ **Accounts:** The company accounts have to be prepared to high standards to comply with the Companies Act. Accountancy fees for organising your books and accounts are, as a result, much higher. Life's much simpler when you're self-employed – you don't have to send in accounts to HMRC and, if your turnover is less than £15,000, you only have to fill in the three-line part of the tax return showing your turnover, your total allowable expenses, and your *net* (turnover less expenses) taxable profit.

- ✔ **Capital gains:** If you leave profits in the company until you wind up or sell, you may well have invested this money to gain interest. If so, the taxman treats this interest as an investment asset and charges capital gains tax (CGT) of up to 40 per cent on it for the tax years up to and including 2007–8 (up to

5 April 2008) and 18 per cent from 2008–9 (from 6 April 2008). (Refer to Chapter 6 for an explanation of CGT.) The tax relief on good will (the value of your customers) and other assets is also more favourable for sole traders and partnerships than for companies.

✔ **Costs:** Experts estimate that it costs between £350 and £500 in accountancy fees to incorporate a sole trader's business. The standard registration fee for companies charged by Companies House is £20 (£15 for electronic registration), or £50 for same-day registration. You also have to pay an annual filing fee of £30 (£15 for electronic filing). HMRC must be informed of an incorporation for corporation tax and VAT purposes (if applicable), and you should inform your customers and suppliers, and must inform your insurance company. All these tasks carry cost implications and you need to be sure that the costs involved don't outweigh any tax savings.

✔ **Disclosure:** After incorporating everyone knows your business. As a limited company you're required to disclose lots of information about your business, profits, and your own salary. Although small companies don't have to file full accounts, lots of information is still available should your customers or suppliers want to see it. They can discover your margins and profits and may push you on price. If you're a lot of cash in the company, you become more susceptible to being sued.

✔ **Flexibility:** You generally have more flexibility in dealing with the tax authorities over income tax and NICs matters as a self-employed individual rather than as a company director, because no separation exists between self-employed people and their business, whereas companies are separate from directors. In addition, self-employed people have instant access to their profits, whereas strict rules apply to a limited company meaning that you can't simply take money out of the company whenever you feel like it.

✔ **Loss relief:** A big difference exists between the treatment of losses for unincorporated businesses and incorporated companies. Losses of companies can generally be used only against profits of the same company, whereas the losses of unincorporated businesses can be set off against other income of the sole trader or the partners as the case may be. A particularly valuable relief for sole traders and partners is the ability to carry back losses made in the first four years of a business's life against personal income (for example, a salary from a previous employment) of the three years before the business started, which often creates a repayment of tax. (Refer to Chapter 16 for details on relieving your losses.)

✔ **National insurance contributions (NICs):** As a limited company you have to pay NICs as both employer (secondary contributions) and employee (primary contributions), which can often work out more expensive. (Refer to Chapter 12 for more on NICs.) If you're self-employed, you make only one set of payments.

✔ **Paperwork (and lots of it!):** Administration is the main downside to forming a limited company. Not only do you have to submit annual accounts and returns to Companies House (the organisation that looks after the register of limited companies) and run a PAYE salary scheme, but you also have to complete both a corporation tax return and your own personal self-assessment tax return.

✔ **Pensions:** Pension arrangements schemes can sometimes be less flexible for limited companies and more expensive to administer.

Sole traders may want to consider adding a limited company to their business as a partner, thereby forming a partnership. This arrangement enables you to retain all the benefits of an unincorporated business and still qualify for corporation tax rates on part of your profits. No limited liability protection is gained but adding a corporate partner is less expensive than incorporating a whole business and no more expensive when dealing with compliance issues; in addition, unincorporating a part of your business is easier if you want to switch back to self-employed status.

Examining the upside of company status

Although disadvantages apply to incorporating your business, the lower tax rates and other reliefs currently on offer still make it an attractive proposition. Here are a few reasons why you may want to turn your business into a limited company:

✔ **Dividends:** When you own a company you're the company director and also a shareholder, which means you can pay yourself *dividends* (payments known as *distributions* made out of the profits of the company to the shareholders) based on the profits made by the company. NICs aren't payable on dividends. Dividends may also be a good way of repaying people who back your business but who don't have any part in the day-to-day running of it.

✔ **Inheritance tax:** A sole trader business (but not a partnership, which has to be brought to an end on the death of a partner) can simply be left in a will to a successor. Therefore, the trade can simply continue albeit under new ownership. In incorporated companies, although shares can be left to whoever the shareholder chooses, the *Articles* of the company (the company rules) may give the company the right to refuse to register owners. This arrangement may give some protection, one shareholder dies and leaves his shareholding to someone with whom the surviving shareholders don't want to work.

✔ **Investment opportunities:** If you want to raise money for investment in your business, a number of tax-efficient schemes are currently on offer to incorporated companies. The Enterprise Investment Scheme (EIS), for example, gives a number of tax-saving incentives to people who are willing to invest cash in your company in return for some shares. (Refer to Chapter 6 to find out more on the EIS.)

✔ **Limited liability:** As an incorporated company you can have your liabilities limited to the value of the company's assets if you wind it up at some time in the future. This is usually the key reason for forming a limited company. Shareholders aren't personally responsible for the company's debts, but directors may be asked to give personal guarantees of loans to the company (for example, a bank may ask a director to use the equity in his home as security against a loan being made to the company).

✔ **Lower tax rates:** If you incorporate, you can pay yourself a mixture of salary and bonuses, and/or dividends. Salaries and bonuses are allowable against the company's profits (that is, taken off turnover to work out the amount of corporation tax due) so they can help reduce the company's tax bill. No NICs are payable on dividends, which again can help reduce company costs. (See Chapter 12 for more on NICs for directors.) Any profits left after deducting all the allowable costs are taxed at corporation tax rates (21 per cent for small companies with profits less than £300,000 from April 2008), which are generally lower than income tax rates payable by the self-employed (which can be as much as 40 per cent). (The self-employed also have to pay NICs.) See the later section 'Minimising the company's corporation tax liability' for more details on corporation tax.

✔ **Saleability:** Incorporation may make your business easier to sell when the time comes. Investors and buyers tend to prefer incorporated companies, because their accounts are usually drawn up to a higher standard and well maintained.

Putting the options into practice

Choosing between self-employment and incorporating can be tricky, with pros and cons on both sides of the fence. In this section, I outline the basic business structures for a self-employed business and two limited companies, in order to help you compare and contrast the different options, and make the right choice for you.

Anita, Baldev, and Charlie start their art and crafts businesses on the same day. Each of them needs £100,000 to help get started. For the sake of example, each of them has the same turnover, the same costs, and makes a £2,000 profit in the first year. Things pick up in the second year of trading and they each make a £20,000 profit. So how do their different businesses progress? Read on to find out. . . .

Anita's Arts Academy

Anita sets herself up as a sole trader. She uses £20,000 of her own savings and borrows £80,000 from her bank at an annual interest rate of 6 per cent.

In her first year, Anita makes £2,000 profit (income less expenses). However, she has to pay £4,800 bank interest and therefore ends up with a net loss of £2,800 for the year. She can claim relief for this loss against her other income, in the current year or in the previous three years. Therefore, she may receive a refund of tax of up to £1,100. She doesn't have to pay any NICs because her income is well below the current thresholds for both Class 2 and Class 4 NICs.

In her second year of trading, Anita's net profit is £20,000. Once she pays the bank interest and the amount from her self-assessment tax return, she ends up with around £12,300 in her pocket after tax and national insurance.

Anita expands her business in the third year. She can offset some of the money she spends on her new premises against her income.

Many years later, Anita decides to retire to the South of France. She has to pay CGT on any profits she makes but this payment may be at the maximum rate of 18 per cent and she may also be able to claim entrepeneurs' relief. (Refer to Chapter 6 for more on CGT and entrepreneurs' relief.)

Baldev's Booty Basement

Baldev forms a limited company – Baldev's Booty Basement Ltd – and pays himself a small salary and dividends from his profits (see the later section 'Deciding How to Pay Yourself' for details on how you can take money from limited companies). Baldev borrows

£80,000 from his bank, again at the interest rate of 6 per cent per annum, and uses £20,000 of his own savings to buy shares in the limited company. He decides to pay himself a small salary of £5,000 per year and larger dividends as and when profits grow.

In the first year, his profits are only £2,000. After paying his salary of £5,000 and the bank interest of £4,800, the company makes a net loss of £7,800. Baldev can't offset this loss against other earnings from the current or previous years; it can only be carried forward and used once the company starts to make profits. The £5,000 salary is below the tax and national insurance thresholds and so Baldev can be paid his salary in full.

In the second year, the company makes a £20,000 profit. Baldev still takes £5,000 as a salary, which is below the tax and national insurance threshold and so no deductions are to be made. The company would normally pay corporation tax of around £3,100 (see the later section 'Minimising the company's corporation tax liability') but the loss from the previous year can now be offset against these profits reducing the liability by £1,638 (£7,800 loss from earlier year at 21 per cent).

The balance of £13,362 is paid to Baldev as a dividend. As tax has already been paid on this money through corporation tax, and Baldev isn't liable to the higher rate of tax, he has no more income tax to pay, which means his take home income is roughly £18,440.

Looking further ahead, Baldev is able to claim allowances on any equipment and assets he buys out of the company's retained prof-its (money left in the company) and by doing so he can cut the company's corporation tax bill. However, he shouldn't forget that dividends can be paid only from taxed company profits (that is, they are paid out of any profits left after the company has paid out everything it owes each year). Also, dividends don't count as earn-ings for pension contributions purposes (see Chapter 9 on pension contributions), certain state benefits (because you don't pay NICs on them – see Chapter 11 for more), or for most mortgage loan applications (because bank managers often refuse to accept that dividend income is regular and guaranteed income).

Many years later, Baldev decides to sell up and retire to the South of France. If the company grows in size during the time Baldev owns it, so too does the value of his shares. He has to pay CGT on the increase in this value, although he may also be able to claim entrepreneurs' relief against this. (Refer to Chapter 6 for more on entrepreneurs' relief.)

Charlie's Crafty Crafts

Charlie forms Charlie's Crafty Crafts Ltd and decides to pay herself a steady salary of £20,000 each year. She borrows £80,000 from her bank, at an annual interest rate of 6 per cent, and uses a further £20,000 from her savings to buy shares in the company.

Charlie's company is allowed to offset the £4,800 bank interest against her £20,000 salary so her taxable pay is cut to around £13,000 after national insurance and the loan interest deduction. The company however makes an overall loss of £18,000 in the first year because it pays the £20,000 salary but makes a profit of only £2,000. This loss can be offset against future profits.

In the second year, the £20,000 profit has to pay not just Charlie's salary, but also the employer's NICs of around £1,725. Charlie has to pay tax and national insurance on the £18,275 giving her a net salary of around £14,240.

As the company grows, she needs to think about increasing her salary or retaining money in the company to spend on expansion. She also has to weigh up the pros and cons of paying corporation tax on profits against income tax and national insurance on her salary. She may then decide to pay herself a mixture of salary and dividends.

Later on, Charlie decides that she wants to join Anita and Baldev in the South of France. She decides not to sell her company but thinks that she may do better to just sell the company's assets. This way she pays corporation tax on the profits, which may be a better deal than the CGT she may have had to pay. She may, of course, pay no corporation tax because she may still have losses available from previous years to set against the amount she receives for the company's assets. (See the later section 'Selling Your Company' for an explanation of how you sell assets to close down a company.)

Deciding whether to incorporate

Taking all the pros and cons of incorporation into account, you may come to the conclusion that you're best to carry on your business as a sole trader or partnership in the early years. This situation may be particularly relevant if you envisage making losses in the early years of trading, because you can carry back losses made in the first four years against personal income of the three preceding years, often resulting in a substantial refund of tax becoming due. However, don't miss out on the opportunity of forming a limited company later on when the benefits of company status may be more valuable.

You don't have to engage an accountant to incorporate your business – doing so is not a legal requirement. However, you should think about it carefully. If you do decide to do the paperwork yourself, you can find details of how to do it on the Companies House Web site at www.companieshouse.co.uk. If you decide to engage an accountant, Chapter 19 tells you how to find professional advice.

Making the Transition in Your Accounts

When you form an incorporated company for tax purposes, your existing business (whether sole trader or partnership) effectively ceases. The result may be a long accounting period unless the existing business has a 31 March or 5 April year-end (refer to Chapter 16 for details on accounting dates). If the company has a 30 April year-end in, say, 2007 and you form the company on 1 January 2009, your tax assessment for 2007–8 is based on your accounts to 30 April 2007. Your tax assessment for 2008–9 is based on your profits for the year ending 30 April 2008 and on the accounts to 31 December 2008 – a period of 20 months. These profits may obtain some relief for earlier overlap profits (see Chapter 16), but the long period may involve some 40 per cent tax that may not otherwise have been incurred.

When you incorporate your business, you effectively stop and start again. If you made a loss in the 12 months before incorporating your business you can carry it back and offset it against any profits you made in the previous three tax years. This offset can result in a repayment of tax that you're already paid against those profits, a process known as making a claim to *terminal loss relief* (Chapter 16 explains this relief in more detail). Regardless of whether or not you claim terminal loss relief, any losses you have in your business prior to incorporation can usually be offset against the profits you make from the new company. Certain restrictions do apply to the rules, however, so if you think you may be affected, seek professional help from an accountant or speak to you local HMRC office (see www.hmrc.gov.uk for contact details).

Don't forget that the initial setting-up costs involved, as well as the continuing costs such as the annual filing fees with the Registrar of Companies, and the accounting and audit fees, can all be offset against the profits of the company and so reduce the company's overall tax bill.

Forming a Limited Company

More than 2 million limited companies are registered in the UK and more than 300,000 new companies are incorporated each year. Setting up a limited company is actually easy. Chapter 15 guides you through registering your new business with Companies House (the organisation that controls limited companies in the UK) and sorting out your tax responsibilities (NICs and VAT). The following sections explore the basics for getting your limited company off the ground.

Understanding the legal framework

The Companies Act allows one or more people or companies to form a company for lawful purposes. Under the Act they must agree to the company's *memorandum of association*, a set of rules that governs the way in which a company is run and records its profits and/or losses.

The law requires each limited company to have a company director and a company secretary, but from October 2008 the secretary is no longer essential. In general terms anyone can be a company director. However, you can't be a company director if you're an undischarged bankrupt (someone legally declared as being unable to pay their debts) or disqualified by a court from holding a director-ship (unless given leave to act in respect of a particular company or companies).

No minimum age limit exists in the Companies Act for a director to be appointed in England and Wales. However, the person must be able to consent to his or her own appointment. In Scotland, the Registrar refuses to register the appointment of a director under the age of 16 years old (a child below that age doesn't have the legal capacity to accept a directorship in Scotland). Seek legal advice if you intend to have a young person as a director of your company.

All companies must inform Companies House of any changes, such as appointments and resignations of shareholders, within 14 days of each event.

Drawing up the paperwork

To incorporate a limited company yourself, you need to file the following documents:

✔ **Articles of Association:** This document gives details of the share capital of the company (including, for example, the number and type of shares issued). Each shareholder needs to sign it.

✔ **Memorandum of Association:** This document states the company name, the situation of the Registered Office (to be England and Wales, Scotland, or just Wales), the objects (usually the assets) of the company, and its limited liability.

✔ **Company register:** This register shows all members (shareholders) of the company, even if the company is incorporated with just one shareholder.

✔ **Form 10:** This document contains the intended situation of the Registered Office (the statutory address) of the company, and personal information (date of birth, occupation, and details of other directorships they have held within the last five years) relating to the consenting secretary and director(s) – who must be different people.

✔ **Form 12:** This document is the declaration of compliance with the Companies Act 1985. When the memorandum and articles of association have been completed, the solicitor engaged in the formation of the company, one of the directors, or the company secretary, must sign this form in the presence of a solicitor, Commissioner for Oaths, Notary Public, or Justice of the Peace.

Companies House (www.companieshouse.gov.uk) provides the forms you need to incorporate free of charge, and can give guidance on how to fill out the forms. Companies House can't, however, provide or advise on the memorandum of association. You can also get specimens of these documents from legal stationers, accountants, or solicitors.

Ready-made companies are available from company formation agents whose names and addresses appear in the Yellow Pages, usually costing between £100 and £200 or thereabouts. An *off-the-shelf company* essentially gives you the go-ahead for company status. You can change the company name, the Registered Office, and the names of shareholders and company secretary to match your own company. This option is quicker than having a company set-up specialist (often your accountant) forming a new company just for you.

Communicating with HMRC

HMRC says that companies must notify it when 'they first come within the charge to corporation tax', which is usually when trading starts. The company must tell HMRC within three months after the beginning of the first accounting period. The penalties for failing to do are quite severe and can be up to 100 per cent of any tax unpaid after 12 months.

Companies pay corporation tax on their profits through the corporation tax self-assessment (CTSA) system, which means that they have to pay corporation tax nine months and one day after the end of the accounting period to which it relates. The company must then file a CTSA tax return for that period within 12 months of the end of the accounting period for which the tax paid relates.

Getting the family involved

As a company director you have control over your business. And as a taxpayer, you can manage how you take the money out of the company in the most tax-efficient way. To this end, you may consider employing members of your family to help reduce the overall tax bill for your household. Chapter 16 explains how taking on family members is generally tax efficient, but remember that a specific benefit exists when you run a limited company: If your spouse or civil partner is a shareholder in the company, and is also employed in it, you can pay yourselves a mixture of salary/bonuses, benefits, and dividends, thereby reducing your overall tax bills quite considerably.

The tax benefit of employing family members is best shown in an example: Note that for simplicity I haven't taken the company costs (for instance, employer's NICs) into account.

Stephen runs his own company and wants to (and has the means to) take £50,000 a year from the business. This amount is well into the 40 per cent tax rate bracket (which applies to taxable income over £36,000), so regardless of whether the amount is paid as salary or dividends, a 40 per cent tax bill applies on the top slice of his income.

James also runs his own company but his wife Susan is also a shareholder and she holds 99 per cent of the shares issued by the company (called the *share capital*). Susan doesn't have earnings from anywhere else. James and Susan want to (and have the means to) take £50,000 a year from the business.

The £50,000 required can be divided up so that James receives £30,000 in salary. He pays income tax only at the basic rate along with NICs. However, the other £20,000 can be paid out as dividends. Because Susan holds 99 per cent of the shares, she gets 99 per cent of the dividend, that is, £19,800. James receives only £200, being the value of his 1 per cent shareholding. The £19,800 that Susan receives is well within the basic rate threshold so she doesn't have to pay any additional tax on the dividend received. James's share of the dividend doesn't push him into the 40 per cent bracket, so overall, none of their combined income for the year is taxable at 40 per cent.

An alternative would be to pay Susan £20,000 in salary. She would have to pay total tax and NICs of £4,512 (in 2008–9). Although this method leads to more tax being paid than going the dividend route, it still works out a good few thousand pounds less than paying the £50,000 salary straight to James.

Keeping a beady eye on 'husband and wife' companies

HMRC increasingly questions 'husband and wife' company arrangements. HMRC has recently lost a legal case in the House of Lords (*Jones versus Garnet* otherwise known as 'Arctic Systems'). HMRC had previously lost this case in the Court of Appeal and as a result appealed to the House of Lords. The case concerned dividends payments made by a company to Mrs Jones through which Mr Jones provided IT consultancy services. HMRC's view was that the tax law treated the dividends received by his wife to be Mr Jones' for income tax purposes. The House of Lords, however, ruled in favour of Mr Jones. Of course, following the outcome of this case, HMRC is currently working on changing the law, which will eventually entitle it to a much larger tax take in this type of situation.

For the moment, however, the 'husband and wife' arrangement is still a good one, but HMRC does check to make sure that the paid spouse really does work for the company and that duties are commensurate with remuneration – don't try paying your spouse £20,000 per year for an hour's work a day, if the commercial rate is a lot less.

Abiding by anti-avoidance legislation

The government is increasingly determined not to allow small businesses to choose between self-employment (where you trade as a sole trader or in partnership; see Chapter 15) and incorporation simply to reduce liability to income tax and NICs. Over recent years, various anti-avoidance measures have been introduced to try and stop this perceived abuse.

Cracking down on personal service companies

Before 6 April 2000, contractors (particularly in the IT industry) were able to avoid being taxed as employees on payments for services and paying Class 1 NICs by providing those services through a *personal service company*, which is a one-man (or woman) company that supplies labour services. Instead, the worker took the money out of the company in the form of dividends instead of salary. Because dividends aren't liable to NICs, the worker ended up paying much less in NICs than a conventional employee or a self-employed person.

To prevent people paying less tax and NICs by using personal service companies, HMRC introduced the 'IR35' rules, named after the number of the HMRC Budget Press release in which they were first announced. The strict anti-avoidance rules generally apply where, but for the service company, the income arising from an engagement or contract would have been treated as employment income of that person. The rules ensure that, if the relationship between the worker and the client would have been one of employment had it not been for an intermediary such as a service company, the worker pays tax and NICs.

Not all IT contractors are caught by the IR35 rules. Those who genuinely work for different businesses and people, have bought their own equipment, can control their own working hours, and risk making a loss, can often continue to qualify as companies and carry on enjoying the tax breaks that come with that status. But the IR35 rules can apply in any business sector. Examples of occupations where people work through service companies run right across the board, including medical staff, chief executives of large PLCs, teaching professionals, legal and accountancy staff, construction industry workers, engineering contractors, clerical workers, press officers, night club bouncers, and many others. The IR35 rules were also extended from 9 April 2003 so that income received by domestic workers, such as nannies, gardeners, and butlers, who provide their services through limited companies, is also caught by the net.

Alan is a sole trader gardener who has many clients and is paid directly by his customers. HMRC is quite happy that Alan is self-employed and he pays tax accordingly. Alan's sister, Jenny, is also a gardener, but she works full-time for one customer, forms a limited company, and invoices that customer for her services each month. HMRC treats any money that Jenny takes out of her company (including dividends) as salary, and Jenny and her company have to pay PAYE tax and NICs on the income.

For more information on the IR35 rules, take a look at HMRC's guidance 'Intermediaries Legislation (IR35) – Working through an intermediary, such as a service company', which is available online at www.hmrc.gov.uk/ir35/index.htm.

Targeting managed service companies

Even after expanding the IR35 rules (see the previous section 'Cracking down on personal service companies'), the government still felt it was missing out on a chunk of money, mainly from NICs. So, from 6 April 2007, even more anti-avoidance rules exist that apply to *managed service companies* (MSCs), which are companies often set up to provide invoicing and accounting services for contractors.

Generally, MSCs are split into composite companies and managed personal service companies (MPSCs):

- ✓ **Composite company:** In this company, several (typically 10 to 20) otherwise unrelated workers are made worker-share holders of the company. The size of the company is restricted to ensure that profits don't exceed the threshold for the small companies' rate of corporation tax (21 per cent from April 2008). Each worker usually holds a different class of share in the company. This arrangement enables the company to pay different rates of dividend to each worker, and in practice the dividend received is directly related to the company's income from the end client for work undertaken by that worker.

- ✓ **MPSC:** In contrast to a composite company, in this scheme the company engages only one contractor. The MSC scheme provider performs similar functions for MPSCs as for composite companies (for example, invoicing, administration, and accounting services).

Hiding behind a MSC and paying yourself dividends doesn't save you tax. If you work as a contractor through an MSC, all your earnings (even if you call them dividends) are automatically treated as earnings from employment and you have to pay PAYE tax and NICs on them. If the company doesn't pay the tax and NICs, HMRC can recover anything owed from other sources, usually the MSC's director and the person who provided the company to the individual.

Deciding How to Pay Yourself

Once you're set up a limited company, you need to decide what to do with your profits – how much of the profits do you take out of the company and how? Generally, you can distribute profits in two different ways:

- ✔ Use the profits within the company.
- ✔ Pay profits out, through salaries, bonuses, and dividends.

The decision as to whether to take the profits out of your company or keep them often depends on what route produces the most overall tax-effective benefit for you (but not always, because good business reasons exist for keeping money in the company). So keeping tax-efficiency in mind, the following sections help you decide how to handle your company's profits.

Keep in mind that how you distribute your profits isn't set in stone. If the financial structure you put in place turns out to be the wrong one for you, you can always change it later on.

Minimising the company's corporation tax liability

Limited companies pay corporation tax on their profits. Companies pay tax under self assessment (known as corporation tax self assessment (CTSA) just like any other unincorporated business. Tax is payable on the company's taxable profits, which is turnover less expenditure (including salaries, pensions, and employer NICs). If any profit is left after taking off the expenses (called *retained* or *distributable profit*) and paying the corporation tax, the company may pay a dividend to its shareholders.

The rate at which corporation tax is payable depends on the amount of a company's profits for the financial year in question. Corporation tax for the tax year 2008–9 is as follows:

- ✔ From 1 April 2008, for profits over £1,500,000, you pay 28 per cent corporation tax (30 per cent prior to this date).
- ✔ From 1 April 2008, for profits of up to £300,00, you pay 21 per cent corporation tax (20 per cent before this date) (called the *small companies' rate*).

✔ For profits between £300,000 and £1,500,000, a special formula exists for working out the corporation tax rate payable (called *marginal rates*).

If the company is liable only to the small companies' rate of corporation tax, paying directors by way of dividends is usually more beneficial. Paying a dividend won't reduce the company's tax liability further but the director's overall tax and national insurance liability on dividends often works out lower than if the same money is paid as a salary. Where the full rate of corporation tax applies, payment by way of salary produces greater relief from corporation tax – salaries are an allowable expense for working out corporation tax because you deduct them from turnover before working out the amount of corporation tax payable. (Skip to the next section 'Paying yourself out of the profits' for more on dividends and salaries.)

Often, the most efficient tax planning strategy is to pay out as much of the company's income as possible, rather than retaining it in the business, so that you pay the least amount of corporation tax. Tax planning for small companies traditionally involves ensuring that profits fall outside marginal rates and into the small companies rates. Popular strategies for avoiding marginal rates include:

✔ **Advancing company expenditure:** If the company is thinking of buying some equipment, it may be beneficial to buy it sooner rather than later so that tax relief can be claimed in the most beneficial accounting period.

✔ **Giving bonuses:** Bonuses are allowable expenditure for tax purposes so they are taken off turnover to work out the corporation tax charge.

✔ **Deferring income:** It may be possible to reduce turnover (and therefore reduce the company's corporation tax liability) if you can put off receiving income from customers, for example, until the start of a new accounting period.

✔ **Making pension contributions:** As a director of a limited company, you can deduct from your profits the amount of contributions the company pays into your personal pension policy, thereby reducing the company's corporation tax bill. Remember, however, to be deductible, company contributions must actually have been paid, not merely provided for in the accounts. Check out Chapters 9 and 10 for full details on pensions.

You can't take profits out of the company by way of a loan because of strict company law restrictions and certain tax disadvantages.

Paying yourself out of the profits

You take money out of the company by paying salaries, bonuses, or dividends. Each method is governed by different tax rules, and each results in different amounts of cash being available to you, the company director, at different stages throughout the business's lifetime. The tax effects of these two routes can be contrasted as follows:

- ✔ **Dividends** aren't deducted in arriving at the taxable profits, because they are paid out of the profits left in the company each year once everything else has been paid out. Tax on dividends is covered in detail in Chapter 6; in general, the company pays this tax over to HMRC and they pay any additional income tax liability themselves based on their level of income. NICs aren't payable on dividends.

- ✔ **Salaries and bonuses** are deducted in arriving at the taxable profits of the company as long as the amount is justifiable. However, HMRC rarely challenge the size of the directors' salaries paid by trading companies where the directors are full-time working directors. The recipient pays income tax and NICs through the PAYE system.

Take the following factors into account when considering your options:

- ✔ **Be careful of paying very low salaries:** National minimum wage legislation applies to directors under contracts of employment as well as employees. (Take a look at Chapter 12 for info on the minimum wage.) In addition, a low salary may result in decreased NICs, which affects entitlement to certain earnings-related social security benefits. If your salary falls under the NICs threshold, you can pay voluntary NICs (see Chapter 11 for details).

- ✔ **Bear in mind the impact of paying no salary:** The lack of a salary charge in the company's accounts may impact future valuations of the company.

- ✔ **Think about where the payments come from:** Dividends can only be paid out of *distributable profits* (that is, the amount of profits left after certain factors have been taken into account) whereas, at least in theory, salaries can be paid out regardless of the level of profits.

✔ **Consider the shareholders:** Give some thought to the following points:

- Dividends are payable to shareholders in proportion to their holdings in the company, which may not necessarily correspond to the relative efforts of the shareholders in earning the profits. Dividend waivers (when a shareholder agrees to give up his right to receive a dividend) may assist in these circumstances, but care must be taken – company law is strict and often complex. If you're in any doubt, seek professional advice

- Shareholders are subject to income tax on dividends that they receive (refer to Chapter 6 for an explanation of the dividend income tax rules); dividends are charged at 10 per cent for lower or basic rate taxpayers and at 32.5 per cent for those taxable at the higher rate (in both cases covered by a 10 per cent non-repayable tax credit) when the dividend is paid. If a shareholder's total taxable income for a particular tax year is near the higher rate threshold (say between £35,000 and £40,000 before personal allowances) the timing of the dividend may push the shareholder into higher rates for that year.

- Individual needs of shareholders may differ – some may require income, others may be more interested in the long-term growth in the company and therefore the growth in the value of their shares. These conflicting interests may be met by the issue of separate classes of shares with differing distribution rights. For example, some shareholders may receive 'A' type shares and some 'B' type shares. The company is then able to pay a dividend to holders of, say, A-type shares but not those holding B-type.

Overall, the best policy is to extract profits using a mixture of salary, bonuses, and dividends, which can be varied according to individual circumstances.

Your company can provide you with a wide range of extras ranging from a private healthcare plan to a company car. All non-cash items are collectively known as *benefits-in-kind*. The company is usually allowed to deduct the cost of the benefits from its turnover in working out its corporation tax bill. The downside is that you usually have a personal income tax and NIC liability to pay on the provision of such benefits. However, some items, such childcare and medical check-ups, are tax and/or NIC exempt and you can use your company to provide such items in a tax-efficient way. (Chapter 13 covers the expenses and benefits that companies may pay.)

Selling Your Company

Selling your business is usually more straightforward than starting in terms of administration, but it can have as many tax implications. Chapter 16 examines shutting down a business in general – from informing employees and HMRC to calculating your final tax bill. The following sections lead you through the specifics for selling a limited company.

A number of options exist for winding up a limited company, including selling, liquidating, and striking the company off. No two companies are ever the same, and seeking advice from an account-ant or tax practitioner before going ahead is always worthwhile.

Minimising your tax bill

After you decide to sell your company, your overriding objective must clearly be to maximise your net after-tax proceeds of sale. You can achieve this aim through a combination of the following:

- ✔ **Optimising the company's value before sale:** Make sure that everything to do with the company is up-to-date and in order (for example, chase up any outstanding debts).

- ✔ **Planning carefully for capital gains tax (CGT):** Reduce the value of the company before sale (for example, by removing assets from it) to minimise the overall chargeable gain payable. Also, where feasible, defer as large a proportion of the tax bill as possible: for example, by reinvesting the sale proceeds in an Enterprise Investment Scheme (EIS) company. (See Chapter 6 for more on EIS and CGT.)

The following sections highlight things to consider for a tax-efficient sale.

Planning ahead

The extent to which pre-sale tax planning is possible or effective depends to a significant extent on the time available for it. Clearly, much less can be achieved where the owners take advantage of a good 'out of the blue' offer than when they plan their exit from the company over a period of years.

But if you know that you're going to sell your company in the fore-seeable future, you should ensure that the company's 'housekeep-ing' is adequate and order. In particular, you need to ensure that all company expenditure, probably going back over many years, is properly recorded so that, where assets are being sold, appropriate CGT calculations can be made.

Using your losses

If your company has been making losses you may think that the new owner wants to take on those losses in order to claim loss relief – and obtain a repayment of tax – against another source of income. (See Chapter 16 for an explanation of what losses are and how you can claim tax relief for them.) But HMRC makes handing over tax losses to the new owner of a business difficult.

Anti-avoidance legislation allows HMRC to challenge the availability of losses in the hands of a new owner, sometimes several years after the purchase transaction. Therefore, buyers are understandably reluctant to pay for a company that has been making losses, because they may not be allowed to claim loss relief further down the line. So, in general, both sides of a potential company sale transaction prefer the 'old' owner (you) to arrange for the losses to be used prior to the sale.

Paying dividends

Your overall aim is to maximise the net after-tax proceeds of the sale in your hands. You may therefore arrange for part of the value of the company to be paid to you before you sell it, as a pre-sale dividend. The rationale for this tactic is to take advantage of a more favourable tax regime on dividends than on capital gains. The rules governing tax on dividend income ensure that higher rate taxpayers suffer an effective tax rate of 25 per cent on dividends they receive. CGT by contrast is payable at 18 per cent for 2008–9 onwards. (Check out Chapter 6 for the full story on how HMRC taxes dividends and how CGT works.)

Whether a pre-sale dividend is worthwhile depends on the effective rate of CGT you would have to pay on the eventual sale of your shares, which in turn depends principally on

- ✔ The base cost of your shares (that is, the price you paid for them, if any) and the amount you received for them when you sold them

- ✔ The availability of the various reliefs from CGT (notably entrepreneurs' relief and EIS reinvestment relief – turn to Chapter 6 for explanations of these reliefs)

The same rationale determines whether owners selling shares rather than assets should attempt to make use of the provisions for repurchasing the company's own shares, which are briefly reviewed in the later section 'Selling your shares back to the company'.

Don't 'overdo' the pre-sale dividend. HMRC may seek to invoke anti-avoidance legislation, particularly where the dividend payment is being made from profits in a company about to be sold.

Transferring your pension

If the company has a pension fund, its treatment in the sale transaction may well have a significant influence on the agreed price. You need to take specialist advice on pension arrangements at the earliest opportunity.

Receiving termination payments

You may be able to pay yourself a tax-free termination payment of up to £30,000 when your employment with the company comes to an end (remember that directors are considered to be employees). However, assuming that the exemption automatically applies is generally unsafe. For example, HMRC can argue that a lump sum termination payment to a major shareholder is disguised proceeds from the shares. HMRC may also consider whether the termination payment constitutes general earnings.

However, genuine redundancy payments (statutory or otherwise) are generally accepted to be subject to the £30,000 exemption. Certain termination payments are exempt without limit, including contributions to a tax-exempt or HMRC-approved personal pension scheme. Skip to Chapter 12 for the tax and NICs rules governing termination payments.

Deciding what to sell

When you sell your company you can choose between selling the assets of the company, or the shares (or both). Whatever route you take, you effectively sell the company – for example, if you sell the assets of your window cleaning company (your buckets, ladders, and so on) but not the shares, you're still sold your business because without assets your shares are worthless.

Often the sale route that best suits the vendors is inappropriate for the buyers, and vice versa. Therefore, whether the transaction ultimately concerns shares or assets is mostly a matter for negotiation between you and your potential buyer, and reflects the relative strength of your negotiating positions.

From the standpoint of you as the seller, the positive aspects of selling assets rather than shares are the following:

- ✔ Guarantees that you're probably obliged to give on those assets are minimised, and therefore you're exposed to less financial risk after the transaction is completed.

- ✔ Where assets are sold at less than their tax written-down values, the company may benefit from balancing allowances (writing-down allowance and balancing allowances are explained in detail in Chapter 16).

- ✔ You can choose exactly what to sell and what to retain, selling sets of assets to more than one purchaser, if desired.

These advantages are balanced by a number of disadvantages, however:

- ✔ When you sell your company you may receive a mixture of cash, and assets and shares in another company. If you sell assets you may have to pay CGT immediately. However, if you sell shares in your company and receive shares in a new company, you may be able to defer paying CGT until a later date. (Chapter 6 has more on CGT.)

- ✔ If you sell the company assets but keep the company you also keep the potential liability for any future claims made against the company (for example, from aggrieved former customers).

No definitive answer can be given as to whether a sale of just assets or the company's share capital is more appropriate. Often a *hive-down* (the technical term used for the sale of a business and its assets to a new owner) of some of the business assets and the trade that goes with those assets provides a compromise solution that the buyer and seller both find acceptable. You (and your adviser, if you use one) need to negotiate the best deal for you.

Selling your shares back to the company

A company repurchasing its own shares may be seen as an alternative to a 'normal' sale. The difference is that only one side is really involved in the transaction. In general, you sell your shares back to the company in return for all the value in that company. The company secretary then applies to Companies House (www.companies house.gov.uk) to have the shares cancelled because they no longer hold any value (because you've just taken all the money out of the company).

Although not limited to these situations, two types of transaction are particularly suited to the share repurchase approach to a 'sale':

- ✔ Passing a family company from one generation to the next, particularly where the younger generation has insufficient money of its own.

- ✔ The acquisition of a company by a management team who already own shares in it; control is passed to them by the repurchase of the controlling shareholder's holding, leaving control with them.

In both cases, the company usually borrows where it doesn't already have the cash resources to fund the entire repurchase. Nothing in company law prevents a company from borrowing to fund a share repurchase, so effectively the new management, whether the younger generation of a family company or otherwise, is able to fund purchasing a controlling interest in the company from future profits.

The repurchase of its own shares by a company falls within the definition of a *distribution* (a payment made by a company), which means that, in the hands of an individual, the funds received are subject to income tax. Although circumstances do exist in which the repurchase may be treated as a *capital disposal* (that is, a disposal of wealth, where CGT may be payable), treatment as a distribution (and therefore income tax treatment) is the default position.

Part VI
The Part of Tens

In this part . . .

This part contains three vital chapters. I start by pulling together the ten most popular tax-saving tips from the rest of the book, so that you can go through them one-by-one and ensure that you take advantage of the tax breaks on offer. The next chapter looks at dealing with HM Revenue and Customs (HMRC). Many people don't have any direct contact with HMRC, but if you do need to deal with the taxman face-to-face you want to be prepared. Finally, the last chapter sums up some of the most important issues and tips to bear in mind when you run your own business.

Chapter 18

Ten Tax-Saving Tips

*N*obody enjoys handing over hard-earned dosh to the taxman, and most people love the idea of reducing their overall tax bill. However, tax law is complicated and tax calculations can be tricky. I'm sure that you don't have the time, or the energy, to wade through the rules and regulations to make sure that you're making the most of the tax breaks on offer. But help is at hand – this chapter looks at ten simple ways to help you arrange your affairs in the most tax-efficient way.

HM Revenue & Customs (HMRC) wants to receive only what's correctly due to it and you're fully entitled to arrange your affairs to minimise your tax bill legally. But when organising your affairs to reduce the amount of tax you pay, please always remember that tax avoidance is legal, tax evasion is not!

Optimising Your Personal Allowance

Everyone is entitled to a *personal allowance* – the amount you can earn before tax – from birth. In the 2008–9 tax year, this amount stands at £5,435. Make sure that you claim yours!

If you have a grandchild (and you're feeling generous), you can give her money to put in her savings account and the interest it earns remains tax free up to the child's personal allowance. However, for parents, things aren't quite as simple – you pay tax on any money you give your children that earns interest. As if you needed another reason to refuse the mammoth 'loan' your son asks for! Check out Chapter 4 for more about personal allowances.

Keeping an Eye on Age Allowances

From the year in which you reach the age of 65 onwards, you're entitled to an increased personal tax allowance (£9,030 for 2008–9). However, after your income reaches a certain limit (£21,800 for 2008–9) you pay a much higher tax rate on every extra pound of income you receive. If you're married or are in a civil partnership and your annual income is close to the level at which age allowance reduces, consider transferring any income-producing assets or investments to a lower-earning spouse or partner. You can find more about age-related allowances in Chapter 10.

Income from savings such as Individual Savings Accounts (ISAs) and National Savings Certificates is tax free and doesn't count against your total income for age-related tax allowance purposes.

Using Your Capital Gains Tax Exemptions

Each year you're allowed a capital gains tax exemption (£9,600 for 2008–9). Broadly speaking, this exemption is the amount of profit you can make each year, for example from the sale of shares, without having to pay any capital gains tax. This amount can be worth up to £1,728 (for 2008–9).

The allowance is a use-it-or-lose-it allowance – if you don't use the allowance in one tax year, you can't carry it forward into the next tax year. So if you're thinking about selling, say, a bundle of shares, consider selling some at the end of one tax year and some at the beginning of the new tax year. In this way you can use the capital gains exemptions for two years and save up to £3,456 in tax.

Chapter 6 covers capital gains tax issues in more detail.

Tracking the Offsetting of Your Losses

If you've lost money on the stock market recently, you can carry your capital losses forward and offset them against any capital gains that you may make in future years.

You should also be able to claim tax relief for any losses that you make in your business. If you make losses in the first few years of trading and you were employed before that, you may be able to get back some of the income tax you paid as an employee. Turn to Chapter 16 for help on this aspect.

Sharing the Wealth With Your Partner

If you're married or in a civil partnership, I have good news – you can take advantage of certain tax benefits. For starters, if you're in a civil partnership or marriage and you pay tax at a lower rate than your partner/spouse (or perhaps don't work at all), put savings accounts in your name. Then as a couple you pay a lower rate of tax, or even none at all, on your savings.

You can also do some clever juggling with assets to minimise your tax bill. You can use both your capital gains annual exemptions by sharing assets that have built up a capital gain, ensuring that the person paying tax at the lower rate has the higher taxable gains.

And on top of that, the taxman ignores asset transfers between partners and spouses for inheritance tax purposes. You can transfer assets between yourself and your partner or spouse in order to optimise your zerorate tax allowance band – called the *nil-rate band*. Each spouse has a £312,000 nil-rate band for the 2008–9 tax year. Chapter 8 covers saving inheritance tax in this way.

Helping Your Kids Avoid Inheritance Tax

If you're thinking about leaving money or other assets to the next generation in your will, consider making the gift sooner rather than later. Your children, or grandchildren, are entitled to the assets free of inheritance tax as long as you survive for seven years after making the gift.

 Don't forget that everyone has an annual inheritance tax gifts exemption of £3,000. Therefore, every time you give £3,000 away, the value of your estate for inheritance tax purposes is reduced. And if you forget to use the exemption one year, you can carry it forward to the next. Have a look at Chapter 8 for more information on inheritance tax.

Claiming Household Expenses When You're Self-Employed

If you run your own business from home, you miss out on significant tax savings if you don't claim your full expenses entitlement. Many people are unaware that they're eligible to claim a proportion of the household expenses against their business income, such as heating, lighting, and telephone calls.

For example, when you get your gas bill simply work out the proportion of the bill to claim on the basis of the number of rooms used for the business against the total number of rooms in your house. You can claim any eligible expenses through your self-assessment tax return by simply adding these bits of your household bills to your other expenses and deducting them from your income. Chapter 16 looks at expenses in more detail.

Getting Your Employer to Cough Up for Home Expenses

If the terms of your employment contract require you to work from home, your employer can pay you up to £2 per week, free from tax and national insurance contributions, towards your household costs. And you don't even need to keep any supporting evidence to obtain this income tax exemption. So if you fit into this category and your employer doesn't already pay these expenses, ask her to – that £2 per week saves both you and your employer tax.

If you're an employee and you work from home, you need to consider your tax position if your employer agrees to pay for your home telephone bills. You can claim tax relief only for the cost of your business calls, and not on the line rental or other fixed charges. If your employer reimburses you for the cost of your private telephone calls, this money is classed as a taxable benefit and you may end up having to pay tax on it. Chapter 13 has the low-down on employee expenses.

Making the Most of Your Savings

From April 2008, you can save up to £7,200 each tax year in an Individual Savings Account (ISA) and you don't have to pay any income tax or capital gains tax on any interest, dividends, or capital gains you receive – it's all tax free. But remember, this limit works on a use-it-or-lose it basis each year (if you put less than £3,600 into the account in one year you can't carry over the unused amount to the next year), so make sure that you use your entitlement each year if you can.

 Don't forget that if you're a non-taxpayer you can reclaim any tax deductions made on savings accounts. This rule applies to children who are non-taxpayers too (and most are!). You don't get your money back if you don't claim though, so make sure that you claim as early as possible – Chapter 6 tells you how.

Plumping Up Your Pension

Even though the tax rules on pensions recently changed, paying into a pension policy can still be one of the best ways of cutting your tax bill while planning for your future retirement. Chapter 9 looks at pensions in more detail.

Regardless of whether you pay tax or not, you can get tax relief on payments of up to £3,600 a year. This means that for 2008–9 onwards you can pay £2,880 into your pension and the pension company actually invests £3,600 on your behalf. That sounds like a good deal to me!

 When you reach state retirement age – currently 65 for men and 60 for women – you don't have to pay national insurance contributions any more. If you're over the state retirement age and still working, check your payslip to make sure that your employer has stopped deducting for national insurance.

Chapter 19

Ten Tips for Dealing with HM Revenue & Customs

In This Chapter

▶ Keeping your paperwork in order

▶ Knowing your rights

▶ Satisfying HMRC requirements

▶ Finding professional advice

*M*any people go through their entire working life and have no direct contact whatsoever with HM Revenue & Customs (HMRC). Their affairs are simple, they pay tax and national insurance contributions under the PAYE system, and they don't have to fill in a self-assessment tax return. For other people, however, things aren't so straightforward.

This chapter gives you some tips on how to get along with the taxman – from organising your records and knowing your rights, to avoiding enquiries and penalties, making complaints, and getting advice.

Organising Your Paperwork

If you're self-employed then to get your tax return correct, and to make sure that you can answer any questions from the taxman, you must pay careful attention to your paperwork. You need to keep records of your transactions, not only to help your business run smoothly, but also so that you can easily fill out your self-assessment return at the end of each tax year.

 Have a look at page 8 of HMRC's SA103 notes on completing the self-employment pages of your tax return (www.hmrc.gov.uk/worksheets/sa103-notes.pdf). The notes give you an idea of the sort of things you can claim for against your business income for tax purposes. This helps you to devise a filing system to keep proper records that you can give to the taxman if requested.

The less time you spend on sorting out messy paperwork, the more time you have to spend developing your business. And tax officers are known to give an organised person who produces good quality, complete records more credibility than someone who produces an old shoebox full of scraps of paper. Flick to Chapters 15 and 16 for more on setting up and running your business.

Keeping Hold of Records

Everyone has to keep personal financial records for one year past the annual 31 January filing date. However, if you work for yourself, and that includes any spare-time earnings, you have to keep records for five years after the 31 January filing date – making a total of six years. Chapter 2 covers HMRC's record-keeping rules.

Finding the Facts to Help You

The legal framework behind the tax system is complex and often difficult to understand – tax accountants have to train for several years to gain their professional qualifications, and even then, many can only specialise in certain areas. Therefore, before you send in any tax return getting help and advice is a good move.

HMRC sends out a comprehensive set of notes, guidance, and fact-sheets with self-assessment returns. Make sure that you read through the guidance and check the HMRC Web site for any new information (www.hmrc.gov.uk). If you don't understand anything, call one of the many HMRC helplines (these helplines are listed for you in the Appendix) for clarification.

Use the search engines on the Internet to find information. Many Web sites offer free advice from tax experts who normally charge very high fees. Do remember, though, that not all the information you find applies to you, and often certain rules only apply in certain circumstances. You need to look at the whole picture.

Chapter 2 covers the legal framework behind the UK tax system and gives you a good grounding in the basics.

Discussing Your Tax Affairs

You can discuss your tax affairs or get tax information at any tax office or at one of the many HMRC Enquiry Centres located around the country. HMRC can answer questions on your rights and obligations on direct tax matters (income tax, capital gains tax, inheritance tax, and national insurance), and give information to help you with self-assessment returns, claims to reliefs, repayments, and appeals.

Knowing Your Rights

As I outline in Chapter 3, you have certain rights as an individual and as a taxpayer and you need to understand these rights. Although it's HMRC's job to make sure that you pay the right amount of tax due to the state, the taxman must at all times treat you with respect and dignity. As long as you keep your records in order and do everything required of you, you shouldn't have to exercise any of your rights.

Making a Complaint

If you feel that HMRC treats your unfairly, you may choose to make a complaint. A HMRC factsheet (C/FC) called 'Complaints and putting things right' tells you what to do when you're unhappy with the service you get from HMRC. You can download the factsheet from the HMRC Web site at www.hmrc.gov.uk/factsheets/complaints-factsheet.pdf.

The best way to complain is to contact the complaints manager at the local tax office you deal with. You can file a complaint in writing, by phone, by fax, or in person.

HMRC has strict customer service procedures and targets. You're entitled to be treated in a fair and courteous way – but remember, good manners work in both directions.

Notifying Chargeability

Under the self-assessment tax system, the law requires that everyone must notify HMRC of *chargeability to tax* for the previous tax year. Broadly speaking, this means that if you have a new source of income in one year, on which you may be liable to pay tax, you must tell the taxman the following year.

This requirement may be particularly relevant, for example, if you arrived or returned to the UK during the tax year, you received an inheritance payment, or you have income from savings and investments (for example building society interest). Chapter 6 deals paying tax on investments in more detail.

You must let the taxman know if you're chargeable to tax by 5 October following the end of the tax year (5 April) in which the chargeability first arose.

Avoiding Enquiries

An enquiry into your tax affairs can be extremely time-consuming, costly, and worrying. Making upfront disclosures to the tax office helps to avoid the likelihood of an enquiry.

If something in your accounts is likely to prompt HMRC to make an enquiry (for example, an unusually large business expense), provide an explanation when you send in your tax return – this precaution can influence the decision whether to investigate a case that the HMRC computer flags as suspicious.

Staying on the Right Side of the Law

HMRC knows that tax is complicated and that people make mistakes, so they always try to help you to steer your way through paying the correct amount of tax. However, when a problem with your tax affairs does come to light, make sure that you co-operate fully with the authorities from the start.

Never try to hide any sources of income or savings – if you get found out, you have to pay larger penalties, and in some more serious cases, you may even face a prison sentence.

HMRC is introducing a new system to calculate penalties for understating your tax liability, which applies to tax returns filed for the tax year ending on 5 April 2009. From this date, the following factors determine whether a penalty is due for understating your tax liability:

- ✔ The amount of tax understated
- ✔ The nature of the behaviour that led to the understatement (was it a genuine mistake or was it deliberate?)

✔ The extent of disclosure by the taxpayer (did you tell the tax authorities everything as soon as you became aware of your mistake, or did you try to hide a large bundle of cash in an off-shore bank account and 'forget' about it?)

The maximum penalty you can be charged is 100 per cent of the extra tax you owe. The penalty can, however, be reduced right down to nil in certain circumstances, so make sure that you come clean as early as possible, work with the taxman to put things right, and organise things so that this situation doesn't happen again in the future. A penalty may be 'suspended' if you can show the tax authorities that your compliance with the tax system has improved over a specified period.

If you fail to complete and send in your tax return by the required filing date (generally 31 January following the end of the tax year), you're charged an automatic flat penalty of £100. In extreme cases, you may also be charged a penalty of up to £60 for each day that the failure continues. These penalties can quickly mount up and prove to be very costly, so get organised and get your return in on time.

Finding Professional Advice

If your tax situation gets complicated, or you find yourself in the middle of an enquiry with HMRC and you don't know how to resolve matters, consider getting some professional advice from an accountant or tax practitioner.

Ideally, you find an accountant by recommendation from a friend or colleague, but you can also go through the Yellow Pages or search the Web. Speak to several professionals before committing yourself to one in particular – fees and attitudes vary considerably.

Choosing an accountant can be daunting, but if you look for someone who is a member of one of the professional tax and accountancy bodies, you can be reasonably confident that he is honest and competent. The main professional bodies are as follows:

✔ The Association of Chartered Certified Accountants (ACCA) – www.accaglobal.com

✔ The Chartered Institute of Taxation (CIOT) – www.tax.org.uk

✔ The Institute of Chartered Accountants in England and Wales (ICAEW) – www.icaew.co.uk

Accountants may charge by the hour, but many now understand that a small business requires just some basics and so are happy to fix an annual fee, paid monthly. Check with the accountant what this fee covers.

The accountant may ask you about how you plan to keep your financial records (sales information, purchases, receipts, and so on). He usually charges you according to how much work he has to do in order to use those records. So when you keep your records electronically in a spreadsheet or software package, the accountant can access your records easily and so charge you less than when you give him mountains of paper. Generally, the better organised you are, the cheaper the service.

Chapter 20

Ten Tips for Starting and Running Your Own Business

*Y*ou may find the whole process of starting and running a business somewhat daunting. However, don't be put off at the first hurdle. A whole range of free help and advice is on offer – you just have to track it down and use it to your best advantage.

This chapter looks at things you can do to make the process of starting and running your own business as simple and straightforward as possible. Of course, my main emphasis is on tax, but if you want more details on starting and running a business, check out *Starting and Running a Business All-in-One For Dummies* by Matthews *et al.* (Wiley).

 Spend some time planning ahead right from the start. When you set everything up correctly from the beginning, you soon find that you can spend less time on your paperwork and more time working on your business.

Engaging an Accountant

When you start and run your own business you need to understand the basics of tax – which is no doubt why you're reading this book. With basic knowledge of the UK tax system you can handle at least part of your business accounting, and if your business is straightforward you may be confident filling in your self-assessment tax return yourself.

However, it can often prove cost-effective and sensible to appoint an accountant for the fiddly elements of your business. Whatever the size of your business, an accountant can help with business plans and strategy, setting up your business as a sole trader or limited company, and the associated tax and Value Added Tax (VAT) positions. Chapter 15 contains guidance on accountants.

Getting Free Advice

Business Link (www.startupanswers.co.uk) is a great place to start. Funded by the government, Business Link aims to make starting-up as easy as possible and to help small businesses reach their potential and flourish. Business Link runs a programme of user-friendly 'Starting your own business' workshops, free of charge, to anyone with a clear business idea. If you don't have access to the Web site, you can call Business Link on 0845 600 9006 and request a starter pack.

The HM Revenue & Customs (HMRC) Web site is also a good place to get free information and help. Check out www.hmrc.gov.uk/businesses, where you can find details of how to do the following:

- ✔ File a company tax return
- ✔ Get help with VAT
- ✔ Register your new business for tax and VAT
- ✔ Register for the construction industry scheme

The 'Tell me about. . .' section offers a whole host of information that may be of interest to anyone starting their own business. Topics include:

- ✔ Construction Industry Scheme
- ✔ Employment or self-employment
- ✔ Keeping VAT records and accounts
- ✔ Self assessment
- ✔ Starting up a business
- ✔ Tax credits
- ✔ VAT

If you don't have access to the Internet, you can call the HMRC Newly Self-Employed helpline on 0845 915 4515.

Registering As Self-Employed

When you start your own business, you need to register with HMRC for tax and national insurance contributions (NICs) as soon as possible. In any case, you must register within three months of starting your business. The three-month period starts from the last day of the month in which the business begins. If you don't register within this period, HMRC charges you a penalty of £100. Chapter 15 tells you how to register.

If you expect your annual turnover to be over the current registration threshold (£67,000 for 2008–9), you also need to think about VAT. See the section 'Registering with the VAT man', later in this chapter.

Thinking about National Insurance

Anyone who is aged between 16 and state pension age – currently 60 for a woman and 65 for a man – may have a liability to pay NICs. If you run your own business as a sole trader, or in partnership, you usually pay Class 2 and Class 4 NICs and need to register with HMRC accordingly. Chapter 15 tells you more about these contributions and how to register.

If you trade through a limited company, HMRC usually treats you as an employee and so you pay Class 1 NICs (usually called primary contributions). The company also has to pay NICs on your earnings (called secondary contributions). Chapter 12 covers these contributions in more detail.

A self-employed person can be excepted from Class 2 NICs liability if their net profit is expected to be less than the Small Earnings Exception (SEE) limit (£4,825 for 2008–9). To obtain a SEE exemption certificate, contact HMRC National Insurance Contributions Office, Self Employment Services, Benton Park View, Newcastle-upon-Tyne, NE98 1ZZ.

If you're over the state pension age, you don't have to pay Class 1 or Class 2 NICs. You can apply for an Age Exemption Certificate by contacting HMRC National Insurance Contributions Office, Contributor Caseworker, Longbenton, Newcastle-upon-Tyne, NE98 1ZZ.

Registering with the VAT Man

Generally you need to register for VAT if your annual turnover reaches the current annual registration threshold limit (£67,000 for 2008–9). This threshold operates on a month-by-month basis, so you need to check at the end of each month to make sure that you haven't gone over the limit in the previous 12 months. You also need to think about whether you're going to go over that limit in the following 12 months. If you think you may, you probably need to register.

You can register for VAT even if your turnover is below the threshold and you may actually save tax by doing so, particularly if your main clients or customers are organisations that can reclaim VAT themselves. Turn to Chapter 15 for more information on voluntary registration for VAT.

You must register with HMRC within 30 days of being aware that you're going to exceed the threshold. If you fail to register, HMRC charges a penalty that can eventually be up to 15 per cent of the VAT owed. This amount is in addition to the actual VAT due, so make sure that you register on time and avoid incurring costly penalties.

Paying Your Tax Bill

If you run your business as a sole trader or in partnership with someone else, you need to pay any tax due by 31 January after the end of the tax year covered by your self-assessment tax return.

You may also have to make two payments on account of your total tax liability before the return for that year is due. You make payments on account on 31 January in the tax year and on 31 July after the end of the tax year (six months later). If these two payments are less than the total amount that you owe for that year, you have to pay the balance by 31 January in the following year. If it turns out that you paid too much on account, you get a repayment as soon as you send in your self-assessment tax return.

Make sure that you budget for your tax bill. A sensible plan is to put money aside each month to cover the payments, because you may find it tricky coming up with a huge lump sum when your bill is due. Chapter 3 has more details on paying your tax bill.

Using Up Loss Reliefs

If you have earnings from a PAYE employment or a pension, receive dividends and interest, or have any taxable capital gains, you may be able to set off any losses made in your new business against these amounts.

If you make a loss in any of the first four years of a new business, you can offset this loss against tax on your employment earnings in the three years before your business started. You have to prove that you do in fact intend to make a profit in the future and that your business isn't just a 'hobby'.

You have to claim the loss relief within 12 months following 31 January after the end of your loss-making business year. Claiming loss relief in this way may mean that you receive substantial repayments of tax, which can help put your business back on course.

Chapter 16 tells you more about getting tax relief for your business losses.

Becoming an Employer

You need to register as an employer when you start employing somebody (or take on subcontractors) and one or more of the following situations apply to your employee:

- ✔ He already has another job.
- ✔ His earnings are equal to or above the PAYE threshold (£105 per week for 2008–9) and liable for deductions of tax.
- ✔ His earnings are equal to or above the national insurance lower earnings limit (LEL) (£90 per week for 2008–9).
- ✔ He receives benefits-in-kind from you (for example, a company vehicle or expense allowances).

You can register your employee up to four weeks in advance of his first payday.

HMRC produces a useful booklet entitled 'Thinking of employing someone?', which tells you all you need to know. You can download it from the HMRC Web site at www.hmrc.gov.uk/employers/employing-someone.pdf. You can also call the New Employer Helpline on 0845 607 0143 for more information.

Chapter 16 discusses taking on employees.

Growing the Business

If you're a sole trader and things really take off, you may want to consider turning the business you run into a limited company. As well as giving yourself the title of company director and being able to separate the business finances from your personal life, you may also benefit from the low rates of corporation tax currently available.

Although the government abolished the zero-rate of corporation tax, you can still use a limited company to help reduce your tax bill. Chapter 17 looks at incorporating your business and the benefits that this move may bring.

Thinking of Moving On

When you trade as a sole trader, stopping a business is much simpler than starting one. You need to let HRMC know as soon as possible and, if you're registered for VAT, you also have to go through the VAT de-registration process. Also, if your profits are caught by the 'overlap' rules relating to when you started out, now is the time to claim the relief due. Chapter 16 contains guidance on this overlap scenario.

Winding up a limited company usually involves a little more work because a number of possible exit routes exist and each company situation is different. In general, however, the directors usually sell their shares to someone else, who continues to run the business, or sell their assets and shut down the company.

If the company is worth something, engaging an accountant to advise you on the best way of winding things up is a good idea. In some cases, you may even think about disposing of the business gradually over several years.

Appendix

Further Information

• •

*T*his Appendix helps you find further information from HM
Revenue & Customs (HMRC) and the Pension Service, and
guides you through the state benefit rates.

HMRC Helplines

This section lists various HMRC helplines, which are open during
the normal weekday hours (9am to 5pm). The HMRC Web site
(www.hmrc.gov.uk) also provides a wealth of information.

Charities Helpline (0845 302 0203): Issues charity forms and
leaflets that assist with registration for Gift Aid and charitable
status. The helpline also provides information about VAT reliefs for
charities or disabled people, community amateur sports clubs, the
completion of limited company or trust and estates tax returns,
repayments, Gift Aid, payroll giving, and order enquiries.

Child Benefit Helpline (0845 302 1444): Provides help and advice
on all child benefit claims.

Child Trust Fund (0845 302 1470): Handles all queries concerning
Child Trust Funds.

Construction Industry Scheme (0845 366 7899): Offers help and
advice for subcontractors and contractors within the Construction
Industry Scheme, and provides related forms, leaflets, and sta-
tionery.

Contracted Out Pension Helpline (0845 915 0150): Answers
enquiries from pensions providers, scheme administrators, members of the public, authorised third parties, and Department of
Work and Pensions offices with regards to contracting out of the
State Second Pension (formerly State Earnings Related Pensions,
known as SERPS).

Customs Confidential (0800 59 5000): A free 24-hour, 7-day per
week hotline for you to report anything suspicious to HMRC (for
example, cigarettes that look a bit dodgy).

Deceased Estates Helpline (0131 777 4030): Provides information about the income tax and capital gains tax liabilities of deceased estates arising after the date of death.

Employer Helpline (0845 714 3143): Gives advice to employers on PAYE, national insurance contributions (NICs), statutory sick pay (SSP), maternity pay, tax credits, stakeholder pensions, student loan repayments, and Construction Industry Scheme matters. Employees asking their employer for advice on their own tax affairs should be advised to contact their HMRC office as shown on their most recent correspondence.

How to Pay Helpline (0845 366 7816): Provides help and advice on self assessment and PAYE payment.

Individual Savings Accounts (ISAs) Helpline (0845 604 1701): Advises on the tax rules for ISAs. You can also look at the HMRC factsheet available online at www.hmrc.gov.uk/leaflets/isa-factsheet.pdf.

IR35 Contract Advice Line (0845 303 3535): Provides help for customers with general enquiries and background information about the IR35 intermediaries legislation.

National Benefits Fraud Hotline (0800 854 440): Deals with reports of benefit fraud. Call this confidential line if you suspect that someone is defrauding the benefits system. You can also make a report online at https://secure.dwp.gov.uk/benefit fraud.

National Insurance – Deficiency Helpline (0845 915 5996): Deals with enquiries from people who've been notified that they have a shortfall in their NICs records.

National Insurance Enquiries for Individuals Helpline (0845 302 1479): Provides assistance with queries regarding national insurance, including age exemption, Home Responsibilities Protection (HRP), Married Women's Reduced Rate Election (MWRRE), statement requests, Class 3, automated refunds, and deferment renewals.

National Insurance – Registrations Helpline (0845 915 7006): Advises young people aged from 15 years 9 months to 20 years who've not yet received their national insurance number, and gives information relating to the registration of a national insurance number for adults and people who want to work in the UK.

National Minimum Wage Helpline (0845 600 0678): Provides help and advice to employees and employers on the national minimum wage rules, and deals with complaints from workers who are being paid below the threshold.

New Employer Helpline (0845 607 0143): Provides new employers with help on PAYE, NICs, statutory sick pay (SSP), maternity pay, tax credits, stakeholder pensions, student loan repayments and Construction Industry Scheme matters.

Newly Self-Employed Helpline (0845 915 4515): Registers self-employed people for national insurance, income tax, and VAT, and arranges free workshops with HMRC's Business Support Teams.

Probate and Inheritance Tax Helpline (0845 302 0900): Advises customers who require information on Probate and/or inheritance tax following a death.

Residency – National Insurance Contributions for those abroad (0845 915 4811 or +44 191 203 7010 from outside the UK): Answers questions about national insurance status and entitlements, pension status, and health care provisions for people under UK pension age who live or work abroad.

Residency – Tax Matters for those Not Resident in the UK (0845 070 0040 or +44 151 210 2222 from outside the UK): Assists with queries regarding income tax and capital gains tax for customers who live or work abroad.

Self-Assessment Helpline (0845 900 0444): Provides help and advice to customers completing their self-assessment tax returns and associated pages. Also provides general advice on self assessment.

Self-Employed Helpline (0845 915 4655): Deals with enquiries from the self-employed who need help with Class 2 NICs.

Shares and Assets Valuation Helpline (0115 974 2222): Assists with the valuation, for tax purposes, of unquoted shares (shares of companies that are not quoted, listed, or traded on the stock exchange) and other assets such as copyrights, goodwill, bloodstock, chattels, foreign land, and underwriting interests. The helpline can't give advice relating to specific tax matters or charges such as capital gains tax, income tax, stamp duty (for example, stock transfer forms), or inheritance tax.

Stamp Taxes Helpline (0845 603 0135): Handles initial enquiries relating to stamp taxes payable on the purchase of land, property, and shares, or on the leasing of land and property. For a bespoke service for same-day stamping (for those who must have documents stamped urgently), call 0121 616 4513.

Tax and Benefits Confidential (0845 608 6000): Offers confidential guidance to people operating in the hidden economy to help them put their affairs in order.

Tax Credits Helpline (0845 300 3900): Gives information about tax credit, including working tax credit and child tax credit.

Tax Evasion Hotline (0800 78 8887): Aims to catch people who avoid paying income tax, corporation tax, capital gains tax, inheritance tax, VAT, and NICs. Call this hotline to report your suspicions of someone, or make a report online at www.taxevasionhotline. co.uk/html/formhome.htm.

VAT National Advice Service (0845 010 9000): Answers all general questions relating to Customs and Excise and Value Added Tax (VAT) matters.

Welsh Language Helpline (0845 302 1489): Provides information for those who prefer to discuss problems and ask questions in Welsh. Many HMRC leaflets are also available in Welsh.

Pensions Guidance

This section guides you through the various leaflets, guidance, and claim forms that are available from the Pension Service (telephone 0845 6060 265; www.thepensionservice.gov.uk).

Guides for planning ahead

BM01: Backdating membership of an Occupational Pension Scheme

BR19: State pension forecast

BR19L: Understanding your state pension forecast

BR33: State pension – the options available to you

CPF5: Your pension statement

Over50?: Are you over 50?

PM2: State pensions – your guide

PM3: Occupational pensions – your guide

PM4: Personal pensions

PM5: Pensions for the self-employed

PM6: Pensions for women

PM7: Contracted-out pensions – your guide

PM8: Stakeholder pensions – your guide

PM9: State pensions for parents and carers

PTB1: Pensions: the basics. A guide from the government

SERPSL1: Important information for married people – inheritance of SERPS

SPD1: Your guide to state pension deferral: Putting off your state pension to get extra state pension or a lump-sum payment later

SPD2: How to get extra weekly state pension or a lump sum payment: Your introduction to state pension deferral

Guides for pensioners

DPL1: Direct payment giving it to you straight

GAA5DWP: Going abroad and getting your benefits

GL24DWP: If you think a decision is wrong

PC10S: A guide to pension credit

PG1: Pensioners' guide England

PG2: Pensioners' guide Wales

PG3: Pensioners' guide Scotland

RM1: Retirement – a guide to benefits for people who are retiring or have retired

WFPL1: Your guide to winter fuel payments

Claim forms

BF225: State pension – dependents' allowance

BR1: State pension – use this form to apply for state pension if you're less than four months away from state pension age

BWV3: Winter fuel payment claim form for UK residents

PC1: Pension credit application form

WFP1R: Winter fuel payment claim form for UK for past winters 1997–8, 1998–9, and 1999–2000

WFP2: Winter fuel claim form – EEA and Switzerland for past winters

General guides

D49: What to do after a death in England and Wales

D49S: What to do after a death in Scotland

GL12: Going to hospital?

GL13: Separated or divorced?

GL18: Help from the Social Fund

GL24: If you think a decision is wrong

GL29: Going abroad and social security benefits

GL32: Prisoners and their families

HB2: Vaccine damage payments

IB203: Incapacity benefit

SD1: Sick or disabled

SD4: Caring for someone?

WIDA5DWP: Widowed?

Benefit Rates

In this section I provide the various weekly rates of state benefits payable from April 2007 and April 2008. (You can find more on state benefits in Chapter 11.)

Non-taxable state benefit rates

Benefit	Weekly rate from (£)	
	April 2007	April 2008
Attendance allowance		
Higher rate (day and night)	64.50	67.00
Lower rate (day or night)	43.15	44.85
Child benefit		
For the eldest qualifying child	18.10	18.80
For each other child	12.10	12.55
Disability living allowance (care component)		
Higher rate	64.50	67.00
Middle rate	43.15	44.85
Lower rate	17.10	17.75
Disability living allowance (mobility component)		
Higher rate	45.00	46.75
Lower rate	17.10	17.75
Incapacity benefit (short term)		
Lower rate:		
under pensionable age	61.35	63.75
over pensionable age	78.05	81.10

Taxable state benefit rates

Benefit	Weekly rate from (£)	
	April 2007	April 2008
Bereavement allowance	87.30	90.70
Carer's allowance	48.65	50.55
Dependent adults		
with retirement pension	52.30	54.35
with carer's allowance	29.05	30.20
with severe disablement allowance	29.25	30.40
Industrial death benefit		
Widow's pension		
Permanent rate:		
higher	87.30	90.70
lower	26.19	27.21
Invalid care allowance		
Standard rate	48.65	50.55
Incapacity benefit (long-term)	81.35	84.50
Increase for age:		
higher rate	17.10	17.75
lower rate	8.55	8.90
Incapacity benefit (short-term)		
Higher rate:		
under pensionable age	72.55	75.40
over pensionable age	81.35	84.50
Non-contributory retirement pension		
Standard rate	52.30	54.35
Age addition (at age 80)	0.25	0.25
Retirement pension		
Standard rate	87.30	90.70
Age addition (at age 80)	0.25	0.25

Widow's pension

Pension (standard rate)	87.30	90.70
Widowed parent's allowance	87.30	90.70

You pay income tax on all these benefits. Also, bereavement allowance replaced widow's pension from 9 April 2001 for all new claims by widows and widowers.

Index

FOR DUMMIES®

Do Anything. Just Add Dummies

FOR DUMMIES®

Do Anything. Just Add Dummies

HOBBIES

Poker
978-0-7645-5232-8

Knitting
978-0-7645-5395-0

Drawing
978-0-7645-5476-6

Also available:

Art For Dummies
(978-0-7645-5104-8)
Aromatherapy For Dummies
(978-0-7645-5171-0)
Bridge For Dummies
(978-0-471-92426-5)
Card Games For Dummies
(978-0-7645-9910-1)
Chess For Dummies
(978-0-7645-8404-6)

Improving Your Memory
For Dummies
(978-0-7645-5435-3)
Massage For Dummies
(978-0-7645-5172-7)
Meditation For Dummies
(978-0-471-77774-8)
Photography For Dummies
(978-0-7645-4116-2)
Quilting For Dummies
(978-0-7645-9799-2)

EDUCATION

Psychology
978-0-7645-5434-6

The Koran
978-0-7645-5581-7

Anatomy & Physiology
978-0-7645-5422-3

Also available:

Algebra For Dummies
(978-0-7645-5325-7)
Astronomy For Dummies
(978-0-7645-8465-7)
Buddhism For Dummies
(978-0-7645-5359-2)
Calculus For Dummies
(978-0-7645-2498-1)
Cooking Basics For Dummies
(978-0-7645-7206-7)

Forensics For Dummies
(978-0-7645-5580-0)
Islam For Dummies
(978-0-7645-5503-9)
Philosophy For Dummies
(978-0-7645-5153-6)
Religion For Dummies
(978-0-7645-5264-9)
Trigonometry For Dummies
(978-0-7645-6903-6)

PETS

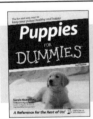

Puppies
978-0-470-03717-1

Dog Training
978-0-7645-8418-3

Cats
978-0-7645-5275-5

Also available:

Aquariums For Dummies
(978-0-7645-5156-7)
Birds For Dummies
(978-0-7645-5139-0)
Dogs For Dummies
(978-0-7645-5274-8)
Ferrets For Dummies
(978-0-7645-5259-5)
Golden Retrievers
For Dummies
(978-0-7645-5267-0)

Horses For Dummies
(978-0-7645-9797-8)
Jack Russell Terriers
For Dummies
(978-0-7645-5268-7)
Labrador Retrievers
For Dummies
(978-0-7645-5281-6)
Puppies Raising & Training
Diary For Dummies
(978-0-7645-0876-9)

Available wherever books are sold. For more information or to order direct go to www.wiley.com or call 0800 243407 (Non UK call +44 1243 843296)

FOR DUMMIES®

The easy way to get more done and have more fun

GUAGES

Spanish
DUMMIES

978-0-7645-5193-2

French
FOR DUMMIES

978-0-7645-5193-2

Italian
FOR DUMMIES

978-0-7645-5196-3

Also available:

Chinese For Dummies
(978-0-471-78897-3)

Chinese Phrases
For Dummies
(978-0-7645-8477-0)

French Phrases For Dummies
(978-0-7645-7202-9)

German For Dummies
(978-0-7645-5195-6)

Hebrew For Dummies
(978-0-7645-5489-6)

Italian Phrases For Dummies
(978-0-7645-7203-6)

Japanese For Dummies
(978-0-7645-5429-2)

Latin For Dummies
(978-0-7645-5431-5)

Spanish Phrases
For Dummies
(978-0-7645-7204-3)

Spanish Verbs For Dummies
(978-0-471-76872-2)

SIC AND FILM

Guitar
DUMMIES

978-0-7645-9904-0

Filmmaking
FOR DUMMIES

978-0-7645-2476-9

Piano
FOR DUMMIES

978-0-7645-5105-5

Also available:

Bass Guitar For Dummies
(978-0-7645-2487-5)

Blues For Dummies
(978-0-7645-5080-5)

Classical Music For Dummies
(978-0-7645-5009-6)

Drums For Dummies
(978-0-471-79411-0)

Jazz For Dummies
(978-0-471-76844-9)

Opera For Dummies
(978-0-7645-5010-2)

Rock Guitar For Dummies
(978-0-7645-5356-1)

Screenwriting For Dummies
(978-0-7645-5486-5)

Singing For Dummies
(978-0-7645-2475-2)

Songwriting For Dummies
(978-0-7645-5404-9)

LTH, SPORTS & FITNESS

Fitness
FOR DUMMIES

978-0-7645-7851-9

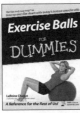

Exercise Balls
FOR DUMMIES

978-0-7645-5623-4

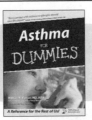

Asthma
FOR DUMMIES

978-0-7645-4233-6

Also available:

Controlling Cholesterol
For Dummies
(978-0-7645-5440-7)

Diabetes For Dummies
(978-0-470-05810-7)

High Blood Pressure
For Dummies
(978-0-7645-5424-7)

Martial Arts For Dummies
(978-0-7645-5358-5)

Menopause FD
(978-0-470-061008)

Pilates For Dummies
(978-0-7645-5397-4)

Weight Training
For Dummies
(978-0-471-76845-6)

Yoga For Dummies
(978-0-7645-5117-8)

FOR DUMMIES®

Helping you expand your horizons and achieve your potential

INTERNET

978-0-470-12174-0

978-0-471-97998-2

978-0-470-08030-6

Also available:

Blogging For Dummies
For Dummies, 2nd Edition
(978-0-470-23017-6)

Building a Web Site For
Dummies, 3rd Edition
(978-0-470-14928-7)

Creating Web Pages
All-in-One Desk Reference
For Dummies, 3rd Edition
(978-0-470-09629-1)

eBay.co.uk
For Dummies
(978-0-7645-7059-9)

Video Blogging FD
(978-0-471-97177-1)

Web Analysis For Dummies
(978-0-470-09824-0)

Web Design For Dummies,
2nd Edition
(978-0-471-78117-2)

DIGITAL MEDIA

978-0-7645-9802-9

978-0-470-17474-6

978-0-470-14927-0

Also available:

BlackBerry For Dummies,
2nd Edition
(978-0-470-18079-2)

Digital Photography
All-in-One Desk Reference
For Dummies
(978-0-470-03743-0)

Digital Photo Projects
For Dummies
(978-0-470-12101-6)

iPhone For Dummies
(978-0-470-17469-2)

Photoshop CS3 For Dummie
(978-0-470-11193-2)

Podcasting
For Dummies
(978-0-471-74898-4)

COMPUTER BASICS

978-0-470-13728-4

978-0-470-05432-1

978-0-471-74941-7

Also available:

Macs For Dummies,
9th Edition
(978-0-470-04849-8)

Office 2007 All-in-One Desk
Reference For Dummies
(978-0-471-78279-7)

PCs All-in-One Desk
Reference For Dummies,
4th Edition
(978-0-470-22338-3)

Upgrading & Fixing PCs
For Dummies, 7th Edition
(978-0-470-12102-3)

Windows XP For Dummies,
2nd Edition
(978-0-7645-7326-2)

Available wherever books are sold. For more information or to order direct go to www.wiley.com or call 0800 243407 (Non UK call +44 1243 843296)